AFTER APOCALYPSE

AFTER APOCALYPSE: FOUR JAPANESE PLAYS OF HIROSHIMA AND NAGASAKI

Selected, Translated, and Introduced by
DAVID G. GOODMAN

COLUMBIA UNIVERSITY PRESS
NEW YORK   1986

Library of Congress Cataloging in Publication Data
Main entry under title:

After apocalypse.

   Contents: The Island / Hotta Kiyomi — The head of
Mary / Tanaka Chikao — The elephant / Betsuyaku
Minoru — [etc.]
   1. Japanese drama—20th century—Translations into
English.   2. English drama—Translations from Japanese.
3. Hiroshima-shi (Japan)—History—Bombardment, 1945—
Drama.   4. Nagasaki-shi (Japan)—History—Bombardment,
1945—Drama.   I. Goodman, David G., 1946–   .
PL782.E5A37   1986   895.6'25'080358   85-17051
ISBN 0-231-06226-5

Columbia University Press
New York   Guildford, Surrey
Copyright © 1986 Columbia University Press
All rights reserved
Printed in the United States of America

This book is Smyth-sewn.

Designed by Ken Venezio

To the Memory of My Father

CONTENTS

Illustrations appear as a group following page 104

I was sitting in John Hall's room in the Ginza Tōkyū Hotel. It was August 27, 1966, the day after I had arrived in Japan for my first stay. Hall, then A. Whitney Griswold Professor of History at Yale, was the man most responsible for my being in Tokyo. As my instructor in Japanese history, he had stimulated my interest in the country, and he had gone out of his way to find me a job as an English teacher in the provincial city of Okayama. He had stepped out momentarily and had left me to wait for him in his room.

As I waited, a maid entered. She carried the usual paraphernalia, but across her nose and mouth was a white gauze mask secured by loops over her ears. I had never seen a mask like it before, and my first reaction was, "My God, she's a survivor of Hiroshima!" I was convinced that the mask—which in reality was only meant to protect her from the dust—concealed horrible scars left by the bomb.

When I returned to Yale a year later, I approached Robert Lifton, professor of psychiatry in the medical school, to arrange for a tutorial in psychohistorical approaches to Japan. It was 1967, the year *Death in Life,* Lifton's monumental study of the survivors of Hiroshima, was published. Lifton agreed, and thereafter we met on a weekly basis, reading Cassirer, Langer, Erikson, and of course Lifton himself. It was intellectually one of the most important experiences of my life.

Tsuno Kaitarō and I had been drinking for some time at Hashimoto Ken'ichi's Ryōzanpaku in Kyoto, and it was late. We began to discuss Tsuno's 1980 book *Theatre and the Plague (Pesto to gekijō),* which Tsuno felt had been misunderstood. The book is a treatise on the relationship between the modernization of theater architecture and modern theater's inability to deal with complex phenomena like the plague. I frankly had been uncomfortable with the book myself, but as we talked I realized how badly I had misunderstood it. The plague had been an extended metaphor for all those things that theater in its modern form had lost the ability to treat. As we talked, I realized that what Tsuno had ultimately been trying to do was discover the roots of our modern incapacity to give effective artistic expression to the plaguelike mixture of myth and reality surrounding nuclear weapons that has infected every aspect of our lives, the contemporary malady Lifton calls "nuclearism."

Ever since he first introduced me to Satoh Makoto in the spring of 1968, Tsuno has been the principal influence on my thinking about theater. The process of coming to terms with his ideas has been a consistent challenge and a constant reward.

From the outset, the atomic bomb experience has been an integral part of my concern with Japan; this book is a natural outgrowth of that concern. Without John Hall, Robert Lifton, and Tsuno Kaitarō, it would not have been possible.

AFTER APOCALYPSE

Part of the horror of thinking about a holocaust lies in the fact that it leads us to supplant the human world with a statistical world; we seek a human truth and come up with a handful of figures. The only source that gives us a glimpse of that human truth is the testimony of the survivors of the Hiroshima and Nagasaki bombings.
JONATHAN SCHELL, *The Fate of the Earth*

As they introduce four different perspectives on Hiroshima and Nagasaki, the plays collected in this anthology also illustrate the evolution of postwar Japanese playwriting. *Shingeki,* the Japanese version of Western modern theater, began to develop in the first decade of the twentieth century. It was above all a realistic, secularizing movement that sought to emulate the theater of Henrik Ibsen and Anton Chekhov. The irrationality and penchant for the supernatural that had characterized traditional *kabuki* were anathema; the ideal was a purely realistic form of dramatic presentation in the spirit of Stanislavsky's Moscow Art Theater.[1]

By the 1930s, this ideal had been achieved. The psychological realism of Kishida Kunio (1890–1954) and the socialist realism of Kubo Sakae (1901–1958)[2] marked the high points in the dramatic writing of the orthodox shingeki movement; and modern theater in the postwar years, from 1945 to 1960, was in many respects an extension of the shingeki movement of the prewar period. Personalities like Kishida and Kubo, their disciples, and their troupes dominated the modern theater scene. Shingeki became an orthodoxy, the main tenets of which were a commitment to proscenium-arch realism, humanism, and a tragic dramaturgy.[3]

The real break with the orthodox shingeki movement came around 1960 and developed out of political and literary differences that arose during that year's demonstrations against renewal of the United States-Japan Mutual Security Treaty. The issue of the demonstrations was whether U.S. military bases should be allowed to remain on Japanese soil and whether Japan should remain under the U.S. "nuclear umbrella." During the demonstrations, younger actors and playwrights began to feel that orthodox shingeki dramaturgy was as inadequate to deal with current realities as orthodox Marxist politics. The transition from modern to postmodern drama in Japan was thus integrally related to the question of nuclear weapons.

While the plays translated here depart in significant ways from shingeki orthodoxy, Hotta Kiyomi and Tanaka Chikao themselves represent the two streams of the orthodox shingeki movement. Hotta belongs to the "political" stream of Kubo Sakae, Tanaka to the "literary" stream of Kishida Kunio. Hotta began his theater career after the war writing plays for his fellow workers at a Hitachi Electric factory and was discovered by theater professionals as an up-and-coming proletarian dramatist. Tanaka, on the other hand, was a disciple of Kishida Kunio and a devotee of the "literary" approach to the theater. He began writing plays professionally in the 1930s and has written and taught widely on the literary aspects of dramatic composition.

By contrast, Betsuyaku Minoru and Satoh Makoto are representative playwrights of the postmodern movement. Their plays break decisively with shingeki tradition. Moreover, unlike Hotta and Tanaka, who were born in Hiroshima and Nagasaki respectively, Betsuyaku and Satoh have no organic relationship with the atomic bombings. Their concern with the atomic bomb experience derives from growing up in postwar Japan, where nuclear weapons were a pervasive concern.

The plays collected here thus illustrate the transition from modern to postmodern playwriting. They also reveal how intimately the theme of Hiroshima and Nagasaki is related to the development of postwar Japanese drama. These plays by four of Japan's leading dramatists demonstrate the important role the need to formulate the reality of atomic holocaust has played in the quest for new playwriting techniques and perspectives.[4]

FORMULATION, MASTERY, AND TRANSFORMATION

The best source of information on the *hibakusha* (survivor) experience is Robert Jay Lifton's magisterial work, *Death in Life: Survivors of Hiroshima*.[5] I refer often to Lifton's work in my introduction to each play, but three of his concepts deserve explanation here.

Formulation is the process of coming to terms with the experience of the bomb, giving it some form or expression, either explicit or tacit and intrapsychic. Formulation is the process of breaking out of the state of muteness—what Lifton calls "psychic closing off" or "psychic numbing"—that a major, traumatizing experience like the bomb imposes and arriving at some potentially enunciable formula to explain what happened.

Mastery is a question of who is master of the survivor's existence, bomb or man? Who governs the survivor's life, that moment on the morning of August 6 or 9, 1945, or the survivor himself? The question of mastery is the question of the extent to which the experience of the bomb continues to overshadow and control the life of the survivor or the extent to which he has succeeded in integrating it into his normal psychic existence.

Transformation implies that in the process of formulation, the raw data of experience are necessarily altered in some more or less meaningful way. Transformation implies that formulations are not fixed but may be altered in ways that either enhance or retard mastery, and it is therefore possible to rank formulations according to the degree to which they facilitate or inhibit mastery.

Works of literature and art are formulations made openly in the public domain; they make the unarticulated images of survival, the inchoate "A-bomb philosophy" of the individual survivor, manifest in a communal forum and facilitate communal mastery of the experience. As with the private formulations of individual survivors, atomic bomb art and literature represent formulations from which varying degrees of mastery may be inferred. Concepts like formulation, mastery, and transformation are therefore useful tools in dealing with works about the atomic experience. They allow us to better understand individual works and how they relate to one another.

FOUR FORMULATIONS

Each of the plays presented here offers a different formulation of the A-bomb experience. Each play moves farther away from a realistic recitation of events and presents a more radically transformed image of the atomic bomb experience than its predecessor. Each image or formulation is a more probing foray into the mysteries surrounding Hiroshima and Nagasaki, and each employs a wider variety of techniques. That does not mean that the earlier plays are less legitimate formulations, but only that no formulation is definitive. The plays comprise a developmental continuum, but taken together they also suggest four complementary perspectives on the conundrum of life and death in the atomic age.

Hotta Kiyomi's play *The Island* (1955) attempts to realistically portray the impact of the Hiroshima bombing on Japanese society. The island in the Inland Sea near Hiroshima where the play takes place is a microcosm of provincial Japan, and the people of the island are the uncomplicated common folk of the country. In Hotta's formulation, Hiroshima survivors have two alternatives, hopelessness or faith, but not action. Manabu, the central character of the play, embodies these alternatives. He longs for some kind of personal fulfillment through work or marriage, but both are denied him because of his atomic bomb experience. Denied a personal future, he must choose between despair and faith. Explicitly, that faith is the religion of humanism. Manabu is a teacher, and he wagers his immortality on his ability to inculcate in his junior high school students the values that will prevent a future holocaust and guarantee humanity a peaceful future. Implicitly, Manabu's faith is in the absolute saving grace of Amida Buddha as expounded by the True Pure Land sect of Buddhism. It is no coincidence that, as the final curtain falls, Manabu faces a clearing western sky. Ultimately, the playwright suggests, he will be redeemed in Amida's Western Paradise.

The Head of Mary (1958) by Tanaka Chikao is a Catholic drama that views the bombing of Nagasaki as a theophany, that is, as a manifestation of God's will in history. The play describes a conspiracy by a group of atomic bomb survivors to steal the remains of a statue of the Virgin Mary that had stood before the Urakami Cathedral in Nagasaki at the time of the bombing. They want to reconstruct the statue in their own poor sanctuary as a special object of veneration. Tanaka regards the survivors' experience in religious terms, but his formulation is more complex than Hotta's. If Nagasaki were indeed a manifestation of God's will in history, then the event was not meaningless; it was part of a divine plan. Why else should God have singled out Japan's most Christian city for destruction? But what conceivable purpose could such a holocaust have served? The problem for Tanaka is to describe the complex relationship between an inscrutable God and His imperfect human flock.

Both *The Island* and *The Head of Mary* denigrate political action. Written in the wake of the 1960 demonstrations, Betsuyaku Minoru's *The Elephant* (1962) is a more activist work, although on the surface this may not be readily apparent. The play centers on the conflict between two Hiroshima survivors, an invalid and his nephew. Though he is hospitalized and dying from radiation aftereffects, the invalid is committed to movement and action, while his apparently healthy nephew is convinced of the futility of life and committed to passivity and stasis. Unlike the plays of Hotta and Tanaka, *The Elephant* is an existentialist drama that describes a world where God is absent. Betsuyaku's play finds the root of hope implicit in the human situation and advocates action simply because the alternative is so unpalatable.

Satoh Makoto's *Nezumi Kozō: The Rat* (1969) can be read as a third alternative, neither strictly religious nor entirely existential in conception. Satoh sees the bombings, not as theophanies, but as revelations of the human imagination in history. Instead of viewing them as isolated and unique events, Satoh construes Hiroshima and Nagasaki as the most recent and terrible manifestations of mankind's impulse for self-destruction. For Satoh, the problem of Hiroshima and Nagasaki is not the problem of nuclear weapons per se, but a problem of the dynamics of the human imagination, which invents and employs machines of ever increasing destructive power. Since Hiroshima and Nagasaki are repetitions of an archetypal ur-holocaust innate in the human mind, there is no reason to believe that they will not be repeated in the future with even more terrible results. Satoh's purpose in writing is therefore to influence the human imagination in order to obviate future holocausts. Like Betsuyaku, his view is existential, but the divine also plays a decisive role in his work, not as an objective force in history, but as an undeniable and eminently powerful aspect of the human mind. As with Betsuyaku, action is justified for Satoh because the alternative is unacceptable; but like Hotta and Tanaka, action must be in relation to the metahistorical dimension man symbolizes as the divine.

HIROSHIMA/NAGASAKI, SYMBOLIC IMMORTALITY, AND THE POST-SHINGEKI MOVEMENT

Shingeki began as a realistic, secularizing movement in Japanese modern theater. The revolt against it, on the other hand, has consistently sought to reinject a transcendent and often overtly religious dimension into the theater. It is no coincidence that this movement has been closely linked to attempts by playwrights to deal with Hiroshima and Nagasaki, for in order to make the instantaneous deaths of hundreds of thousands of people meaningful, those deaths had to be integrated into a transcendent order that afforded the victims a kind of symbolic immortality. In *The Island*, it is order of Pure Land Buddhism and the promise of redemption in Amida's Western Paradise. In *The Head of Mary*, it is the eschatology of Catholicism and the promise of salvation through Mary's saving grace. In *Nezumi Kozō*, it is the perilous metahistory of the human imagination and a unique secular messianism. Only in *The Elephant* are we presented with the image of a disintegrating and paralyzed man utterly adrift in absurdity.

Attempts to formulate Hiroshima and Nagasaki in a dramatic medium led ineluctably to a revolt against shingeki orthodoxy because shingeki's principal tenets—realism, humanism, and tragedy—were inadequate, if not inimical, to the sorts of religious and quasireligious formulation necessary to ensure symbolic immortality to the victims. That religion in its many forms should play such a prominent role in these plays and in the entire post-shingeki theater movement is thus no coincidence. As Lifton points out, "Religion has been the primary source of man's overt symbolization of immortality."[6]

But formulations of the atomic bomb experience are not limited to the overtly religious; they have also been political. To treat Hiroshima and Nagasaki on the stage has been a means to overcome the political passivity imposed on the theater by shingeki orthodoxy and made palpable by the traumatic experience of 1960. Particularly in the years since 1960, the theme of Hiroshima and Nagasaki has been linked to attempts to restore the sense of movement and political potency that the Security Treaty debacle denied. For many writers, including the playwrights whose work appears in this anthology, coming to terms with Hiroshima and Nagasaki has been a means to overcome the sense of psychic and political paralysis that had come to characterize their daily lives.[7] The plays in this anthology thus contribute to our understanding, not only of postwar Japanese dramatic literature, but Japanese literature in general in the postwar period.

TRANSLATING THE PLAYS

Translating plays presents certain unique difficulties, for while plays are literature, they are also meant to be performed. In translating these plays, my principal concern has been to render them faithfully into English, and I suppose my translations will therefore be regarded as literary. However, I have adapted and directed at least one of these plays (*The Elephant*) and I am convinced that with imaginative direction, all of them can be successfully staged in English. Speaking of his radical reworking of Peter Weiss' *Marat/Sade,* Satoh Makoto once argued that direction *is* adaptation, and I would agree.

All Japanese names are given in their original order, surname first.

THE ISLAND

The Island: Orthodox Realism

Hotta Kiyomi's *The Island* was the first play about the atomic bombings to receive national attention in Japan. Hotta won the 1955 Kishida Prize for Playwriting for the play, and Naitō Taketoshi, who played the role of Manabu, received two separate awards for his performance.

THE PLAYWRIGHT

Hotta Kiyomi was born in Hiroshima prefecture on March 13, 1922, and was educated at the Hiroshima Commercial High School. At the time of the bombing, he was working in the Osaka area and thus survived the destruction of his city. After the war, Hotta worked at the Kameari factory of the Hitachi company, where he became a leader in the workers' theater known as the Self-Reliant Theater Movement (*Jiritsu engeki undō*), which was sponsored by labor unions and flourished in work places around the country after the war.[1] In 1950, Hotta was dismissed from Hitachi during the "Red Purge," the Occupation's version of McCarthyism in Japan that cost more than 20,000 suspected Communists and fellow travelers their jobs.

Hotta joined the Mingei (People's Art) troupe in 1955 and served as an assistant director on its productions of *Death of a Salesman* and *The Diary of Anne Frank.*[2] He left the troupe in the early 1960s and has not been active in theatrical activities since.

Hotta's original motivation for becoming involved in the theater and the impulse behind the Self-Reliant Theater Movement are best described in his own words:

I didn't really begin writing plays because I thought I'd like to be a playwright. In the factories caught up as they were in that state of meaninglessness after the war, we young people who had been brought up to believe that "All is for the Emperor!" shared the sense that now at last we could build our own lives as we saw fit; and "Let us live our own lives!" was a slogan that really excited us.[3]

Hotta's participation in the workers' theater immediately after the war and his later affiliation with the Mingei troupe places him squarely in the mainstream of the orthodox shingeki movement, and *The Island* displays all the main features of orthodox shingeki dramaturgy: a commitment to proscenium-arch realism, tragedy, and humanism. The play is a thoroughly realistic work that seeks to inform, uplift, and exhort its audience through an encounter with its tragic hero, Kurihara Manabu.

THE TRAGIC HERO

The play takes place on an island in the Inland Sea near Hiroshima toward the end of the Korean War (1951–1952). Manabu, a *hibakusha* (survivor) who is employed as a junior high school teacher despite his college training as an engineer, is struggling to reconcile his sense of mission as a survivor with his need for personal fulfillment. On the one hand he wants to inculcate the young with values that will preclude another holocaust; on the other he wishes to put his education to work in the world beyond the island. Despite the trauma of his exposure to the bomb, Manabu seems to have mastered his experience quite effectively. He nevertheless lives with the persistent fear of delayed radiation effects.

Manabu has achieved a remarkably healthy formulation of his experience of nuclear war. He views it as something that happened and that is now behind him. He has trouble believing rumors that the United States will use nuclear weapons in Korea, but he contends that even if they do, the human instinct for survival will inevitably prevail. Manabu's idol is Mahatma Gandhi; he gives a plaque inscribed with the words of Pascal to a former student; and his proclamation, "The future belongs to mankind!" epitomizes his humanistic philosophy.

Ironically, the bomb has permanently denied this altruistic man, with his profound faith in man's ability to shape his own future, an acceptable future of his own. He briefly fantasizes that he will marry a former student; but almost simultaneously, Kawashita Kin, another *hibakusha* on the island, learns that she has leukemia and dies. Manabu has also developed signs of malignancy, and he realizes that he can never marry. The ineluctable consequences of radiation exposure—cancer, premature death, and potential genetic impairment—disqualify him as a prospective mate. Despite his humanism and heroic optimism, Manabu is tragically flawed: he is a *hibakusha* and will be denied in perpetuity the future he foresees for mankind.

THE KIYOMORI FESTIVAL

The great strength of *The Island* is its realistic description of the society affected by the bomb. Particularly important in this respect is the motif of the Kiyomori Festival, an annual observance commemorating a man punished for the hubris of having harnessed the power of the sun. The festival brings together the strands of historical fact, myth, and religion that form the basis of provincial Japanese culture and relates them to contemporary attempts by the people to formulate their experience. Hotta's device of the festival allows us to understand how the Japanese perception of the atomic bomb experience has been mediated by their culture.

Taira Kiyomori (1118–1181) was leader of the Taira (or Heike) clan at the time of its disastrous war with another powerful warrior family, the Minamoto (or Genji) clan. The war ended in 1185 with the decisive victory of the Minamoto. Many battles between Taira and Minamoto forces were fought along the shores of the Inland Sea as the Taira fled west by ship and were pursued by the Minamoto on land, and so the people who live along the shores of the Inland Sea feel a special affinity with the Taira clan. Indeed, many of them, like the Kido family in the play, consider themselves descendants of Taira warriors who settled in the region.

The defeat of the Taira clan is recounted in *The Tale of the Heike (Heike monogatari)*, one of the monuments of classical Japanese literature.[4] This epic evolved from a number of documentary and oral sources and was popularized by blind, itinerant priests known as *biwa hōshi,* who chanted it to the accompaniment of the lute-like *biwa* and infused it with a Pure Land (*Jōdo*) Buddhist message: salvation does not come through individual merit but through the saving grace of Amida Buddha (Amitābha). The Taira, though defeated, will be saved through Amida's mercy. *The Tale of the Heike* thus establishes a profound connection between the Taira clan and the eschatology of Pure Land Buddhism.[5]

Buddhism in Japan is not an unalloyed religion. It exists almost always in a syncretic relationship with Shinto, the indigenous religious system. In fact, until 1868, when the government ordered that they be clearly distinguished, Buddhist and Shinto divinities were closely identified and frequently indistinguishable. The myth of the love affair between Taira Kiyomori and the goddess of Miyajima that forms the basis for the Kiyomori Festival is an example of a Shinto legend that became inextricably associated with the Taira clan, the Inland Sea, and the notion of redemption in Pure Land Buddhism.

The Kiyomori Festival, a longstanding observance on the island,[6] takes on added significance as the islanders struggle to come to terms with the experience of the Hiroshima bombing. Manabu's mother Yū and Kawashita Kin are better able to deal with Manabu's experience (and their own) by likening it to Kiyomori's. Through comparison with the Taira chieftain, they are able to tie their experience into a historical continuum, thus denying its uniqueness and reducing its threat. Something like the bomb had happened before and to someone they know. That is reassuring. Second, by recalling the divine retribution visited upon Kiyomori, Kin and Yū are able to formulate their resentment toward those who had unleashed the power of the sun on them, and they also reassure themselves that the transgression will not go unpunished. Finally, because of the Pure Land Buddhist associations of the Taira clan, formulating the atomic bomb experience in terms of the Kiyomori Festival links it to the promise of salvation through faith in Amida's mercy.

THE ISLAND AS SOCIAL MICROCOSM

The Island presents a social microcosm of Japan. The lingering structure of dependency and paternalism revealed in the relationship between Ōura and the Kawashita family, for example, remains a consistent feature of Japanese society today. And the ritual complexities of choosing a marriage partner in the circumscribed confines of Hotta's island remain a typical gauntlet for many in his island nation.

Perhaps the most interesting facet of Hotta's realistic description of island society is the moral ambiguity of its people. The first sentence of the play indicates the close relationship between the peaceful life of the island and the work most of its inhabitants performed during the war at the Kure naval base. Pacificistic Manabu's brother Tsutomu seems to have died as a suicide pilot. And even at the time the play takes place, the fishermen of the island make more money collecting scrap metal needed to prosecute the war in Korea than they do with their nets. People find themselves hoping that Japan will rearm so that the Kure naval base will reopen and the islanders will once more be employed; and they become panicky when a Korean cease-fire is announced and rumors spread that American forces, the major employers in the area, will be returning home.

Hotta depicts the people of the island with sympathy and affection, but he views them as ineluctably compromised by the avaricious life-style to which capitalism commits them. It made them accomplices in the war and continues to visit their lives with tragedy. Kawashita Kin's husband Shichirō, blown to smithereens while attempting to disarm a torpedo he had hoped to salvage for scrap, is only the most recent casualty of the cycle of desire and damnation in which all are trapped.

Significantly, no political solution to this situation is proposed in the play. Instead, resignation and salvation through the loving grace of the Buddha Amida is proposed. Shinran, founder of the True Pure Land sect of Buddhism (*Jōdo shinshū*) had proclaimed: if Amida loves and is willing to save the good man, how much more will he be to save the bad man incapable of saving himself;[7] and Hotta believes that the victims of the atomic bomb, like the defeated Taira, will only truly be redeemed through the power of Amida. As the play concludes, Manabu faces a gradually clearing western sky with renewed hope. He is facing Amida's Western Paradise (*saihō jōdo*), and it is in resignation and faith in ultimate salvation through Amida's mercy that Manabu finds hope.

THE LIMITATIONS OF REALISM

The detailed description of the social microcosm of the island and the use of the Kiyomori Festival are brilliant devices that contribute importantly to our appreciation of the provincial milieu into which the bomb was dropped, but they do not necessarily contribute to our understanding of the *hibakusha* experience as such. In an important sense, the experience of nuclear holocaust defies the kind of realistic description Hotta attempts in this play. "It was beyond words!" is the most frequent caveat of survivors talking about their experience. Realism reduces experience to quotidian dimensions, but the most salient characteristic of the atomic bomb experience was the way it radically departed from "reality." As Lifton observes, "The most striking psychological feature of [the] immediate experience was the sense of a sudden and absolute shift from normal existence to an overwhelming encounter with death."[8]

Shingeki realism equates *historical* experience with *individual* experience. Critic Saeki Ryūkō has observed that in shingeki we are expected to extract historical meaning from our encounter with individuals straining and inevitably crushed under the weight of their historical experience.[9] This is the tragic perspective endemic to shingeki, and this is the perspective of *The Island.* Manabu and Kin are struggling with the consequences of their atomic bomb exposure; and inevitably they are destroyed by it, even as they protest their undying faith in humanity. Through our encounter with these tragic individuals, we are expected to experience vicariously their suffering and learn something from their ordeal.

This is the shingeki formula. And that is the problem. There are numerous plays in the shingeki repertory that are not about the atomic bomb experience but that nonetheless follow precisely this same pattern.[10] It is a kind of formulaic writing, and what comes across most strongly is not the unique experience of the atomic bomb but the tragic formula. The satisfaction we receive from the play derives largely from our fulfilled expectations: when you come right down to it, even an experience as terrible as atomic holocaust conforms to familiar patterns! But what if anything was unique about the atomic bomb experience? The shingeki stage is crowded with tragic characters crushed by the weight of history but filled with faith in human prospects. What distinguishes Manabu and Kin from this multitude? Even the long-term radiation effects unique to the atomic bomb experience are virtually indistinguishable from the long-range tragic consequences of the encounter with major historical events described in other shingeki dramas.

It is hard not to perceive a link between the realistic shingeki dramaturgy of *The Island* and its apolitical message of resignation and faith. Because shingeki heroes are foredoomed to failure, they lack from the outset any substantial prospect for effective action. Without in the least impugning Hotta's religious beliefs, it is nonetheless true that some such rationale for resignation and inaction is called forth in *The Island* by the structure of the play, which precludes the possibility of meaningful action.

Thanks to the realistic description in *The Island*, we have a better appreciation of the nature of provincial Japanese society and how it dealt with the atomic bomb experience; but we are not necessarily closer to an understanding of that experience and its unique mystery, nor does the play tell us what sorts of action might be available to us in a nuclearized age. It was for other playwrights to deal with these questions.

THE ISLAND
A PLAY IN THREE ACTS

by Hotta Kiyomi

The Island (Shima) was first performed in September 1957 by the Mingei troupe under the direction of Okakura Shirō. This translation is from the text found in *Nihon no genbaku bungaku*, vol. 12 (Tokyo: Horupu, 1983).

CAST OF CHARACTERS

Kurihara Yū
Kurihara Manabu (Yū's son)
Kurihara Fumi (Yū's daughter)
Ōura (Yū's younger brother)
Kawashita Kin
Kawashita Kikuo (Kin's eldest son)
Kawashita Kunio (Kin's younger son)
Shintani Tadashi
Shimizu Tokuichi
Mōri (middle school drafting instructor)
Mr. Yamaoka
Kido Reiko

TIME AND SETTING

The action takes place on an island near Kure from the spring of 1951 to the spring of the following year.*

---

*Kure is a port city near Hiroshima. During the war, it was the site of a major naval base and arsenal.

ACT ONE

SCENE I. THE KURIHARA HOME, LATE MARCH.

The Kurihara home. The rock garden set off by the low brick wall at stage right was built by the late patriarch of this family with stones he carried here from the surrounding shores and hills on his days off from work at the naval arsenal at Kure. In addition to a maple tree that has grown out of all proportion to its miniature surroundings, there are azaleas, jasmine, and other flowering shrubs. The blossoms of the peach tree near the wooden gate at the back of the garden are particularly beautiful. To the left as one goes through the gate, stone steps lead down the hill upon which the house sits; and so standing in its garden and looking over the thickly clustered roofs below, the Seto Inland Sea with its brisk maritime traffic will be visible. Across the water to the left would be part of what remains of the naval arsenal; and to the right would be an inlet and then the open sea leading toward Iyo.*

An open tatami room with an L-shaped veranda faces the garden. On the veranda is an old wicker chair. To the left as one faces the room is an alcove that now contains Manabu's overflowing bookshelf. On the wall, a T-square and a triangle. On top of the book-shelf, a radio and a globe. A low desk stands in front of the alcove. To the right of the alcove are two pairs of hinged paper doors upon which a quotation from Shinran has been written in bold strokes.† The large and elaborate Buddhist altar behind these doors strengthens the impression that this family are devout believers in Shinran's True Pure Land sect of Buddhism.‡ Mounted above the altar on the crossbeam are a portrait of the

---

*Iyo is an archaic name for Ehime prefecture in northwestern Shikoku.

†Shinran (1173–1262), a major Japanese religious thinker, founded *Jōdo shinshū*, the True Pure Land sect of Buddhism. The words here are taken from his "Hymn to the True Faith of the Nembutsu" (*Shōshin nembutsu ge*), which sums up the basic tenets of the Pure Land faith. A translation of the "Hymn" may be found in Wm. Theodore de Bary, et al., eds., *Sources of Japanese Tradition* (New York: Columbia University Press, 1958), pp. 212–216.

‡The word used here is *Aki-montō*, literally "believers from Aki (Hiroshima)." It suggests that the Kurihara family have been believers in the True Pure Land sect for centuries. *Montō* are known for their elaborate altars, and the term is thus sometimes used derogatorily, to refer to people whose religious understanding does not match their ostentation.

family's deceased patriarch dressed in a formal black kimono and a photograph of Tsutomu dressed in his Navy pilot's uniform.* Next to this room is the living room. In the middle is a kotatsu, *a charcoal brazier set in a hole in the floor and covered with a table and lap blanket. The entrance to the house is upstage and to the left as one faces this room, and to its right is a corridor leading to the kitchen, which has both a wooden floor and a lower, earthen-floored section for the hearth. On the wall to the right are a closet and sliding doors leading to a bedroom.*

It is a late March evening bathed in the gorgeous light of a crimson sunset. Sitting beside the kotatsu, *Yū is occupied sewing fishing nets, work she does for extra income; and Mōri is winding thread from a spinning wheel onto a bamboo spindle. The diverse sounds of ferry boats, expressing the sentiments of people on their way home after a hard day's work; of fishing boats hastening out to sea for night fishing; and of passenger ships sounding their horns as they pass through the Inland Sea can be heard now near, now far—and amidst it all is the voice of a woman hawking sardines as she hurries down the road.*

YŪ: Actually, the Kiyomori Festival is supposed to be held on leap years, on the third day of the third lunar month, the day of the high tide.† When poor Tsutomu was a first grader, he won a chance to ride on a horse in the parade. He played the part of an adviser to a feudal lord. A little girl played the part of the lord and rode in a palanquin. It was so cute!

MŌRI: Sort of "history on parade," is that it?

YŪ: I'm sure I put the photo album around here somewhere. . . . *(She searches the alcove.)*

Kin peers out from the kitchen. She is a hard working woman with a certain masculine hardiness about her. At the moment, she is about eight months pregnant.

KIN: Mizz Kurihara . . . Oh, Mr. Mōri, you helping? Brought some sardines. Want me to fix them for *sashimi*?

YŪ: Manabu won't be home tonight, so maybe I'll braise them.

---

*Tsutomu had volunteeed as a "pilot trainee" (*hikō yoka renshūsei*). Many of these young men died as suicide (*kamikaze*) pilots.

†According to Hotta, the third day of the third lunar month fell on April 22 in 1985. The text here has been altered slightly at the playwright's suggestion.

KIN: Mr. Manabu away?

YŪ: He was invited to the Morita wedding.

KIN: How does he know the Moritas?

YŪ: Classmates. The celebration's turned into a real fancy affair, just like the old days. I don't know what they're trying to prove.

KIN: Just want to show off their money. Morita's putting on airs because he made a killing in the steel business. Big deal. Should hear the things people say behind his back.

YŪ: It'll be a while before us poor folk can afford to celebrate like that.

KIN: Wife's a farmer's daughter from Iyo, come loaded down with furniture and all the trappings.

YŪ: Is that right?

KIN: Just take one look at her! Anyway, I'll take off the heads for you. (*She has apparently gone to the kitchen sink.*)

YŪ (*speaking to Mōri of Kin*): Her husband was a horse groom who made private first class in a transport division. Good looking he was and really knew how to handle horses. We called him Shichi the groom. . . . You know, this is the first time since the war broke out that they've held the festival. I wonder how long that makes it? After all, during the war, everyone in town was working at the arsenal in Kure—or at least it seemed that way—and the fishermen, come spring those that could afford it headed for Korea to catch sardines, and those that stayed behind on the island headed out toward the coast of Kyushu to fish. I hear that next year Representative Kaneda from the prefectural assembly is going to try to get us some money from the government for the festival. Why, in the old days the Kiyomori Festival was a big attraction—people would come all the way from Osaka to see it. Of course, everybody contributes, but at fifty yen per family and a thousand families, what does that make it, 50,000? Only a few families can afford to contribute even a hundred yen.

MŌRI: What's the point of the festival, to propitiate the spirit of Taira Kiyomori?

YŪ: Couldn't say really. Best I can remember, they used to do it so the fishing would be good. The divinity of Kiyomori's Tomb is a white snake, if that helps.

MŌRI: I see.

YŪ: Must be a god of the sea. . . . They say it was Taira Kiyo-mori who dug the Inland Sea. (*Pause.*) Next year, bring your parents to see the festival. They'd enjoy it.

MŌRI: I'm sure they would. They've never been out of their village.

KIN: Fish are on the sink. Be careful the cat don't get them.

YŪ: Kin, maybe you know. What's the Kiyomori Festival sup-posed to be about?

KIN: Festival for Kiyomori. You see, Taira Kiyomori fell in love with the goddess of Miyajima,* and she promised to marry him if he dug out the Inland Sea in a single day. Well, soon as the sun came up, Kiyomori started digging, but just when he was about to finish, the sun set behind the mountains to the west. (*She points to the western sky.*) Just about this time of day it was. Even Kiyomori couldn't hold back the sun. But he was so much in love with the goddess that he climbed onto a rock, unfurled his fan, and began shouting, "Come back! Come back!" to bring the sun back into the sky. And you know what? The sun stayed in the sky until he was finished digging. "All right, marry me as you promised!" he said. But the goddess of Miyajima shook her head. "I can't marry the sort of man who'd call back the sun." Kiyomori turned red with rage and flourished his sword; and with that the beauti-ful goddess turned into a dragon and tried to devour him. Kiyomori ran for his life. He got away all right, but then he was struck down with a raging fever for having called the sun back into the sky. They used hundreds of pounds of ice but couldn't bring the fever down. They say he died in terrible pain. Of all the gods and Buddhas in the world, none's so powerful as the sun. Kiyomori sinned by invoking the power of the sun against the laws of nature. A noble and powerful

---

*Miyajima is a popular name for Itsukushima, an island in the Inland Sea near Hiroshima famous for its Shinto shrine and large, crimson gate (*torii*) that is enveloped by the sea each day at high tide. The picturesque shrine is a favorite tourist attraction and is hailed as one of the three most beautiful sites in Japan. Three female divinities are enshrined at Miyajima, one of whom is the subject of the Kiyomori legend.

man he was, but he got what was coming to him. They'd set a cake of ice on his forehead and watch it turn to steam before their eyes.

YŪ: Today it'd be like the fever people got from the bomb.

KIN: Exactly!

YŪ: I remember the fever Manabu had when we brought him back from Ninoshima. He was delirious, and . . . .

KIN (*to Mōri*): Thought there was something wrong with the thermometer, so I went and bought a new one. Had a fever over 104° for almost a month!

YŪ: It wasn't that long.

KIN: So involved with nursing him you didn't even know what day it was. I'm telling you! Couple of times his heart stopped altogether. (*Pause.*) Mr. Manabu pulled through, but it was all because of his mother's loving care. Take my word. What she did, no ordinary person could do. Really something. Why, her husband died the year Fumi began school, and she raised three children without a man in the house. . . .

YŪ: Will you stop blubbering and get to the point?

Kin stops and looks questioningly at Yū.

YŪ: I thought you were telling us about the Kiyomori Festival.

KIN: Oh! (*She laughs generously.*) Sometimes I just don't know what I'm going to do with myself!

YŪ: It's people like you give women a bad name!

KIN: Your fault. You interrupted me!

YŪ: Where did she get off the track?

MŌRI: I think it was where she was saying that Kiyomori was punished for calling back the sun and died of a high fever. That's where she began talking about the bomb.

KIN: See! Told you it was your fault!

KUNIO (*from the kitchen*): Mother, the rice is ready.

KIN: And I thought I'd only stay a minute! (*So saying, she exits.*)

KUNIO (*entering*): Here, let me. (*He takes the spindle from Mōri. He is considerably more skilled than the older man.*)

YŪ: Kunio, you don't know how lucky you are to go to high school. You have to study hard and take some of the burden off your mother. You've got a big family, after all.

KUNIO: Why'd she have to go and have so many children, anyway. What's the point?

YŪ: Will you listen to that? Kids these days are really on the ball.

KUNIO: Probably didn't know how to stop.

MŌRI: Kunio, what do you want to be when you grow up?

KUNIO: How should I know. I just passed the exam to go to high school. A lot of people get killed because they're in too much of a hurry. What I'd really like to do is work and go to college at night, but. . . .

YŪ: Now, don't get greedy.

Shimizu appears in the garden.

SHIMIZU: It's been a long time.

YŪ: Who is it?

SHIMIZU: Shimizu. Shimizu Tokuichi.

YŪ (*surprised*): Toku! (*She hastens to the veranda.*)

SHIMIZU: How have you been?

YŪ: It seems like forever since I've seen you! (*She looks him over from head to foot.*)

SHIMIZU (*looking in the house and around the garden*): The old place hasn't changed a bit.

YŪ: When did you get back?

SHIMIZU: A little while ago. I must've gotten to Kure about 2:30, I think. It's so much easier to get here now!

YŪ: The bus drives right through the the arsenal now.

SHIMIZU: That really caught me by surprise. It's the first time in my life that I was inside. You didn't used to be able to go through because it was a navy base. You know, it's already six years since the war ended.

YŪ: Well, don't just stand there, come in!

SHIMIZU: Is everyone well?

YŪ: Tsutomu was killed in the war. . . .

Shimizu is silent.

YŪ: He went for training, and. . . . That picture was his last. (*She goes and stands beneath the photo, looking up.*) He was so happy when I bought him a sword, he sent me this picture right away.

SHIMIZU: What a shame. He was a fine young man.

YŪ (*pointing to Kunio*): They would have been about the same age.

SHIMIZU: I'd like to pay my respects.

YŪ: If Tsutomu were alive, he'd have been so happy to see you! (*Repeating the* nembutsu,* *she opens the altar.*) Tsutomu, Toku's here.†

Shimizu seats himself before the altar and brings his hands together in prayer.

YŪ: "Mother, even if I don't come back alive, don't you cry. After all, my life was only entrusted to you temporarily by the Emperor. We'll meet again at Yasukuni Shrine."‡ That's what he said. He probably felt bad because he'd kept it secret about being accepted for pilot training. Life would be so much easier if he were still alive. . . . (*Pause.*)

SHIMIZU: You haven't changed a bit.

YŪ: I've become an old woman.

Fumi returns. She is an intelligent-looking girl, although not a raving beauty. She peeks at the altar.

YŪ: You remember him, don't you, Fumi?

FUMI (*kneeling and bowing formally, her hands on the floor*): Welcome home.

SHIMIZU: What a fine young woman you've become!

Fumi goes inside to change. Kunio is staring at Shimizu with interest.

YŪ (*taking some sweets down from the altar*): These are just some sweets the temple shared with us.§ Come and help yourself.

---

*The nembutsu is a short doxology: "Namu Amida-butsu," "Hail, Amida Buddha!" Although a belief in Amida (known as Amidism) had existed earlier in the syncretic systems of the Tendai and Shingon sects, it was not until Hōnen (1133–1212) and Shinran that Pure Land Buddhism was established in Japan as an independent sect. The principal tenet of Pure Land belief is that salvation comes from the saving grace of Amida (*tariki*) and not through the merit of the believer (*jiriki*). By intoning the *nembutsu*, the Pure Land believer seeks salvation by throwing himself upon Amida's mercy.

†For a description of Japanese relations with the dead, see Robert J. Smith, *Ancestor Worship in Contemporary Japan* (Stanford: Stanford University Press, 1974).

‡Located in Tokyo, Yasukuni Shrine is the central shrine dedicated to the souls of soldiers who lost their lives in Japan's wars.

§It is not uncommon for a family to partake of an offering after it has been presented to the deceased. In this case, the offering was originally made to the local temple on the occasion of *higan*, a seven-day semiannual Buddhist festival falling on the spring and autumn equinox, when cemetery visitations are

(*She goes to the* kotatsu. *Pointing to Mōri*): Don't mind him. He's just an art teacher at the middle school.

Mōri bows.

MŌRI (*taking some papers from his briefcase*): Give these to Manabu,* will you?

YŪ: Why don't you stay a while?

MŌRI: My landlady'll have supper ready. I don't want to keep her waiting. (*To Shimizu*): It was a pleasure. (*Exits.*)

KIN (*coming from the kitchen*): Kunio, a guest?

YŪ: It's Shimizu . . . Tokuichi.

KIN: Oh! (*To Shimizu*): How have you been? Understand you've made something of yourself in the city. Where you living now?

SHIMIZU: In Tokyo.

KIN: Remember me?

SHIMIZU (*laughing*): Of course I do.

KIN: Kunio, this gentleman was a classmate of Mr. Manabu since grade school. Studied hard and made a success of himself. (*To Shimizu*): Boy's just passed the test for high school. Can't afford to let him go, life the way it is and all, but Mr. Manabu says, "It's a waste, let him go." Was on the student council and everything, so. . . . Kikuo says. . . .

FUMI: You have to say who Kikuo is.

KIN: Older brother. Anyway, Kikuo only graduated from junior high school, so he says, "We're sending him no matter what!" Won't hear otherwise. Maybe you can help him find a job

---

made. The offering was subsequently divided among the parishioners, including the Kurihara family, who now share it with their guest.

*Here and elsewhere in the play, Manabu is called *Pika* or *Pika-san,* a sobriquet that derives from the word *pika-don,* literally "flash-bang," which is a Japanese diminutive for the atomic holocaust and the atomic bomb. By calling the bomb the *pika-don,* the Japanese have engaged in the same kind of psychological game U.S. planners played when they named the Hiroshima and Nagasaki bombs "Little Boy" and "Fat Man," attempting to bring them down to human scale. The nickname *Pika* is an ironic term of endearment, because it stigmatizes him by identifying him with the weapon and the event that have so hobbled his life. Regrettably, I have not been able to come up with an English equivalent of *Pika-san,* and so Manabu is referred to by his name throughout.

when he's finished. (*She bows respectfully.*) Kunio, you too. Get your head down, will you! (*She forces his head down.*) Really a country boy, you see. Doesn't even know the proper way to pay his respects. Done for if we don't send at least one boy up to Tokyo to make good. And your wife, is she from Tokyo?

SHIMIZU (*laughing*): I'm not married.

KIN: Still single? Single, really? (*Looking at Fumi*): You'd be just right for Fumi here.

FUMI: Please!

KUNIO: Mother!

KIN: Stay around for a while, all right? No reason to rush off. Got some delicious flounder to feed you. Fish from the Inland Sea's especially good. And flounder's at its best this time of year.

KUNIO: Mother!

KIN: Look after my boy, will you? Hard to find a good job around here. Man's got to go out to the city if he's going to make something of himself. Mr. Manabu made it all the way through Hiroshima Technical College, and he'd be section chief in some company by this time if it hadn't been for the bomb. Right, Mizz Kurihara? (*To Shimizu*): I remember how the two of you competed to be first at everything.

Shintani enters from the garden.

SHINTANI: Toku!

SHIMIZU: Oh!

KIN: See what a success he is!

YŪ: If Tsutomu were alive, he'd be the same age as you, Tadashi.

FUMI: Cut it out, Mother. There's no point in going on about the dead.

KIN: Mother's had a hard time of it. She's entitled to complain.

SHIMIZU: After the bomb and all, is Manabu all right?

YŪ: It's been more than three years since he had any symptoms.

SHIMIZU: It's wonderful how he survived.

KIN: I'm the one came back from Hiroshima with the news.

SHIMIZU: Then you were there, too?

KIN: No. Actually it was my sister. Killed by the bomb she was.

Close to the epicenter. Looked for her for two days. Never did find her.

SHIMIZU: Her school was just around the corner from the bus stop at Miyuki Bridge, wasn't it?

YŪ: Manabu was walking between Takanohashi and Daigakumae when the bomb fell. They say if he'd been just a little closer to the center, he'd never have made it.

SHINTANI: Takanohashi's almost exactly a kilometer and a half from the epicenter. According to statistics, everyone within a radius of one kilometer was killed; and up to four kilometers, your chances were fifty-fifty. Only the lucky ones survived.

YŪ: Thanks to the Buddha's saving grace.

KIN: What do you mean? Thanks to you! Mr. Manabu wouldn't be alive today if it weren't for you. When he got back from Ninoshima, he hardly looked human. Breath faint as some insect, and. . . . Skin on his back peeled off in sheets; maggots grew in the raw flesh.

YŪ: I get chills whenever I think about.

KIN: It was so terrible to look at, you couldn't walk in Hiroshima with your eyes open. Can't believe I spent two whole days there. Wouldn't do it again for all the money in the world. (*Pause. A shiver runs through her and she knits her brow.*) Looked into the face of every person I met. Weren't human.

SHIMIZU: You went there the day of the bomb?

KIN: Day after. On the evening of the sixth, the clog maker came back covered with wounds. An officer in the Second Army he was, so he got a ride back in a truck far as Kure. I took the first boat on the morning of the seventh, and when I got to Ujina, the wharf looked like something, you know, out of this world. Spent those two days, that day and the next, walking around Hiroshima looking for my sister.

SHIMIZU: And the radiation hadn't dissipated yet, either, had it?

KIN: No, must've breathed my share, too. Was there two whole days.

SHINTANI: A month later, the clog maker vomited blood and died.

YŪ: Plenty of people died on this island. The Enomoto sisters died—they were staying in the prefectural women's dorm—and Mr. Nakatani went on the fifth to see his son. He said he'd be right back, but he decided to stay the night. Just unlucky, I guess.

KIN: Could go on like that forever, but what's the point? Any normal person would faint if they saw the number of corpses scattered around that town. People who died with their bellies split open and their guts in their hands and all. . . . There's just no way to describe it. There were mothers died suckling their babies, and the children just went on sucking, not knowing. . . . (*She covers her face with both hands. An anguished sigh. She rubs her abdomen.*) I'd give anything to know no child of mine would meet a fate like that!

Pause. The sun is setting behind the mountains to the west, and the sky alone is red.

YŪ: It was unforgivable what America did. (*Pause.*)

SHINTANI: Now they've developed a bomb hundreds of times more powerful than the one they dropped on Hiroshima. A hydrogen bomb they call it.

KIN: Why do they build these things? Somebody should drop one on them and see how they like it. Then they'd understand.

YŪ: It doesn't matter who's the target, they must never use bombs like that again! How can they get away with it?

SHIMIZU (*to Fumi*): How was it your brother survived?

FUMI: Mother brought him back from Ninoshima.

KIN: Mr. Manabu? I'll tell you how. I'd been searching for my sister without any luck. Hadn't eaten anything and was a total wreck. Morning of the ninth, I was waiting for the ferry on the wharf at Ujina when someone working there says to me, "I'm supposed to tell someone from the island that a student from the Technical College named Kurihara went over to Ninoshima on the evening of the sixth. Ever heard of him?" Well, I forgot all about my sister and hightailed it back here. Early the next morning, Mizz Kurihara hired a small fishing boat and went by herself to get him. When she got back, I thought her eyes were going to pop out of her head: "If you're going to bring back stories, get them straight!" she says and starts crying and bawling me out. Don't think I've ever resented her the way I did then. There I was, crazy with grief because I couldn't find my sister, and here she comes only worried about herself!

YŪ: That's what you say, but I was beside myself! I spent all day every day just sitting in front of the altar. Manabu's voice kept ringing in my ears, calling me. So I thought I'd go looking for him one more time. This time the three of us went, Kin and Fumi and me. But we couldn't find him. "He probably died before he got to Ninoshima," the soldier there said and wouldn't pay us any mind. All he could say was Manabu's name didn't appear on his list.

KIN: No way to describe the way that place smelled, either.

FUMI: Their faces were all swollen, and—I don't know what you'd call it—they were moaning or groaning, and the ones with their eyes open glared at me as if they were ghosts and I was the one who'd damned them to hell! Oh, let's not talk about it anymore. I'll have nightmares for sure.

KIN: But you know mothers! Finally, she goes over to where they're burning this mountain of corpses and starts going through them with her hands like this. (*She imitates the movements.*)

YŪ: It was no way for human beings to meet their end. They were burning them like so much trash. (*She clasps her hands and intones the* nembutsu. *Pause.*) Well, I thought I'd try one last time, so I called, "Manabu! Manabu!" And you know what? This voice called back, "Mother!" (*Cries.*) And he raised his hand. . . . (*She is unable to go on. Pause.*)

KIN: Never been happier in our lives than we were at that moment. (*She also wipes away her tears.*)

SHINTANI: How dramatic!

YŪ: It's all because we've made regular temple pilgrimages. The Buddha led us to him.

KIN: Hah! Don't make me laugh. Then it must've been the Buddha let people suffer in the first place, just so's he could lead them out of suffering! Who needs Buddhas like that in the world?

YŪ: Go ahead and talk. You'll be sorry when you find yourself in hell.

KIN: No matter where I find myself once I'm dead, the point now is to live. Right, Fumi? (*Laughs.*)

KUNIO: Mother! (*He yanks her sleeve.*)

KIN (*pushing Kunio's head*): Seen and not heard, remember?

KIKUO (*from the kitchen*): Mother, come on, let's eat already.

KIN: Eat by yourself, you're not a child anymore. What have you got two hands for? Mother this and Mother that, can't I have a minute's peace? (*To Shimizu*): Well, guess I'd better. . . . Drop by and let's chat some more.

SHINTANI: Hey, Kikuo! Tomorrow all right?

KIKUO: No, I've got to work.

SHINTANI: Tomorrow's Sunday.

KIKUO: Doesn't make any difference.

SHINTANI: Anyway, we're meeting on the middle school field at noon. See if you can make it.

KIKUO: Okay.

All three members of the Kawashita family exit.

SHINTANI: Toku, maybe we should go too. I'm starved. (*He descends into the garden.*)

YŪ: Your grandmother must've been happy to see you! She's always talking about you. After all, she raised you like a wet nurse till your first birthday, you know.

SHIMIZU: Yes. I don't know how I'll ever repay that debt.

YŪ: Come back to the island and look after her.

SHIMIZU: It's not that the thought hasn't occurred to me. But there's no way I could take her up to Tokyo, and. . . . Well, give Manabu my regards.

YŪ: He'll be happy to know you're back.

The two men leave.

Yū sighs. A pause during which the silence becomes palpable, as when the wind has stopped blowing after a storm. The two women do not speak. As if regaining her senses, Yū goes to the altar, lights the evening lamp, and quietly begins to pray. Fumi nimbly ties the strings of her apron and tidies up the net and other implements. It is obvious from her ease and efficiency that she was been well trained by Yū.

YŪ (*closing the altar*): If he's alone all his life, it'll be so hard for him. Being a survivor he's not likely to find a wife, so. . . .
Fumi stares at her.

YŪ: The minute I stop praying, these passions well up in me.* (*She clasps her hands and once again begins intoning the* nembutsu. *Pause.*)

FUMI: You work yourself into such a state! (*Laughs.*) You'd think you actually enjoyed it!

YŪ (*changing her attitude*): Tokuichi's like a changed man!

FUMI: City life makes all the difference.

YŪ: If Manabu were only healthy like . . . .

FUMI: You make it sound like he'll never be able to accomplish anything.

YŪ: He'll be all right as long as I'm alive, but . . . .

FUMI: Mother, don't you think you ought to begin looking at it a little differently?

YŪ: That's what you say, . . .

FUMI: People think you're too hard. Nobody'd marry a man with a mother-in-law like you.

YŪ: Really? I thought it was the sister-in-law who was supposed to cause all the trouble. Anyway, I just wish some fine young woman would come to be Manabu's wife, that's all.

FUMI: Maybe Manabu has his own ideas on the subject.

YŪ (*after a pause*): Fumi, after you're married, I want to live with you.

FUMI: You want your son-in-law to carry on the family name?†

YŪ: That's not the point.

FUMI (*laughing*): Two for the price of one, is that it? It's all right with me if some man will have us.

---

*According to Buddhist doctrine, *bonnō* or passions are the source of man's attachment to this world and the principal obstacle to his release from the cycle of life (=suffering), death, and rebirth.

†It is not uncommon in Japan for a son-in-law to be adopted into his wife's family and to carry her family name, especially when there is no son in the family to do so.

YŪ: Well, for the time being, let's not think about it. Wait your turn a little longer, all right? Sounds like someone's at the door.

FUMI (*going to the entrance*): It's Reiko.

Kido Reiko enters after Fumi.

REIKO (*producing a gift*): My brother passed the high school entrance exam. This is just something to express our appreciation.*

YŪ: Oh, you really didn't have to.

REIKO: My parents say he did well because Mr. Kurihara was his teacher.

YŪ: Well, in that case, we'll accept on Manabu's behalf. Fumi, go buy some cakes or something for our guest.

Manabu returns. Fumi exits.

YŪ: Manabu, look what the Kidos sent.

MANABU: You didn't have to. Will you look at that! While other people are celebrating weddings, we're serving hand-me-downs from the dead! Get rid of that stuff, it's awful!

YŪ: You'll be punished for talking like that. (*But so saying she disposes of the sweets.*)

MANABU (*laughing*): I don't see how I could be punished more than I have been already! It was a real feast, Mother. Let me see, there was *sashimi* of tuna and sea bass, broiled snapper, clear soup, sea eel vinaigrette, and deep fried shrimp and shrimp broiled on skewers. There were shellfish braised in the shell and cuttlefish, too. Then there was a stew and fish and vegetables wrapped in rice and seaweed. Oh, and there was octopus, too.

REIKO: Did you eat all that?

MANABU: I suppose I did. I left early because all the food was gone.

YŪ: You'd better take some stomach medicine right now. I don't know why you can't control yourself.

MANABU: My upbringing, I guess.

---

*The Japanese school year begins in April. Entrance examination results are usually announced in late February and March.

YŪ (*laughing*): The women are probably still talking about you in the kitchen! "And he's a school teacher, too!"

MANABU: It just shows I'm healthy. You ought to be happy!

YŪ: Can I fix you a little tea with rice?

MANABU (*laughing*): See what I mean!

Reiko joins in his laughter. After a moment, Yū realizes what she's said and also laughs out loud.

YŪ: Parents! Just fools for our children, I guess.

MANABU: And here I thought there was no one wiser!

Yū goes to the kitchen.

REIKO: Open it. I'll bet you can't guess what it is. I picked it out myself. In Hiroshima.

MANABU (*opening the package*): Oh!

REIKO: Try it on.

Manabu holds a white turtleneck sweater up to his shoulders.

REIKO: Look! (*She produces a matching sport coat from the box.*)

MANABU (*going to the kitchen*): Mother!

YŪ: My word! Have you opened it already? It must have been expensive! Beautiful. (*She touches it.*)

MANABU (*exaggerating*): Hey, you'll soil it! (*Returning from the kitchen*): Thank your parents for me.

REIKO: Was the bride beautiful?

MANABU: She was really quite something, all decked out in Japanese style like that. I wonder how you'd look dressed like that? A little like a doll, I suppose, Even a homely woman looks beautiful in a wedding kimono.

REIKO: I beg your pardon!

MANABU: Her hair was up in a *shimada,* I think you call it. The only trouble was, it sort of lost its charm when you realized it was a wig.

REIKO: Some women don't have much charm to lose. Us homely ones in particular!

MANABU: What's wrong with you all of a sudden? (*Laughing*): That's not what I meant at all.

REIKO: Who cares!

MANABU: Don't be silly, now. I was talking about Morita's new wife.

REIKO: You shouldn't talk about a friend's new wife like that.

MANABU: But it's the truth. What am I supposed to do?

REIKO: When I was a child, my biggest dream was to wear a bride's hood. "What do you want to be when you grow up, Reiko?" people would ask me, and I'd say, "A bride!" (*She smiles.*) Even now, when I see a woman dressed like that, I get goose bumps all over.

MANABU: We'd better find you a husband, quick.

REIKO: You're awful!

MANABU: But, you know, it's really symbolic how brides wear hoods at their weddings—it's as if they were going out of their way to draw attention to the fact that women are supposed to be jealous creatures with horns.* It's as if they were saying, "Today I'm covering them up, but tomorrow watch out!" They purse their lips and look so innocent during the ceremony, but . . . . Ah, poor, downtrodden male-kind!

REIKO: Don't you think you're overdoing it? You've got to make everything seem so logical or you're not satisfied.

MANABU: I just have this thirst for knowledge, that's all. Let's find out where the idea came from. (*He takes a dictionary from the alcove.*) Let's see. Ah, here it is, "Bride's hood: A type of headdress worn by women in ancient times during temple pilgrimages to signify the suppression of jealousy." See, that's what I said.

REIKO: Terrific.

MANABU: "The word has now come to signify the headdress worn by brides during the wedding ceremony." What do you know, it has its origin in temple pilgrimages. Temple pilgrimages and brides! (*He laughs.*) When you think of it, it's really quite wonderful. If once in her life a women presents a comely, modest appearance, what's wrong with that?

REIKO: Deep down you're really feudalistic, you know that! (*She laughs coquettishly.*)

MANABU (*ducking the criticism with a laugh*): What about you, Reiko? You'll have an arranged marriage, I suppose.

REIKO: I wonder? (*Laughing*): What about you?

---

*The hood worn by Japanese brides is called a *tsuno-kakushi* or "horn concealer."

MANABU: Mine will be a love match, of course. How could I leave something that important to a third party?

REIKO: Even in the case of an arranged marriage, the couple get to know each other for six months or a year before they actually tie the knot.

MANABU: But before they even meet, things have been pretty much decided.

REIKO: Of course. After all, it's a once-in-a-lifetime thing. It can't be left to the whim of a moment.

MANABU: The problem is that too often the focus isn't on the individuals but on the social status of the two families, their finances, and the like. Your family must be like that.

REIKO: Maybe. Nothing's decided without the approval of my grandfather. He's like our own private emperor.

MANABU: I guess that means that even if there was someone you really liked, you wouldn't necessarily be able to marry him.

REIKO: If push came to shove, I wouldn't give in so easily. And if I still couldn't have my way, I'd run away.

MANABU: You would?

REIKO: What kind of a student of Kurihara Manabu would I be if I didn't? (*She laughs.*)

MANABU: Good for you! But it's easier said than done. At the very least it seems clear that the man you're likely to choose is not going to fit the bill as far as your family is concerned.

REIKO: Not necessarily.

MANABU: For example, let's take Mr. Mōri.

REIKO: Mr. Mōri?

MANABU: Just as an example. The first question that will come up is whether he's really a descendant of Mōri Motonari.* Someone will be sent to his home village to investigate. They'll discover that his father is a cabinet maker. And right then and there he'll be disqualified, because regardless of what an outstanding individual he is or how bright his future

*Mōri Motonari (1497-1571) was a warrior chieftain who consolidated much of the Hiroshima area under his control in the sixteenth century.

as a painter might be, the fact of the matter is that no mere
carpenter is likely to be a descendant of Mōri Motonari.

REIKO (*laughing*): And if it were you?

MANABU: I wouldn't last a minute either.

REIKO: Why?

MANABU: Well, for starters, I don't have any money, and my
family can't match yours in status, either. The Kidos are an
old and venerable breed.

REIKO: I suppose so. But how did our old and venerable breed
come to be?

MANABU: Well, maybe you're only half-breeds.

REIKO: I'm serious.

MANABU: So am I. Just consider the history of the island. In the
beginning it was half farmers and half fishermen. Then in the
twelfth century the Heike fled the capital and some of the
warriors came here and fathered children, half-breeds, just
like the Occupation soldiers today. Eventually, their children
and their children's children started lording it over everybody,
claiming they were descendants of the warrior class.

REIKO (*laughing*): You're just making that up!

MANABU: The point is, "old and venerable" really doesn't
mean much of anything. For all we know, "Kido" may only
mean that your ancestors were doormen for the Heike!* (*He
laughs.*)

REIKO: What do you mean?

MANABU (*improvising*): One night . . . a dark, moonless night it
was, Taira Kiyomori disguised himself and went out to have a
little fun with the ladies. As everyone knows, he was a master
of disguise. Well, dawn eventually arrived, and Kiyomori returned home, humming a tune and feeling fine. Just then, as
he was about to go through the gate, the doorkeeper, someone with a nondescript name like Tagosaku or Kichibei,
grabbed him by the scruff of the neck. What a sight! So
Kiyomori says, "Look, keep this secret and I'll reward you
with a surname. From now on your family will be called
Kido!" Maybe that's how your family began!

---

*Kido means "wooden door."

Reiko laughs, amused.

MANABU (*after a pause*): Reiko, what sort of man would you like for a husband?

REIKO (*laughing*): A man like you.

MANABU: Forget about me.

REIKO: Why? Because of our families?

MANABU: Because of the bomb.

REIKO: What difference does that make? What matters are the feelings of the individuals concerned, right? (*She laughs.*) I've got a thing for you, you know. (*She gazes at him coquettishly.*)

MANABU (*taken aback, as if blinded by a bright light*): Ah, to be blessed . . . .

REIKO: What?

MANABU: Hm? Oh, with good students.

YŪ (*entering from the kitchen*): Toku dropped by a minute ago.

MANABU: Who?

YŪ: Tokuichi.

MANABU: Shimizu? Really?

Kunio enters. Fumi brings in tea and cakes.

FUMI: He's become a real gentleman.

REIKO (*to Fumi*): I'm just leaving.

FUMI: Oh, stay a while.

REIKO: I'll be back tomorrow and I'll have more time.

YŪ: Tell everyone we say hello.

Yū sees Reiko out.

FUMI: Manabu, why don't you quit teaching and put your skills to better use.

MANABU: Maybe I should.

FUMI: Reiko's really something. She only went to grade school, and look at her.

YŪ: Why don't you go to work for the NBC, too? The pay's the best around.

MANABU: It's hard consorting with common folk like you. Before you know it, the conversation always turns to money. Right, Kunio?

Manabu takes a fountain pen and a paper plaque from the top of the desk.

MANABU (*to Kunio*): This is in honor of your entering high school. It's my favorite pen.

KUNIO: Thanks!

MANABU: Take this, too.

KUNIO (*looking at the plaque*): "Man is but a thinking reed. Pascal."

MANABU (*after a pause*): Be of good heart, and don't give up no matter what, you hear?

KUNIO: Yes sir.

MANABU: If you've got the ability, there's nothing to be afraid of. Just take things in stride.

KUNIO (*his eyes shining*): Just watch me. You won't be disappointed.

Ōura enters.

ŌURA: Kunio, go get your father and tell him that Mr. Ōura wants to see him.

KUNIO: Father's not home.

ŌURA: What about Kikuo?

KUNIO: He's there. (*Exits.*)

ŌURA: Fumi, rub my shoulders, will you? Congratulations, Manabu. The percentage of students being admitted to high school is up.

MANABU: It was a relief when I found that out. The students who went on the job market also seem to have done reasonably well.

ŌURA: Teachers really have it made: they get a monthly salary and have everyone in their debt as well! (*Fumi is massaging his shoulders.*) That's it, right there. How old are you now, anyway?

FUMI: Twenty-two.

ŌURA: You'd best be getting married soon. Leave everything to me. You just look after your mother.

YŪ: Did your discussion with the chief of police go all right?

ŌURA: It cost me a pretty penny.

YŪ: You'd better be careful.

ŌURA: Yeah, well, they figure it's all in the line of duty. (*He laughs.*) "We'll look the other way. Just see that the job gets done."

YŪ: Don't take any unnecessary chances, you hear?

ŌURA: Just because you're my sister, don't worry yourself. The problem is the people on this island are so low-down. These anonymous letters are the worst of all. Manabu, you have to give your students a better moral education. People misunderstand democracy, that's the problem! I was just joking about it with the Chief today—we live in a world where school teachers go on strike!* Right, Manabu? In the old days, teachers were the most respected people in town. Nowadays they're just a bunch of troublemakers.

Kikuo and Kunio enter from the kitchen.

ŌURA: First they're striking, then they're against the war. Don't they understand that it's because of the war in Korea that Japan is finally getting back on its feet? They spout all these theories when they don't even know the price of rice, but would they work and sweat for a living? Look at my hands. They've known as much honest labor as any pair you're likely to see! Right, Yū?

YŪ: Kikuo's here.

ŌURA: How many torpedoes are there left at Kamegasaki?

KIKUO: Just one.

ŌURA: Things are all set with the police. You can go ahead and dismantle it. It'll be trouble if the Occupation forces come sniffing around.

KIKUO: Okay. But I need a tank of oxygen for the torch.

ŌURA: I'll call Kure right away. Pick it up early in the morning.

KIKUO: What about men to carry it out of the cave?

ŌURA: Just leave it where it is. We've got to keep this a secret or there'll be trouble. Make sure you keep that in mind. Tell your father—you can work on the pieces once you've got the thing apart; the important thing now is to make sure nobody can tell it's a torpedo. (*He takes a thousand-yen bill from his wallet.*) It's not much, but this is for Kunio's matriculation. He's come this far, so I'll do what I can to look after him, but I can't be expected to do everything. If your brother's going to school, you'll have to work twice as hard to cover for him.

KIKUO: Yes, sir. Thank you very much

ŌURA (*following him*): Be careful, you hear!

Kikuo and Kunio exit.

---

*The Japan Teachers Union (*Nikkyōso*) has been one of the most militant unions in postwar Japan.

ŌURA: Kin and Shichirō really know how to raise kids. Those are two fine boys.

KIN (*entering*): Thank you very much for the gift.

ŌURA: That's all right. Anytime you need a little help, just let me know.

KIN: Thank you . . . . Mizz Kurihara, Kojima Ume just got fired by the Occupation.

YŪ: Why?

KIN: Caught her trying to walk off with a bar of brass tied to her leg.

YŪ: I just met her mother the other day at the temple. She was so happy Ume'd finally found a job.

KIN: Been going to Kure for six months as a day laborer before she finally got hired.

YŪ: You see, that's what it means to be mortal: all our effort's for nothing. One day our children make us happy; the next we're drenched in tears.

Pause.

ŌURA: If Shichirō were working for the Occupation, he'd do the same thing.

KIN: Shichi'd never . . . .

ŌURA: Hunger makes thieves of us all.

KIN: One bar of brass more or less ain't going to hurt the United States of America, why'd they have to fire her? Lots of people do it, I guess she was just unlucky. If Shichi got fired now, we'd have to kill ourselves, children and all.

ŌURA: None of this would happen if people'd just do as I tell them.

KIN: They say you're all right if you've got a skill, but Shichi worked for ten years at the arsenal, and I never knew what he did. How was I supposed to know my husband was an expert at disarming torpedoes? Not the kind of work just anyone can do, you know.

ŌURA: You'd better keep your mouth shut about that outside this house.

KIN: A special skill, it is. (*She laughs venally.*) He's worth more than what you're paying him.

ŌURA: Relax. I'll see you don't go hungry.

YŪ: You seem a lot better off these days, don't you, Kin?

KIN: At least we're out of debt. For the Boys' Festival in May, I'm going to cook up two whole pecks of rice and let the kids eat their fill. Going to get Shichi a bottle of good number two sake and let him drink till he's up to his gills, too.

YŪ: Good for you.

KIN: Just wait and see: won't be long before I take you for that pilgrimage to Kyoto.

YŪ: I'm counting on it.

ŌURA: Don't I deserve something after all I've done for you?

KIN: Let me see now . . . maybe I could fix you up with a woman? (*She laughs uproariously.*)

ŌURA: Don't be stupid! (*Laughter.*)

YŪ: You've been working since you were a child. It's about time life got a little easier for you.

ŌURA: Think of me as your boat in troubled waters. Rely on me.

YŪ: You go around hawking sardines with a belly like that—it's a wonder you don't have a miscarriage.

KIN: Wish I would. Had my fill of kids.

ŌURA: People who've had their fill of kids shouldn't get pregnant.

KIN: What can you do? They're a gift from heaven.

YŪ: What about contraceptives? They're all the rage these days, you know.

ŌURA: You'd think you'd be done with the whole business at your age.

KIN: Be year after next exactly.

ŌURA: Forty? It'll be two or three years more than that!

FUMI: How many does this one make?

KIN: Nine, counting the two that died.

FUMI (*involuntarily*): Nine! (*She laughs.*)

ŌURA: Strong as an ox, that's what you are.

KIN: But feeling my age, I am. Lot harder than when I was young. (*She displays her leg.*) Look at this. Varicose veins.

YŪ: Kin, you're covered with bruises!

KIN: First time it happened. (*She rubs her legs.*)

ŌURA (*to Fumi*): That's enough. Thanks. (*To Kin*): I already told Kikuo tomorrow's an early day. All right? Here, this is for the movies. (*He gives Fumi a hundred yen and exits.*)

FUMI (*after a pause*): Don't you think you should have a doctor take a look at your legs?

KIN (*laughing*): Can't be going to the doctor every time I get pregnant! The fuss young women make these days over having a baby, getting themselves admitted to the hospital and all. If you pamper yourself too much, Fumi, you just make it harder. In the old days, people used to work on the beach right up until they started to hurt. (*Pause.*) When you have a minute, take Kunio out to buy his school uniform, will you? Parents got no education. Just have to rely on you.

YŪ (*to Manabu*): Come spring vacation, you stick around and take it easy, too, hear?

KIN: Reminds me of when Mr. Manabu graduated to the First Middle School. So proud I was, like he was my own. Never dreamed a boy of mine would be going to high school! (*Laughing*): Saying the same thing to Shichi last night, and you know what he said? "Kin, you must've got knocked up by somebody beside me!" I could've killed him!

MANABU: Hey, watch your language! I'm still single, you know!

KIN (*referring to Manabu*): Mizz Kurihara, now *there's* something to look forward to!

YŪ: Isn't there some nice young woman around for him?

KIN: Ask me, Miss Kido's got her eye on him.

MANABU (*only half in jest*): You think so too, eh?

KIN: Will you listen to that?! (*She laughs.*)

FUMI: Ah, youth! So carefree!

KIN: Why, Miss Fumi! (*She laughs uproariously.*) Don't make me laugh! The baby's going to move! (*She holds her belly and dissolves into laughter.*)

Yū is about to be infected by the levity, but her expression changes gradually as if she were imagining the trials that lie ahead. She looks at Manabu as Kin continues to laugh.
Blackout.

SCENE 2. A HILLTOP, THE FOLLOWING DAY.

The next day: Sunday morning atop a high hill. Ordinarily one can see the mountains of Shikoku beyond the capes and small islands to the south (upstage center), but today the spring mist obscures the view.

Looking north, to the right are the port of Kure and what remains of its arsenal; while beyond the mountains of Etajima in the foreground, Nijima and Ujina should be visible. It is one of those deforested mountains common in the Inland Sea, but here among the bushes and miscanthus reeds, still covered as they are with last year's withered foliage, the stumps of the pines cut down by the navy during the war are particularly obtrusive. It is spring. The trees are in bud; the lone cherry tree to the right is in bloom; and wisps of mist rise from the ground all around. Amidst the sound of motorized sail boats, their wakes like lines drawn on the surface of the sea, and the calls of larks soaring into the sky, every now and then the calm is pierced by the metallic sound of the Ise, the former flagship of the Imperial Japanese Navy, being torn apart for scrap.

On the slope upstage left, beyond the bushes, Mōri is painting at an easel. On the slope in the foreground, the well-worn path that leads across the stage forks at stage left. Nature, man, and birds all radiate a feverish energy as they compete in reclaiming life long suppressed. As if incited by the larks she has been watching soar into the sky, Reiko, who is seated near Mōri, begins to imitate their calls. Gradually their voices become a symphony, but Reiko cannot compete with the larks, and her voice slowly skews out of tune.

MŌRI: You a lark or a locust?
Reiko stops, looks at Mōri, and bursts out laughing until she is all but rolling on the ground.
MŌRI: Ah, to be young again!
REIKO: Don't make me laugh so much! It hurts! (*She cannot stop laughing.*)
MŌRI (*in a falsetto*): Mommy! (*He gestures like a child who needs to urinate.*)
REIKO: Oh, that hurt! Mr. Mōri, you're so uncouth! How do you expect people to believe you're a teacher?
MŌRI: All right, so I'm uncouth. Kurihara has enough couth for both of us!
REIKO (*sticking out her tongue*): Blah!
MŌRI (*imitating*): Blah yourself!
REIKO: I'll show you! (*She pounces on him.*)
Kawashita Kunio enters stage right, carrying a kettle and a bundle. He is wearing a new school uniform.

KUNIO: Hello! Beautiful spot, Mr. Mōri!

MŌRI: What does a junior high school pupil know?

KUNIO: High school student! Please, show a little respect!

MŌRI: What are you up to?

KUNIO: Filial piety. You know what they say: don't put off 'til tomorrow. I'm different from you, see. I'm looking after my parents while they're still able to enjoy it.

MŌRI (*with excessive gravity*): I'll be more careful in the future, your honor.

KUNIO: Here, have some tea. You must be thirsty.

MŌRI: Thanks.

KUNIO: It's about time you were married, too, Mr. Mōri. Leave it to me; I'll find you a good wife.

Laughing, Mōri pours himself the tea.

KUNIO: That's enough! There won't be any for my father!

MŌRI: Ah! That was good!

KUNIO: What a glutton!

MŌRI: How do you like it?

KUNIO: What's the big deal? All you ever paint is the sea. (*He compares the painting with the landscape.*)

While this has been going on, Reiko has been watching the sea. Shintani and Shimizu enter from stage left, climbing the slope in the foreground. Shimizu stops and takes in the view with obvious pleasure. The only sounds are the larks and a puttering boat in the distance.

SHIMIZU: That's funny.

SHINTANI: What?

SHIMIZU: What happened to all the pine trees?

SHINTANI: The navy cut them down for air raid shelters.

SHIMIZU: Really?

SHINTANI: Sailors from the *Ise* cut them down. (*He points down below.*) They've just about finished dismantling her, but the battleship *Ise* used to be anchored down there off that shore. Beyond the cape, there used to be cruisers, and there were aircraft carriers and submarines off Nekojima. A formation of planes from American carriers sank them all. The planes came in low over Shikoku, and then "Bang!" dive-bombed from here. (*He demonstrates with his hand.*) You should've seen it! (*With both hands.*) Tat-tat-tat–tat-tat-tat!!!! The *Ise* blasted away with antiaircraft fire, but . . . .

Shimizu is staring down below.
There is the sound of hammers from the shore. Kunio looks in the
direction of the voices.
SHINTANI: Feels like we're out on maneuvers.
SHIMIZU: They didn't have to cut down all the trees.
SHINTANI: Yeah, a real waste.
SHIMIZU: We're . . . I mean, what's the point of a park without
   trees? . . . It really makes me mad. It doesn't even look like a
   park anymore!
SHINTANI: And there isn't even anyone to complain to, either.
SHIMIZU: Damn! Wars have no respect for people's memories.
   (*With a self-derisive laugh.*) We used to get drenched with sweat
   playing hide-and-seek up here, and then we'd sit under the
   trees and a cool breeze would blow off the sea . . . . There's
   not even a patch of shade left for god's sake! We used to blow
   bubbles with a mixture made from pine sap and swing from
   the trees like Tarzan . . . .
SHINTANI: You were our leader and got us into all kinds of
   trouble. Digging up potatoes in the farmer's field and eating
   them. . . .
SHIMIZU: I remember that!
SHINTANI: Everything I know about trouble I learned from you.
SHIMIZU: I'll bet.
SHINTANI: My old lady used to bawl me out like you wouldn't
   believe. "Why can't you be more like Manabu!" she used to
   say. To this day, I can't look him in the eye.
SHIMIZU: He sure loved to study!
SHINTANI: It's hard to believe he and Tsutomu were brothers.
   Tsutomu was really gung-ho when he went off for training
   with the navy. "I'm going to blow me a battleship clear out of
   the water!" he said. The two of us came here to sing military
   songs and watch the sun rise the morning he left to join up:
   "You and I, my friend/ Cherry blossoms, blooming together/
   Our great land to defend/ Ready to fall, in stormy weather/
   Dying like men/ Comrades to the end!"
KUNIO: Hey, Tadashi. You been talking to crazy old Yamaoka
   again? (*He twirls his finger at his temple to indicate insanity.*)
SHINTANI (*turning toward Kunio*): Well, look who's here! And
   Mr. Mōri, too. (*As if blinded*): Hey, watch out! You're going to

blind somebody with that insignia! I didn't recognize you decked out like that!

KUNIO (*giving tit for tat*): Just goes to show you, "Clothes make the man!" (*He bows perfunctorily to Shimizu.*)

SHINTANI (*laughing*): You'll get it all dirty before the matriculation ceremony!

KUNIO: What, this old rag?

SHINTANI: You on your way to Kamegasaki?

KUNIO (*affirmatively*): Mm. (*He exits down the slope stage left.*)

SHIMIZU: He must be on cloud nine.

SHINTANI: He's got what it takes, that's for sure. He's the toughest kid around in a scrap, too. And he's captain of the volleyball team. As a matter of fact, he's just like you when you were his age!

SHIMIZU: In my time sons of fishermen didn't go to high school.*

SHINTANI: They're better off now: his father's making a pretty good living disarming torpedoes, and Kin's a real worker, too.

SHIMIZU: Torpedoes?

SHINTANI: They disarm torpedoes over at Kamegasaki.

SHIMIZU: Navy torpedoes?

SHINTANI: Yeah, there's such a demand for scrap metal because of the war in Korea, people on the island will do just about anything for it. The fishermen spend more time looking for scrap than schools of fish.

SHIMIZU: I feel like Rip Van Winkle!

SHINTANI: How old were you when you left the island?

SHIMIZU: Almost eighteen.

SHINTANI: You're the same age as Manabu, right?

SHIMIZU: Yeah, Kurihara was born in 1926. The first kindergarten was started the year before we began school.

SHINTANI: What does that make you, kindergarten pioneers?

SHIMIZU (*laughing*): Not me. I wasn't allowed. I just watched the other children through the fence, standing in a circle,

---

*Shimizu is speaking here of the prewar educational system, where "middle school" was roughly equivalent to the postwar high school and was principally for young men preparing for college.

singing: "Children of Shōwa, Shōwa, Shōwa, all!"* I still remember the song.

SHINTANI: We learned it, too. "Mountain, mountain, Fuji Mountain/ Strong in body, strong in soul!"

He looks at Shimizu, who is trying to hold back his tears.

SHIMIZU: Kurihara's mother deserves a lot of the credit, but it didn't hurt that his uncle's rich, either.

SHINTANI: Ōura paid his way through Technical College, didn't he?

SHIMIZU: I at least wanted to go to high school. Until I was twenty, all I wanted was to be like Kurihara.

SHINTANI: Why until you were twenty?

SHIMIZU: What? Oh, I was twenty when the war ended. After that, the good of the workers became my . . . . (*He stops in midsentence.*) Where are you working these days?

SHINTANI: NBC.

SHIMIZU: NBC? An American company?

SHINTANI: The president is. In the old shipyard. Look, see that ship in the number four dock?

SHIMIZU: They make war materiel?

SHINTANI: No, it's just a regular civilian company. The initials stand for "National Bulk Carrier." It specializes in building tankers. That one there will be ready to launch in May, and is it ever huge! Forty thousand tons. They say the future's in tankers, not passenger ships anymore.

SHIMIZU: Then they must be hiring a lot of people?

SHINTANI: Not exactly. The equipment's different—you know, from Japanese companies. Every now and then they hire part-time people, but otherwise . . . .

SHIMIZU: I wonder if Kurihara wouldn't be better off if he'd quit teaching and go to work for NBC.

SHINTANI: They only take new graduates for technicians. It's hard to get in through the front door. And what about the physical? He may seem healthy, but after all he does have A-bomb disease.

---

*Shōwa is the name of the period of Emperor Hirohito's reign, 1926–.

SHIMIZU: Isn't there some place in the old arsenal he could find a job?

SHINTANI: There are so many people out of work, you know.

. . .

SHIMIZU: What are the people on the island doing for a living anyhow?

SHINTANI: Part-time work for the Occupation mostly. Even at that, people have to commute to the employment office two and three months, sometimes as long as six months, and even then they don't always get hired.

SHIMIZU: How do they make ends meet?

Voices singing a school song are heard upstage left:

Misty island moutains shimmer,
Waking to spring's first glimmer;
Or golden dragon shapes' ballet,
Moonlit waters of the bay.
Our native land, by nature blessed,
You nurture us to do our best,
We who live nestled in your breast!

SHINTANI: Somebody's singing the school song. (*The two men listen in silence.*)

The monotonous sound of a boat's motor and the calls of the larks. And as if to rend the quiet, the sound of hammers. Pause.

SHINTANI: It's so peaceful. Hard to believe the atomic bomb exploded right over there, in the sky over Hiroshima.

SHIMIZU: Instead of dismantling torpedoes and working part-time, if only the old arsenal were still in operation, everyone on the island could work without worrying.

SHINTANI: The economy won't pick up until Japan rearms, that's all there is to it.

SHIMIZU: We should start trading with Red China.

SHINTANI: Toku, you a Communist?

SHIMIZU: Why do you ask?

SHINTANI: The Communist Party used to distribute handbills saying that. Not a bad idea in the long run, but it's not going to put food on the table today.

REIKO: Mr. Kurihara! (*She runs off stage right.*)

SHINTANI: Manabu?

After a few moments, Manabu enters with Reiko.

SHINTANI: Manabu!

SHIMIZU: It's been a long time!

SHINTANI: Toku and I were just on our way to visit Tsutomu's grave.

SHIMIZU: It was terrible he had to die so young.

MANABU: He was in a big hurry to get it over with, I guess.

SHIMIZU: You sure look healthy, though!

MANABU: I'm all right. At least I can still enjoy the fresh air.

SHINTANI: Manabu's the most conscientious teacher in the junior high. Every student in his class got into high school, you know.

SHIMIZU: I had no idea you were teaching junior high school.

MANABU: I got hooked into it because I thought I wouldn't have to work so hard!

SHIMIZU: Maybe teaching is the best job for someone with your condition.

MANABU: You make it sound like all we do is lounge around. I'd better quit before it ruins my reputation completely!

SHINTANI: If you quit, Manabu, the kids are the ones who'll suffer.

MANABU: Keep it up, flattery will get you everywhere! I guess I'm just a sucker for punishment. Tonight, for example, a boy from Kannonzaki is leaving for Osaka, so I'm walking all this way just to say good-bye. All I want is to prevent these kids from winding up like me. I can't help becoming emotionally involved. They're human beings, after all.

SHIMIZU: But you've been all right?

MANABU: All things considered. It's not every man who's been to hell and back as I have. So, what brings you to this neck of the woods?

SHIMIZU: Well, I've been living with my nose to the grindstone since the war, you know, and I thought I'd like to see the island where I grew up, that's all. I had to come as far as Himeji on business anyway, so. . . .

SHINTANI: He says he was setting up a crane.

MANABU: If memory, serves, you were working for Ishikawa-jima.

SHIMIZU: Until last year I was, but I only made it out of electrician's school in Ototane, so . . . . Beginning this year, I'm working for a subcontractor. You graduated from the Technical College. What a waste.

MANABU: The boondocks haven't changed a bit, I'll bet.

SHINTANI: He says he feels like Rip Van Winkle.

SHIMIZU: I wonder if wars accelerate history?

MANABU: I'd better get off, this island, too, before it's too late. You begin to degenerate if you stay on an island like this too long.

SHIMIZU: I remember, it was the day of the Kiyomori Festival. I was a first-year student in higher primary school.* I was part of the festival procession, all dressed up in a black, crested kimono and formal skirt with a sword stuck in my sash. We'd just reached the foot of the temple steps, when you showed up looking dashing in your high school uniform. I ran home like I was on fire and climbed up here and yelled at the top of my lungs, "Kurihara, I'll beat you yet!" (*Laughs.*) Now it seems funny, but I was bawling like a baby. That was twelve years ago.

MANABU: Now you're the one who's shown up looking dashing.

SHIMIZU (*starting to laugh*): To be honest, when I heard you were teaching junior high school, I was sort of relieved—relieved and a little disappointed.

MANABU (*forcing a smile*): Maybe you're the reason I got hit by the atomic bomb—you put a hex on me.

SHIMIZU: Maybe so. (*He laughs with Manabu.*) The saddest thing about coming up here, though, is that there isn't a single tree left. It's as if the navy robbed us of everything we had—and then some. The whole place seems like a gaping wound left by the war.

MANABU: I guess you've got a point. It takes someone from outside to notice. We'll have to come up here and replant, won't we, Tadashi?

---

*In the prewar period, students not going on to college went to higher primary school instead of middle school.

Shintani does not answer.

MANABU: No sense of civic responsibility, that's his problem. (*To Shintani*): No matter what I teach my students, this island's not going anyplace if you grownups don't set an example.

SHINTANI: Worry less and live longer, that's what I say.

SHIMIZU: I can see you've got your work cut out for you.

MANABU: Oh, it's not as bad as all that. We have our ways.

SHIMIZU: In Tokyo, if you protest against the bomb, you get yourself arrested.

MANABU (*laughing*): City folk have a way of letting things get out of hand.

SHIMIZU (*with a laugh*): Maybe so.

MANABU: Tokyoites have a short fuse. At the drop of a hat, they're out in the street waving red flags! There must be a subtler way to protest.

SHIMIZU (*laughing*): Maybe, but one more atomic bomb and we're all done for.

MANABU: Try getting bombed: it makes you patient.

SHIMIZU: It takes two to tango.

MANABU: That's true, but maybe without realizing it you're allowing the other side to lead.

Shimizu is silent.

MANABU: That's what happened in the Red Purge.*

SHIMIZU (*giving Manabu a momentary look*): That . . . America did that because it was getting ready for the Korean War.

MANABU: I wonder if that isn't the problem, always shifting responsibility to the other side like that? (*Laughing*): You've become a real firebrand, though, haven't you!

SHIMIZU: Not really. (*Pause.*) Right now, America's threatening to use the atomic bomb in Korea. What do you think of that, as someone who's experienced the bomb?

---

*The "Red Purge," so named because it involved a reversal of the Occupation's policy of purging Japan's wartime leaders from public life and applied purge techniques instead to Communists and fellow travelers, began in late 1949 in anticipation of the Korean War and continued through 1950, eventually leading to the dismissal of about 22,000 workers in the public and private sector. Manabu's remark here implies that Japanese leftists did not take the initiative in responding to the purge, but simply reacted to Occupation policies.

MANABU: Not everyone who experienced the bomb feels the same. If you're asking my personal opinion, I don't think America will use it again.

Shimizu looks at him dubiously.

MANABU: Maybe they will drop it. I'm no prophet. But the human . . . instinct I guess you'd call it, the instinct for survival that's a fundamental part of human nature will win out in the end, I think.

SHIMIZU: I'm not sure I understand.

MANABU: Maybe you have to have experienced the bomb to understand. As long as country is divided against country, each vying for power, I don't think we'll ever have peace.

SHINTANI: Gandhi's Manabu's idol.

Shimizu is silent.

MANABU: What I'm trying to say is that I don't think people are really reading the constitution, Japan's peace constitution.* Postwar Japan is a pacifist state, you know.

SHIMIZU: But the fact of the matter is Japan's rearming. Don't you have to recognize that?

MANABU: "Nonviolent resistance," "truth and nonviolence": on the face of it it may not seem like much, but in point of fact there's never been a philosophy more deeply trustful of humanity. I think Gandhi was the greatest optimist who ever lived.

SHIMIZU: I wonder if that sort of religious faith is a match for the bomb?

MANABU: I'm not talking about blind religious faith. Look, one of my first students graduated from high school this year, and his father had his heart set on his going to the Defense College and wouldn't listen to anything the boy had to say. So the boy came to see me. I was against the idea, of course, but one thing led to another and he wound up running away from home, and eventually he entered the engineering department at Hiroshima University, which is what he wanted to do in

---

*The postwar Japanese Constitution is known as a "peace constitution" because in its famous Article 9 it renounces war as an instrument of national policy.

the first place. It's in kids like him that I place my hopes. You know: "From a tiny acorn, a mighty oak shall grow"? That's what I believe, so I try to educate the children. The future belongs to mankind, absolutely!

SHIMIZU: That's the whole point of education, isn't it? It seems sort of smug.

MANABU: Smug?

SHIMIZU: This island. The island's junior high school. I sense a certain self-satisfaction in your willingness to accept those limits.

Manabu does not respond.

SHIMIZU: The kid you describe had the economic wherewithal, and that's why things went as they did. But in the real world there are a lot of problems that can't be solved—no matter how much conscientious teachers like you prod and cajole.

MANABU: Of course. I understand that much.

SHIMIZU: Right now, at this moment, there is mist rising from the sea. It's a peaceful spring day. But for all we know, at this instant, beyond the horizon in Korea, thousands of people are being subjected to saturation bombing and running for their lives. How many parents must there be slaving for their children, not knowing that in a matter of hours they'll be killed? What kind of power is it that kills these people? On this island, you're dismantling war ships and torpedoes. You're wielding hammers to make a living. Japan springs back to life while across the sea people are dying in Korea. What's behind all these things?

MANABU: What?

SHIMIZU: The point is, how do you fight it? One false move, and it's the end of the human race.

MANABU: You're in too much of a hurry. You want to think of everything in terms of some fictitious ideal society. Mankind has progressed this far by resolving contradictions one at a time.

SHIMIZU: Until the appearance of the bomb.

MANABU: The appearance of the bomb has made that process all the more crucial. The problem is how to trust in the very human intelligence that released "the power of the sun." After all, atomic energy is a human creation.

SHIMIZU: Maybe . . . .

MANABU: And in the end, humanity will conquer it.

SHIMIZU: How can you be so sure?

MANABU: Human beings have always had an instinct for happiness.

SHIMIZU: And the bomb obliterated it in an instant.

MANABU: But that's the whole point: it wasn't obliterated. There may have been people who thought they could wipe it out, but that's all nonsense. The human life force can never be wiped out with illusions like that. I experienced it with these very eyes, with this body. What is the atomic bomb? It's just one application of atomic energy, right? The delusions and conceits of a few madmen will never obliterate the real potential, the happy future that atomic energy can create for mankind. I believe absolutely in the human love of life, and man's will to live happily. (*Pause.*) You know, when I was on the boat to Nijima after the bombing, the sun setting behind Miyajima was absolutely gorgeous. The shrine was silhouetted by the rays of the sun. As I watched the sun set, I swore to myself that I'd survive! (*Pause.*) At that moment, I became convinced of the power of man's will to live. . . .

Letting his words hang, he gazes at the sun. The people around Manabu, aware of a change in his manner of speech, follow his gaze. Manabu now shifts his eyes to his shadow.

MANABU: The summer sun shone on my scorched back. I looked for a spot that might provide some shade and squatted down. Before I knew it, I was back on all fours. The pain in my back was terrific. But in the sunlight, it hurt all the more, so I started searching for a shady spot all over again. I wished that the sun would go out forever. I would go ten meters and rest, crawl five more meters and rest, until I finally made it to Miyuki Bridge, and then I couldn't move one meter more. My own shadow—I tried desperately to crawl into my own shadow . . . . (*Pause.*) I felt as if I was being sucked into oblivion. If I'm goint to die, I thought, at least I want to leave something on this earth, so I picked up a piece of tile and wrote on the ground, "August 6, 1945. Kurihara Manabu. Age 20." I was ready to die. (*Pause.*) That's when someone

said, "We'll put you on the next boat, so try to hang on!"
Someone on a truck threw me a shirt. "I can still live!" I
thought, and courage welled up inside me. I gritted my teeth,
and I was sure I was putting up a fight, but the next thing I
knew I was on the wharf at Ujina. Even there on the wharf,
there were lots of people who died by jumping into the sea.
Unable to stand the heat, they'd jump into the water even
though they could see the dead who had drowned before
them right before their eyes. The pain was so intense you
couldn't stand it. Worse than the pain, you couldn't breathe!
On that narrow wharf, people were so crammed together
. . . . Some tried to get into the shadow of the person next to
them; others wanted to be the first to get to Nijima and tried
to work their way to the edge of the wharf. We were like
maggots on that wharf. (*He moves his hands, indicating seething
maggots.*) I can't describe the pain when our wounds rubbed
together. . . . A lot of people just got shoved into the sea by
the crowd. I stayed on the wharf by holding onto a rope. I
could see this island, and I thought, "If I can only make it that
far I'll be saved!" I had this feeling that if I could just return to
my mother, I'd live for sure, so I held on for dear life. If this
island hadn't been here, I don't think I could have lasted as
long as I did. It's really nothing this island, you know, just the
place where I was born, but . . . . (*Without realizing it, he has
begun to stroke the earth.*) This island! . . . (*He looks at the sea
and then toward Ujina. Pause. The sound of Reiko weeping brings
him back to the present. To Reiko*): What's wrong?

REIKO: Nothing.

MANABU: People from Tokyo laugh at girls who cry for no
reason.

SHINTANI: What was it like the instant the bomb fell?

MANABU: I don't really remember. I just hit the dust.

SHINTANI: Black rain fell, didn't it? How long after the bomb
was that?

MANABU: Good question. The reason the rain was black was
because of the ashes mixed in. It began falling all of a sudden,
like a cloudburst. I tried to stand but couldn't because my legs
were numb, and I guess I must've been knocked quite a ways

by the wind. My face was all puffed up, and my arms were just hanging uselessly at my sides. I wondered what I had in my hands that was so precious, and when I looked, I saw pieces of skin hanging from my fingers. The first thing I did was look at my hands. (*Looks at his hands.*) They were all right, but my back started to prickle. I reached around, and . . . you know, I thought it was my shirt . . . the skin on my back just slid off in my hand. Ah! They got me too! (*Laughing*): Then I began to lose consciousness again.

SHINTANI (*laughing, after a pause*): Manabu, you should've tried this. (*He gesticulates.*)

MANABU: What's that?

SHINTANI: Kiyomori trying to make the sun *go down!* (*He laughs.*)

MANABU (*also laughing*): Why didn't I think of that?

SHIMIZU: How did you recover?

MANABU: We tried all sorts of things. Whatever we could think of. At first, I was unconscious and really didn't know what was happening. My mother did everything for me.

SHINTANI: In the end, though, moxabustion did the trick. Right, Manabu?

SHIMIZU: Moxabustion? You cured A-bomb disease with moxabustion?

MANABU: Fighting fire with fire!

SHIMIZU: How could that be? Maybe heat increases the cells' resistance. It's hard to believe moxa could cure the effects of the atomic bomb.

MANABU: Moxa and the bomb. (*He laughs.*) You use the most primitive means to combat the power of the most primitive particles in nature. I guess that's another reason I believe in Gandhi.

SHIMIZU (*looking at him quizzically, then laughing*): Oh, I get it!

MANABU: I have to live to a ripe old age and prove that you can't destroy mankind, even with the atomic bomb. (*To Reiko*): You'd better start treating me better. God's given me a mission. As you say, Tadashi, worry less and live longer. By the time our pupils are grown up and we're grandfathers with grey hair, this world will be a different place. Until then we just have to plant one seed at a time, ever so carefully. And when my time comes, God will say I've made my contribution to humanity and call me. . . .

REIKO: Oh! (*Looking at his face, she fumbles for a tissue.*)

MANABU (*putting his hand to his face and realizing that he is bleeding from the nose*): What a doozy. Must be my punishment for taking God's name in vain!

SHIMIZU: Is it because of the bomb?

MANABU: You amateurs are too quick to jump to conclusions. (*Taking the tissue from Reiko and holding his nose.*) I've been out in the sun too long, that's all.

REIKO: You got carried away talking, that's it.

SHINTANI: You're tired.

MANABU: Yes. . . .

REIKO: Maybe you should sit down in the shade?

MANABU: Don't worry so much.

REIKO: How about under that cherry tree?

MANABU: It's stopped already.

REIKO: It's still bleeding. Please lie down. (*She removes her jacket and folds it into a pillow.*) Here. (*She helps Manabu lie down, then positions herself to shade his head.*)

MANABU: You see, teaching has its rewards.

REIKO: Please try to be quiet for a minute.

Pause. A boat's whistle and diesel engine reverbate cheerfully as it traverses the Inland Sea.

SHINTANI: Hey, it's already eleven o'clock. That's the ferry to Iyo.

SHIMIZU: The *Ehime?* So it still passes by here on its way to Ujina at ten and on its way back to Shikoku again at eleven just like when I was a boy. After more than ten years, it was good to see you here where we used to play so innocently. Take good care of yourself. I'm glad I decided to come back to the island. Thank you. (*He squeezes Manabu's hand.*) Don't worry, I'm not giving in to you—I'll beat you yet. Yesterday, when I came across on the ferry, I was thinking I'd get away from it all, you know. How strange. (*Smiling*): I had this illusion that of all the islands in Japan, this island, my home island alone had somehow remained unchanged and unaffected. Somehow I forgot it's postwar Japan here too. Well, take care of yourself. (*He squeezes Manabu's hand again.*) Good-bye.

MANABU: My mother was hoping you'd eat with us tonight.
. . .

SHIMIZU: Yes, I know. But somehow all I can think about after one night in my hometown in ten years is getting back on the train. Maybe it's because I have no family left. The fact that my mother's not here . . . . (*He laughs.*) Here I am twenty-seven years old and wanting my mother!

MANABU: There are times when it's best not to have any family. Try living in the country and you'll see. More often than not, family ties you down.

SHIMIZU: I'll be back for the Kiyomori Festival, I promise. Then let's meet up here again. Tell your mother I'm sorry. And regards to Fumi. (*Exits.*)

Manabu watches Shimizu leave. Pause.

MANABU: I shouldn't have drunk all that wine at the wedding last night.

REIKO: It was all the excitement. You were talking a blue streak, you know.

MANABU: You really think so?

REIKO: Don't you let him get the better of you, all right?

The bald teacher, Yamaoka, enters, stands on a tree stump, faces upstage right, bows deeply, and, as if unrolling a scroll, begins sonorously to recite the "Imperial Rescript on Education." Reiko cries out in*

---

*The Imperial Rescript on Education was promulgated by the Emperor Meiji on October 30, 1890. It was a hortatory document with a strong Confucian flavor that provided the moral basis for the Japanese educational system until the end of World War Two, when it was replaced by the Fundamental Law of Education and other laws inspired by the Occupation. (See note below.) The text reads as follows:

Know ye, Our subjects:
Our Imperial Ancestors have founded Our Empire on a basis broad and everlasting, and have deeply and firmly implanted virtue; Our subjects ever united in loyalty and filial piety have from generation to generation illustrated the beauty thereof. This is the glory of the fundamental character of Our Empire, and herein also lies the source of Our education. Ye, Our subjects, be filial to your parents, affectionate to your brothers and

surprise and clings to Manabu. The recitation continues. Mōri looks on in amazement.

REIKO: What do you suppose Mr. Yamaoka thinks he's doing?

MANABU: Ask him yourself.

REIKO (*laughing*): No point in asking a madman. Don't *you* ever get that way!

MANABU: He's got it easier than I do.

REIKO: Don't be silly! Oh, there's Kunio coming down the path from Twin Pines. (*Standing*): Kunio!

Startled, Yamaoka falls silent and glares at Reiko.

MANABU: Watch out, you've stirred up the hornets' nest!

Reiko looks back at Yamaoka. Seeing the look in his eyes, she shouts, "Mommy!" and collapses. Mōri positions himself to shield Reiko. Yamaoka bows to Mōri and exits. Mōri politely returns the bow.

MANABU: Mōri, it looks like you've won Mr. Yamaoka's respect.

MŌRI: I must have if I can make him stop reciting the "Imperial Rescript"! (*He laughs.*)

REIKO: Is he gone? (*Hesitantly she raises her head.*) I thought I was a goner. My heart stopped beating!

MŌRI (*in a falsetto*): Mommy!

REIKO (*sticking out her tongue*): You're awful!

MANABU: Mr. Yamaoka must have been as startled as you were.

REIKO: It's all Kunio's fault.

---

sisters; as husbands and wives be harmonious, as friends true; bear yourselves in modesty and moderation; extend your benevolence to all; pursue learning and cultivate arts, and thereby develop intellectual faculties and perfect moral powers; furthermore, advance public good and promote common interests; always respect the Constitution and observe the laws; should emergency arise, offer yourselves courageously to the State; and thus guard and maintain the prosperity of Our Imperial Throne coeval with heaven and earth. So shall ye not only be Our good and faithful subjects, but render illustrious the best traditions of your forefathers.

The Way here set forth is indeed the teaching bequeathed by Our Imperial Ancestors, to be observed alike by Their Descendants and the subjects, infallible for all ages and true in all places. It is Our wish to lay it to heart in all reverence, in common with you, Our subjects, that we may all attain to the same virtue.

Quoted in de Bary, et al., eds., *Sources of Japanese Tradition,* pp. 646–647.

MŌRI: Reiko, people like you live forever. (*He goes back to his painting.*)

REIKO (*placing Manabu's hand over her heart*): See how fast it's beating?

Caught off-guard, Manabu allows her to take his hand. Nearby, a lark takes flight. Pause.

REIKO (*coquettishly*): You were so funny last night at Ichirō's matriculation party.

MANABU: Why do you say that?

REIKO: Why? (*Didactically*): The interrogative case. Use your head! God didn't give people heads to have permanent waves and make barbers rich. Heads are to think with, so you'd better start using yours!

Manabu smiles sheepishly.

REIKO: Don't just lie there! (*Laughing*): Everybody laughed so! Even Grandad had to hold his stomach. "The Ōura grandkids take the cake!" he said. He called you a "grandkid"! (*She laughs.*)

MANABU: Well I am his grandchild. So are you.

REIKO: I know, but it's still funny. As if you were really a child. You really monopolized the conversation after that. I think you owe me a treat.

MANABU: You name it.

REIKO: They said it was a waste just to let you go on teaching school. Then my father said he was going to find you a wife.

MANABU: What?

REIKO: You'd better place your order. What sort of wife would you like?

MANABU: Well, let me see. First someone who's healthy, beautiful, never gets moody, is bright. . . .

REIKO: Don't be so greedy! Nobody's perfect!

MANABU: See, someone self-effacing like you would never do.

REIKO: Never mind! Anyway, I've decided never to get married. I'm going to open a dressmaking shop and be independent. I've got it all planned out.

MANABU: Is that so?

REIKO: If you get sick and your wife runs out on you, I'll look after you. After all, you are my teacher.

MANABU: Are you serious?

REIKO: Would I lie to you? Cross my heart and hope to die.

MANABU: You'd look after me?

REIKO: Why you're so self-effacing! (*She laughs.*) Here. (*She takes Manabu's hand and with his finger crosses her heart.*)

MANABU: Reiko, what would you think if I quit teaching?

REIKO: Quit?

MANABU: Don't you think it's a waste of my talent?

REIKO: Let me see. . . . (*She is teasing.*)

Kunio enters up the slope stage left. Hearing the laughter, he pauses. Feigning disinterest, he goes to Mōri.

KUNIO (*in a loud voice*): Mr. Mōri, are you still at it?

MANABU (*getting to his feet*): Is that you, Kunio?

KUNIO: Mr. Kurihara, we decided to have a going away party at your house at noon. Kawaguchi and the others are leaving for Osaka on the night train.

MANABU: It's already noon. Mother's going to be upset with you.

KUNIO: I already gave the beans and sugar for the soup* to my sister and asked her to get things ready. Just leave everything to me.

MŌRI: Am I invited too?

KUNIO: We're asking everybody to chip in a hundred yen apiece. But since you eat so much, we'll make an exception: two hundred yen!

MŌRI: You mean there's a charge?

KUNIO: Listen to that pitiful voice! All right. You probably can't afford it on what you make anyway.

MŌRI: Done! Manabu, I finally finished it. A masterpiece, wouldn't you say? I really had to work to get this color. Neither blue nor green, the soft, warm tone of spring, the special color of the Inland Sea. Sparkling and reflecting the sun's rays when it's actually absorbing the spring sun and sending up wisps of mist, that feeling. This peaceful sky and island and sea . . . .

Pause. Then the dull, drawn-out sound of an explosion.

Zenzai is a sweet, thick bean soup drunk on special occasions.

REIKO: What was that? It sounded like the atom bomb going off.

MANABU: I don't know.

MŌRI: Maybe one of the Occupation's munitions dumps went up. (*He looks in the direction of Kure harbor.*) I don't see any smoke.

Suddenly, Kunio runs off stage left.

MŌRI: Manabu, over there! (*Pause.*) See, yellow smoke. It's Kamegasaki!

Pause.

MŌRI: The torpedo!

The three stand in silence. In the distance, the weird, intermittent shriek of a siren sounds the alarm.

Curtain.

ACT TWO

A night in May. Manabu's house. Only the desk lamp is lit. In the garden, the pale light of the moon. A ship's whistle. Dressed in a kimono, Manabu seats himself at the desk and administers himself an injection of vitamin B₁. Shortly, Fumi returns home. Manabu hastily conceals the syringe under the desk.

FUMI (*turning on the light in the living room*): That uncle of ours, I'm telling you—he was so loud on the bus, I thought I'd die! He was boasting about the fight he had at the tax office: "We have a torpedo blow up in our faces, and all you people can talk about is last year's taxes!" People were laughing at him behind his back. Where's mother?

MANABU: You were so late, she went to the Saeki's to ask about you.

FUMI: There was a general meeting of the workers at the plant. A lot of the temporaries got the axe today, you know. People are worried that if the truce in Korea holds, the Occupation troops will go home. They say that by fall, everyone may be looking for work. The head of our subsection asked us women in particular not to quit without consulting him first, but if the Americans leave, we won't have much choice. Word is that some of them have gone straight back from Korea already. If the Americans leave, what are the people on the island going to do to put food on the table? What should I do if I get fired?

MANABU: We'll cross that bridge when we come to it. Don't worry.

FUMI: Can we get along on your salary?

MANABU: While you're collecting unemployment compensation, you can go to dressmaking school.

FUMI: Will you let me?

MANABU: It's a good opportunity.

FUMI: Girls like Yuki who got involved with soldiers are really going to be in for it. What's she going to do about her child? He'll be an orphan.

MANABU (*laughing*): You're just like your mother! You'd think you'd have enough to worry about without other people's problems.

FUMI: Maybe so, but still . . . . (*She laughs.*) It's a disease. And it's all your fault.

MANABU: My fault? Maybe you're right. I guess I have given you plenty of reason to worry. But never mind, I'll begin paying you back right now.

FUMI: Talk, talk! (*Laughs.*) I'd just be in your way. I'd get married if there was someone decent who'd have me.

MANABU: Get going and look, look!

FUMI: Just because you're all taken care of, you act as if it's none of your business.

MANABU: What do you mean? I'm concerned about you.

FUMI: Really? Listen, spare me the teachers, all right?

MANABU: Why?

FUMI: Why? You mean you have someone in mind?

MANABU: Not exactly. Just asking.

FUMI: I see.

MANABU: Don't women find teachers attractive?

FUMI: Ask Reiko!

MANABU: You'd make one hell of a sister-in-law, I can see that.

FUMI: And you're so perfect.

MANABU (*after a pause*): Fumi, I've been thinking of quitting teaching and getting a job where I can put my knowledge to work.

FUMI: What made you change your mind?

MANABU: I've been teaching for five years. I can't even give you a decent dowry.

FUMI: You want to quit for my sake?

MANABU: For your sake, too. I'm thinking of asking a friend of mine from school to find me a job at Tama Shipbuilding.

FUMI: Tama's in Okayama, right? What about Mother?

MANABU: Don't worry.

FUMI: I'd do anything to make you happy, but . . . .

MANABU: Of course I don't mean to push Mother off on you.

FUMI: Will she go with you, then?

Manabu is silent.

FUMI: Do you think there's a chance they'll hire you?

MANABU: The shipbuilding industry's doing all right just now. Would you do me a favor and sort of sound Mother out?

FUMI: You talk to her yourself. Couldn't you get a job with the Kure Shipyard or NBC?

MANABU: If I'm going to work, I might as well do it for a company with a future.

FUMI: Wouldn't you rather work somewhere you could commute from home?

MANABU: You women are so damned conservative.

FUMI: How are you feeling?

MANABU: Don't keep on about my health. You see me every day for God's sake!

FUMI: I'm sorry. (*Pause.*)

MANABU: Fumi, what do you think of Reiko?

FUMI: Me? I guess I wonder if she considers you a prospective husband. Have you spoken to her—about the future, I mean?

MANABU: I have.

FUMI: That's good. It's one thing to respect someone as a teacher and another to spend your whole life with him as husband and wife.

MANABU: I know that much.

FUMI: After all, she's still a child.

MANABU: You wouldn't understand.

FUMI: I see . . . .

MANABU: If you're against us getting married, come right out and say so.

FUMI: I'm not against it.

MANABU: Try to give me some credit.

FUMI: It doesn't make any difference to me one way or the other. You're the one who's getting married.

Manabu is silent.

FUMI: Are you sure she's up to it?

MANABU: Up to what?

FUMI: Serving mother. Reiko's been so pampered at home.

MANABU: I'll teach her the ropes. What are you getting at?

FUMI: Nothing . . . . (*Pause.*) Aren't you being a little self-centered about this thing?

Manabu does not answer.
Mōri enters from the garden. He is wearing wooden clogs.
MŌRI: No luck today. It's harder'n hell to score when your mind isn't focused.* (*He takes several packs of cigarettes and some caramels from his pocket. He gives the caramels to Fumi.*) I still had twenty-odd balls left, but I gave them to Kunio. I'm a little worried about that kid, you know. He's getting this crazed look in his eyes like the city kids. I'm afraid he's going to turn into a regular pinball maniac.
FUMI: Shall I make some tea?
MŌRI (*making an effort to sound sunny*): I'm eternally in your debt.
FUMI: Of course you are—as long as I'm feeding you. (*Laughing, she exits to the kitchen. Pause.*)
MŌRI (*looking at the desk*): Tests, huh? Try to relax, will you, at least when you're at home. Why don't you talk to the principal and get a few days off?
MANABU: I should have had him relieve me of the ninth grade.
MŌRI: You're too accommodating. People take advantage of you. If you get sick, what are you going to do?
Manabu puts his finger to his lips and stops him. Fumi enters to get the tea cup from Manabu's desk.
MŌRI: How would you like it if I treated you to a movie this Sunday?
FUMI: Sweet talk! I thought you were taking your class to Miyajima to paint the shrine?
MŌRI: Oh, that's right! Then how about if I take you to Miyajima?
FUMI: Not on your life! The goddess of Miyajima's the goddess of divorce!
MŌRI: Heavens! That won't do, will it!
They both laugh. Fumi goes to the kitchen.
MŌRI: I suppose that has something to do with the Kiyomori legend.

---

*Mōri has been playing *pachinko,* a kind of pinball. Players can win prizes, including cigarettes, candy, and canned goods for high scores.

MANABU: I suppose so. (*Laughing*): During the war, the spring before the war ended actually, a friend of mine was going with this girl from the girl's high school, and they decided that since he would eventually be sent to the front they should split up, but no matter how much they talked, they couldn't go through with it. So finally they made a pilgrimage to Miyajima!

MŌRI: As a couple! (*He laughs.*) So what happened? Did the goddess live up to her reputation?

MANABU: The girl started crying and they wound up spending the night together on the island!

Mōri laughs expansively.

MANABU: The girl had beautiful eyes and wore her hair in braids. As for my friend, the last I saw of him was when I left him in the school cafeteria after he'd returned from the nighttime work detail.* (*Pause.*) August 6, 1945. 8:15 a.m. Hiroshima. (*A rather long pause.*) How happy we human beings would be if we could only rewrite history!

MŌRI (*pausing*): The past is to the present what . . . . (*He laughs.*) That's funny, then the future is . . . . I can't quite put it into words . . . . The point is, we only have a sense of happiness when the present is happier than the past, right? . . . Sooo . . . .

MANABU: But what do you do when your past existed totally independent of your will? If you screw things up when you've acted according to your own volition, at least then you can resign yourself to your fate.

MŌRI: So the point is, we've got to live the present more purposefully than the past! Even something as inconsequential as shooting a pinball . . . . (*He tries to obfuscate this comment with a laugh.*)

---

*In the weeks before the end of the war, as a response to the fire bombing of other Japanese cities, labor brigades were mobilized in Hiroshima to work at night clearing firebreaks through the city to minimize potential damage. Because most able-bodied men were in the military, many school children were involved in these brigades.

MANABU: You're a happy man, Mōri. Your whole purpose in life is the pursuit of beauty.

MŌRI: What are you talking about! You're a hell of a lot better off than me. You have a salable skill! I'm a total loss. If I quit teaching, I'd be good for nothing. . . . I'm having one hell of a time finishing that painting. Here it is May, the best season of all and . . . . Sometimes I think that torpedo affected my mind. I try to make some sketches, you know, and all I can think about is Kunio's father being blown to bits, his head and chunks of flesh . . . . Sometimes I think I should turn surrealist and paint poltergeists! (*Laughs.*) I should get blind drunk and blow it all to hell—at least that's what I think sometimes—but that would be running away.

Pause.

MŌRI: But who cares what a junior high school teacher can do anyway? What I'd really like is to go up to Tokyo for some real training. Every now and then, you know, I have this feeling that my not being able to paint is a form of hypocrisy . . . . I'm getting to the point where I can't face my pupils . . . .

MANABU (*laughing*): You too?

MŌRI (*laughing*): If I had money, I'd like to run away to a south seas island.

MANABU: To Bali?

MŌRI: That's it. I'd dance with the daughter of the tribal chief . . . . Wouldn't that be something! I could just live and paint the sea without a care in the world. How beautiful they must be, the coral islands. This island of ours is a real joke. A couple years in a place like this would drive anybody crazy. Sometimes I think my sense of color is going and I get panicky, you know. My students' paintings all seem muddy somehow . . . .

MANABU: You think the quality of their environment is showing up in the colors?

MŌRI: The kids on this island have altogether too few dreams. They have to spend more time exploring the world of their imagination. Just try having them paint something from their imagination: the bottom of the sea, for example. They paint a diver bringing up a torpedo! (*He laughs.*) "I wonder how much I can get for this?" That's all they can think about. They think of everything in the context of their real life. Of course that's important too, but . . . . After all, half those kids can hardly afford to pay their dues to the PTA, so . . . . Even so, I'd like to give them a dream. What about American kids? Or Russians? Chinese? Indians? I'd like to run an exhibition of paintings by children from all over the world. I'll bet you could tell each country's future from their work.

Shintani enters from the garden. He is on his way home from work and wears a suit.

SHINTANI (*taking a card from his briefcase*): Manabu, here's an invitation to the launching of the Little Kure. Come and bring your mother along. You get a souvenir, too. (*He takes out some money.*) I've finally scraped together six hundred and thirty yen. People think nothing of forking over hundreds for pinball or dances, but you'd be amazed at the excuses they come up with when it comes to something like this. "If you want trees planted on the hill, let the village council do it," they say. "Since when do we have a councilman with that much sense?" I tell them, but they just throw it back in my face: "Then you run," they tell me.

MANABU: Don't worry about it. We can start planting with what we've collected so far.

SHINTANI: There were even some who said, "The day Kurihara Manabu comes with his hat in his hand is the day I'll give. Just because he's a teacher, he thinks he's too good for us." They're just jealous because you're popular. There's nothing to be concerned about. The point is to get them to fork over the money. They'll understand when the trees get big. Tonight I thought I'd write to Toku. (*Laughing*): "To treat the wounds of war." You know, if Toku hadn't said that, we wouldn't have gotten the idea to plant trees in the first place. I'll get him to contribute at least five hundred. After all, he's the one who suggested it. Anything you want me to say?

MANABU: Just give him my regards.

SHINTANI: He said he'd be back for the Kiyomori Festival for sure. Well, I'll be seeing you. (*Exits.*)

MŌRI: Shimizu . . . . That was the day it happened.

MANABU: Maybe I should make up my mind to work for some company after all. I wonder what my students would think if I quit teaching?

MŌRI (*consoling him*): What makes you think they care? Maybe that very thought's a form of conceit.

MANABU: Conceit? (*Pause.*)

MŌRI: Just take it easy. There's no point in getting yourself all riled up. You'll just make yourself sick. Things will turn out all right.

MANABU: Maybe you're right. I can't even save Kunio. We're supposed to "esteem individual dignity and endeavour to bring up a people who love truth and peace," right? But in the nature of education, teachers mustn't become involved in politics . . . . (*Pause.*)*

MŌRI: But, Manabu, do you really think that teachers have to be responsible for students who have graduated? The fact is, there's not a thing we can do. If you want my opinion, responsibility has to lie with the nation and national politics. You're taking your responsibility too seriously. You'd need a cat's nine lives and then some to fulfill it. Don't get so excited! "Worry less and live longer," right? (*He laughs, trying to encourage his friend.*)

MANABU (*taking an envelope from a drawer*): You remember the matter I mentioned the other day? Well, actually, I've received an answer from my friend. He wants me to send him my vita right away.

---

*Manabu is here quoting the Fundamental Law of Education, passed by the Japanese Diet in March 1947. The preamble of the law reads: "Having established the Constitution of Japan, we have shown our resolution to contribute to the peace of the world and welfare of humanity by building a democratic and cultural state. The realization of this ideal shall depend fundamentally on the power of education. We shall esteem individual dignity and endeavour to bring up a people who love truth and peace, while education, which aims at the creation of culture which is both universal and rich in individuality, shall be spread far and wide. We hereby enact this Law, in accordance with the spirit of the Constitution of Japan, with a view to clarifying the aim of education and establishing the foundation of education for a new Japan." The full text of the law may be found in the *Journal of Social and Political Ideas in Japan*, December 1963, pp. 122–124.

Despite their activism, the 1949 Special Education Public Service Law, revised in 1954, prohibited teachers (who were civil service employees) from participating in political activities either during or after school.

MŌRI (*taking the letter and examining it*): Go ahead.

MANABU: You think so? After all, it is my life to live.

FUMI (*from the living room*): Tea's ready. Come in here and talk.

Mōri starts for the living room.

MANABU: You go ahead. I'm going to get some air. (*He steps into the garden.*)

FUMI: Mr. Mōri, have you ever been in love?

MŌRI (*after a moment's hesitation*): Yes.

FUMI: What happened?

MŌRI: I got jilted.

FUMI: Really?

MŌRI: I considered suicide. For three years, I had worshiped her from afar, but before I could get up the nerve to declare my love, she went off and married someone else. Ever since, I've been terrified of women, and I decided never to get married.

FUMI: You're kidding!

MŌRI: You can't understand unless you've been in love yourself. When I saw you for the first time, though, I thought I might reconsider.

FUMI: Mr. Mōri! (*They both laugh in embarrassment.*) When was that?

MŌRI: When you were in junior high.

FUMI: I must have been awfully precocious. I can't believe it!

Mōri is laughing.

FUMI: Seriously, though, what do you think about Manabu and Reiko?

MŌRI: Think?

FUMI: Haven't you heard?

MŌRI: I hear all kinds of things.

FUMI: Do you think he's seriously considering marrying her?

MŌRI: I'm not sure he's thought that far ahead.

FUMI: Do you think things will work out?

MŌRI: I suppose they will.

FUMI: Have you heard him talk about quitting teaching and going to work for a company?

MŌRI: Company? Nothing concrete. Has he been offered a job?

FUMI: Don't mention this to him. He'll just get mad. But don't you think this job business has something to do with Reiko?

MŌRI: I couldn't say. (*He laughs.*) You're letting your imagination run away with you. That's the trouble with you Kuriharas—you're too smart for your own good.

FUMI (*laughing*): Maybe you're right! (*Pause.*)

Reiko enters the garden. She is dressed in a kimono and wears a thin layer of makeup.

MŌRI: Well, well! Aren't you a picture! And look at that happy face!

REIKO: I have reason to be happy.

MŌRI: You're at a happy age. As for me, maybe I'll just throw myself over a cliff.

REIKO: Don't be ridiculous!

FUMI: If you see Manabu, tell him Reiko's here.

MŌRI: How about a little gratitude, Reiko? I'm still running errands even as I go to my death! (*Joking*): Adieu! Adieu! Fair damsels, adieu! (*Exits.*)

Pause.

FUMI: That's a beautiful pattern, Reiko.

REIKO: It makes me look like a child, don't you think?

FUMI: Not at all! (*Pause. Fumi begins sewing children's clothes.*) He'll be back right away.

As if drawn out by the moon, Reiko steps onto the veranda.

REIKO (*singing softly*):
Rain is falling
Moon behind the clouds.
When you marry
Who will go with you?
I'll go alone,
Umbrella overhead.

If there's no umbrella,
Who will go with you?
Jingle-jangle, jingle-jangle,
Alone on horseback,
Bells a'jangle,
Damp with rain I'll go.

Pause. Manabu returns through the garden. Fumi exits through the front door.

REIKO (*making no effort to conceal her happiness*): Somebody proposed to me today. He's the son of the manager of the Kure branch of the Bank of Hiroshima. He's twenty-five, graduated from Hiroshima University, and he's working for Mitsubishi Shipbuilding. I saw his picture, and (*laughing*) he has this real serious look on his face! He still looks like a child. (*She laughs out loud.*) Why do people have to have such a serious look on their face when they take their marriage pictures? Mother says that we're just the right age for each other—six years apart—and that if I like him, we can arrange for a meeting. (*She giggles.*) It seems so funny to me, I can't help laughing! (*Laughter.*) Don't you think so? I mean. . . .

KUNIO (*from the kitchen*): Is my mother here?

REIKO (*going to the kitchen*): No, she's not. (*Kunio exists.*)

REIKO: He's turning into a regular delinquent, you know. Why, the other day my brother met him on the wharf on his way back from Hiroshima, and he demanded money, a whole hundred yen! He was afraid of what Kunio might do, so he gave it to him. If he keeps it up, he'll get no sympathy from anybody.

MANABU (*after a pause*): When are you going to meet this young man?

REIKO: Meet him? I'm not going to meet him. You've already forgotten, haven't you. We made a solemn vow on top of the hill. I haven't forgotten. I don't know about you, but I'm not getting married. (*She laughs coquettishly.*)

MANABU: Don't worry about me. You go ahead and get married.

REIKO: Really? May I? (*She laughs.*) You're going to marry me, right? I intend to keep up my end of the bargain. You know, I told my mother about our promise. And you know what she said? "Did Mr. Kurihara bring that up?" (*She laughs.*) She had this real serious look on her face. Then she said, "Mr. Kurihara's not serious either, so don't worry about it." (*Laughter.*) Then she said that you might really like me. But I don't have the qualifications to be your wife, do I? Why are parents so stupid? "You're not a child forever, so be careful!" she says. It's so funny! (*Pause.*) Mother really respects you. "Mr. Kurihara's a real sad case," she says. She says that all the time. "If only he hadn't been a victim of the bomb, he'd really have had pros-

pects," she says. I wonder why you had to be a victim—you'd
have had such prospects otherwise! (*She draws close to Manabu
and laughs coquettishly.*)

MANABU (*taking Reiko's hand*): Reiko . . . .

REIKO: "There's no telling when he's going to develop A-bomb
disease and die," Mother says. She's let this thing develop in
her mind. She's so silly. Don't you go and die now, you hear?
What's wrong?

MANABU: My eyes itch. I must have got something in them.

REIKO: Which eye? If you get something in your eye, the best
way to get it out is with the tongue. (*Looking in his eye*): Let
me see. I'll get it for you.

MANABU: Never mind.

REIKO: Don't be like that. Let me see.

Manabu reels slightly at the scent of Reiko's perfume.

REIKO: What's wrong?

MANABU (*moving away*): I'll go wash it out with water. (*Reiko
follows him as far as the kitchen.*)

REIKO: Is it better?

MANABU (*wiping his face*): Yes.

REIKO (*laughing coquettishly*): I thought for a minute you were
crying! You know, I wanted to show you that engagement
photograph, but my mother wouldn't let me have it. Would
you like to see it?

MANABU (*after a pause*): I suppose.

REIKO: Next time I'll bring it for sure. (*Laughing*): He looks so
serious, you'll laugh, too.

MANABU (*after a pause*): Reiko?

REIKO: Yes?

MANABU: About this marriage . . . .

REIKO: I hate you! I'm never getting married!

MANABU: I've been thinking of getting married myself.

REIKO: You have somebody in mind?

MANABU: You.

REIKO (*laughing*): Really? No, you're just teasing me, trying to
get me married off. I'm right, aren't I? If you're going to get
married, at least find a better wife than me. Promise! (*She
clasps his hands.*)

Yū and Fumi enter through the kitchen.

REIKO: Good night. (*She rubs her cheek kitten-like against Manabu and gets up. To Yū*): Good night. (*Exits.*)

YŪ: There's something about girls from good families, you know—like dolls. Mrs. Kido's an elegant lady in her own right, so . . . . We're going to have to make a kimono for you pretty soon, too, Fumi.

Fumi does not respond.

YŪ: Uncle Ōura promised to help with your wedding preparations, but since that trouble, he can't afford it anymore. And the money I'd saved we spent on Manabu's medicine.

FUMI: I don't need anything.

YŪ (*going to Manabu*): Uncle Ōura wants us to let him use this house as collateral for a loan, but I don't know . . . . If things go wrong like they did last spring . . . . If we lost this house, I wouldn't have a thing to leave you two. I wanted to discuss it with you, so I haven't given him an answer yet, but . . . .

FUMI: If Uncle didn't repay the bank, what would we do? We wouldn't have any place to live.

YŪ: Chances are he won't have any trouble, but . . . .

FUMI: What's he up to this time?

YŪ: Apparently there's some scheme to buy land in Hiroshima and build a hotel. Uncle Ōura wants to go into seafood wholesaling himself, I guess. He says that there are lots of tourists coming to Hiroshima to see where the bomb fell and so the tourist industry will be looking up. He got burnt on his torpedo project, so I suppose this time he wants to get into a legitimate business. He says he wants to find Manabu a wife and have you and me come to live with him in Hiroshima, but I don't want to leave the island at my age. Manabu?

MANABU: Let him use it.

YŪ: You think so?

MANABU: Mother, I've been thinking about quitting teaching and taking a job with Tama Shipbuilding. I was planning to discuss it with you, and this is as good a time as any, I guess. I know I've been a burden to you and Fumi, but now I plan to repay you. That should make you happy. After all, you didn't send me to the Technical College so I'd become a teacher, did you?

Yū is silent.

MANABU: I've been a little confused about this, but I've made up my mind. I'll never get anywhere in the world unless I find work in the city.

YŪ: You know, I'd resigned myself to the idea of your staying on the island, but when I saw Tokuichi last spring, I couldn't help feeling cheated. Living here, of course everybody calls you teacher, teacher, but that's about the only good thing about it.

MANABU: You know, Mother, I didn't think you'd understand. Fumi, I hope you're listening.

FUMI: Then Mother will be going to live with Uncle Ōura?

MANABU: No, she'll come live with me. Then the only problem is what to do about you.

FUMI: Oh, I see. I'm in the way, is that it?

YŪ: Don't be stupid! (*Pause.*) But with unemployment like it is, it won't be easy to find a job.

Manabu is silent.

YŪ: Once you start getting ambitious, there's no end to it. Everything's been determined in our previous life. I'll just be happy to accept my fate.

MANABU: There you go again! That's the problem with you people who spend all your time making pilgrimages. As far as you're concerned, everything's determined by fate.

YŪ: You'll be punished for talk like that! In this world, things don't go as smoothly as you imagine.

MANABU: Oh, just shut up, will you! I'm going to make your life easy, all right? I'm doing all this for you!

YŪ: Pretty soon, we're going to have to look for a husband for Fumi, you know. She's not just some dog or cat. She has to have a proper wardrobe. No matter how bad things might be, she's still an Ōura granddaughter. We can't allow her to become a laughingstock. How could I explain it to your father? (*She glances at her husband's picture.*) Don't just think of yourself—give Fumi some thought, too.

Manabu is silent.

YŪ: I've wanted so badly for you to make something of yourself; I've gritted my teeth and worked as hard as I could. (*Pause.*) Sometimes I complain how everything would be all right if only you hadn't been a victim of the bomb. But that's terrible! Just think of all the people who died! I deserve to be punished for thoughts like that. I ought to be clasping my hands and offering prayers of thanksgiving. I'm unworthy. Once the coolness passes my lips, I forget the heat. . . . Each morning, I pray to the Buddah to let me live this one day without complaining. (*She intones the* nembutsu.)

MANABU: All right! All right!

YŪ: Manabu! (*Pause.*)

FUMI: You spoke to Reiko, didn't you?

MANABU: You keep out of this!

YŪ: What about Reiko?

FUMI: Talk so Mother can understand.

YŪ: Oh, never mind! I just don't care anymore. The two of you work it out between yourselves!

Pause. Manabu goes into the garden. Yū enters the living room.

FUMI: Mother, why do you say things like that? You have to take Manabu's feelings into account.

YŪ: I know that much! How do you think I raised two children? I know exactly what you're thinking.

FUMI: You're always like that. You're always so sure of yourself.

YŪ: And who do you have to thank for raising you so you'd be able to talk to me like that? Soon enough you'll have children of your own. Then you'll understand!

FUMI: You treat us as if we were children.

YŪ: What do you want from me? I've lived my life for you, and watching you grow up has been my only pleasure. Tsutomu wasn't any better, going off like that and enlisting behind my back. If he'd listened to me, he'd be alive today!

FUMI: What's the point of saying that now?

YŪ: I haven't struggled to this day just to do the bidding of my son's wife!

Fumi is silent. Pause.

YŪ: I've been thinking of telling Manabu for some time. No matter how much he and Reiko love each other, they've been brought up differently. A husband and wife aren't like you think. I know what's going to happen down the road, way down the road. I'm not saying that Manabu's never given me a thought. No, from his point of view, he probably thinks that since the Kidos are well off, there won't be anything to worry about if he gets sick because they'll take care of him, but if that's true, he'll spend his whole life under their thumb. Things just aren't so easy!

Kin enters from the kitchen.

KIN: What are you two going on about? Mizz Kurihara, lucky woman to have two such devoted children as Mr. Manabu and Miss Fumi, you are. (*Looking around*): Where is Mr. Manabu?

YŪ: You want something?

KIN: Wanted to see if he could talk a little sense into Kunio's head. Won't listen to a word I say.

FUMI (*from the veranda*): Manabu.

Manabu returns and sits down in the wicker chair. Fumi exits to the kitchen.

KIN: Mr. Manabu, be much obliged if you'd have a word with Kunio. All he wants is to play pinball. "Pa's dead and your brother's in jail, so you'd better shape up and get to work." Tell him that for me. Won't go to work on the sardine nets, neither, no matter what I tell him. "If you don't shut your trap, I'm leaving for good!" Just turns around and threatens me, that's all. Need you to give him a good talking to. Just too much for me to handle.

MANABU: Bring him by.

KIN: Give him a good talking to so's he won't get so desperate. Please! (*She begins to cry.*) If his father was still alive . . . . (*She weeps.*) Kunio was looking forward to going to high school so much, I can understand how disappointed he must feel, but there's nothing I can do for him. (*Pause.*) "I'll see you through!" If Mr. Ōura hadn't built up his hopes like that, he'd have gotten himself a job and everything'd be all right, but ever since Shichi died, Mr. Ōura's turned his back on us, which I don't hold against him. Don't hold it against him, but tell me, what am I supposed to do? (*She weeps.*)

MANABU: Don't cry. I'll speak to the boy.

KIN: You're my only hope. Please! Please! (*She kowtows to him.*) Look out for him like he was your younger brother. Sorry to have barged in on you like this. Please do what you can. Bring him right away I will. (*She exits to the living room.*)

YŪ (*giving her some caramels*): Here, these are for the children.

KIN: Thank you. I don't know how we can ever repay you for all you've done. You and your family are the only thing that stands between us and suicide. My breasts are so full, they ache. If my husband hadn't died, the baby wouldn't have been born early, and . . . .

YŪ: You're lucky the child died. Just imagine what it'd have been like to have a suckling now. You wouldn't be able to work at all.

KIN: Try to console myself thinking Shichi must've called the baby to him. (*She laughs.*) At night in bed I curse him for dying on me like that. Just think of my suffering, Mizz Kurihara. A good mind I have to strangle the kids and hang myself and have done with it.

YŪ: Now don't be so anxious to die. Think of the children. If you go on living, something good's bound to happen.

KIN: What I keep telling myself, but . . . .

YŪ: Eventually you'll be rewarded.

KIN: Born to toil and suffer we are, so what do I expect, huh? Just have to manage the best we can. Nothing else to do. Even when I go selling fish over to Kure, you know, one of my customers gives me clothes for the children and does everything she can for us.

YŪ: That's wonderful. If you do an honest day's work, you're bound to have your day in the sun. The Buddha knows all. (*Pause.*) Kin, for Shichi's sake, take the time to visit the temple.

KIN: Where am I going to find the time to go visiting temples like you? Up at 4:30, work on the sardine nets, run back home, pick up a supply of fish, rush off to Kure to sell them . . . .

YŪ: You know what people say, though. They got punished because they didn't take the time to visit the temple.

KIN: Let them say what they like. Mizz Kurihara, look, there were people who stood by and laughed when my husband died, but now they got fired too. And they deserve everything they get!

YŪ: You shouldn't talk like that.

KIN: Can just go and eat shit for all I care. Let them wait and see! I ain't saying it'll happen, but who's to say that someday they won't be down on their luck and one of my kids won't put them back on their feet.

YŪ: Now you're talking.

Fumi enters from the kitchen.

KIN (*laughing*): Even so, when I get into bed at night, put my hands together and pray I do: "Namu Amida-butsu!" So exhausted, before I know it, I'm fast asleep! (*She laughs. Looking at Fumi's blind-stitched kimono*): Well look at that! Finished! And after your long day's work, too!

FUMI: My pleasure. I'm sorry to have taken so long. If you need anything else done, be sure to bring it by.

KIN: Just like your mother, so kind . . . . The man who marries you'll be the luckiest man in the world! If I weren't a woman, snap you up in a minute, I would!

YŪ: Keep that up and Shichi'll rise from the grave!

KIN: Let him try it—I'll knock him for a loop! (*She laughs.*) Mr. Manabu, I'll bring Kunio by right away. (*Exits.*)

YŪ: I feel so sorry for her. Her life's one trial after another!

Manabu comes to the living room.

MANABU: Mother, I'm going to quit teaching. I may have to neglect you for a while, but be patient. I won't disappoint you.

Yū is silent.

MANABU: And . . . well, I'm thinking of marrying Reiko. I know you won't object. (*Pause.*) This one time, just look the other way and let me do as I like. Please! I'm twenty-six years old. Just once in my life, I'd like to see what it's like to act according to my own lights. (*Pause.*)

Manabu exits through the garden.

YŪ: When I think of how he must feel, it's like a knife in my heart. What a pity! (*Pause.*) How I wish I could trade places with him!

Softly, she wipes away her tears. Fumi is biting her lip and staring at the ceiling.

YŪ: I don't mind letting Manabu do as he pleases, but what'll he do if he's rejected at the physical? It might destroy him—and what would be the point of that? I must have done something awful in my previous life to have deserved this. As for you, Fumi, I haven't been able to send you to high school as I'd have liked. I've done nothing but make you work from the day you were born. Please, don't hold it against me or your brother!

FUMI: Mother, please stop talking like that. If there hadn't been a war, Manabu'd be healthy and Tsutomu would still be alive. We wouldn't have to go through all this! (*No longer able to hold back her tears, she cries out loud.*)

YŪ (*after a pause*): Don't cry. If you start bawling on top of everything else, I feel like I might as well be dead. Come on now, stop.

Ōura enters. His rosy complexion reveals that he has been drinking.

ŌURA: What's wrong?

YŪ: It's Manabu . . . .

ŌURA: Doesn't he feel well?

YŪ: No . . . he says he wants to marry the Kido girl.

ŌURA: The Kido girl? What do you know? And how do you feel about it?

YŪ: If he's bound and determined, I . . . .

ŌURA: Has he proposed already?

YŪ: I don't know. Even if he has, the Kidos will never agree. I'm too old to be shamed like this. You probably don't remember, but once Father borrowed money from the Kidos for the sea bream nets. That year the catch was terrible, and I don't know how many times he had to go and apologize to them.

ŌURA (*laughing*): Well, that's over and done with. Even so, they'll never agree to let Manabu have their daughter. They know all about his condition. I'll have a talk with him. Where'd he go? Fumi, find Manabu for me, will you? It's really your own fault, Yū—you've spoiled him, treating him special because of the bomb. Now he's the one who's got to suffer.

YŪ: Try Mr. Mōri's place.

Fumi exits.

YŪ: While you're at it, he's thinking of quitting teaching and going up to the city. Says he wants to get a job with a company . . . Probably thinks he has to if he's going to marry Reiko.

ŌURA: Let him go.

YŪ: He wouldn't last a year away from me.

ŌURA (*laughing*): I'll bet he's planning to elope!

KIN (*yelling outside*): Go on in! Go on! (*She enters dragging Kunio by the hand.*). Listen to what your teacher has to say! And here's Mr. Ōura, good. Tell him what you said to me!

ŌURA: What are you yelling about?

KIN: Tell him! Talks back and won't listen to a thing I say!

ŌURA: Kunio, what did you say?

Kunio is silent.

KIN: Says we're idiots. Says you tricked us. Says you killed his father, so he's going to kill you. Just like a hoodlum, shooting off his mouth. Drives me crazy!

ŌURA: That's a real mouthful . . . . (*Laughing*): Well, Kunio, go ahead. There's a knife in the kitchen. (*Pause.*) Fool! You ungrateful slime! Who do you think I am? (*To Kin*): It's just as much your fault as his, always complaining about me in front of the boy! That's where he gets it!

KIN: When did I ever say anything against you?

ŌURA: Put yourself in my shoes. If Shichi'd only been a little more careful, I wouldn't be in the spot I'm in now. Only thinking of yourself. Put yourself in somebody else's position for a change. If it weren't for me, who'd look after you? Who paid for the funeral? Who paid for the observance on the forty-ninth day? You pack of idiots!

KIN: All right, I'm an idiot!

ŌURA: There, you see, talking back. Your kid's only following your example. When will you be satisfied? I've been watching out for you all these years! That's what you have to tell your children!

KIN (*tears in her voice*): I do!

ŌURA: If you did, he wouldn't be threatening to kill me! At least a dog'd be grateful. Look after a dog for three days and he never forgets his master. The likes of you are worse than dogs! Starting tomorrow, I don't know you. Don't you dare set foot in my place again, or here for that matter!

YŪ: Don't say that! The poor woman! Kin, you'd better apologize.

KIN: Never! (*Glaring at him through her tears.*) So that's how you feel! Dogs are we! Then act like dogs we will!

YŪ: Kin, be quiet!

KIN: No, we're animals! Worse than dogs! Kunio, I hope you're listening to this. Think I'm weak and defenseless because I'm a widow! Well, who made me a widow? I want my husband back! You and your big talk! Shichi was stupid enough to believe you! Who made him quit his job with the Occupation? Did you send this boy to school for one lousy day? You're nothing but hot air!

ŌURA (*laughing*): You see, just like I said!

KIN: That's right! And you enjoy hearing animals howl, don't you!

ŌURA: Shut up!

KIN (*tears in her voice*): Swore I'd hold my peace no matter what— but not anymore! Now I want Kikuo back. Letting him take the rap when you're the one who should be in jail! And you claim to be a human being! Well, if you're human, then worse than dogs we are and proud of it! (*As if something has snapped within her, she suddenly begins to cry hysterically.*)

Fumi, Manabu, and Mōri enter.

ŌURA: Get out! I don't have the time to carry on with the likes of you!

KIN: Don't worry, I going, but first I want Kikuo and Shichi back!

ŌURA: What! Say that again, you bitch! (*He strikes Kin and knocks her to the floor.*)

Kunio shields his mother and glares at Ōura.

YŪ: Don't!

Kin is calling her husband's name through her tears.

KUNIO: Mother!

This appeal by Kunio only feeds the flames of Kin's anguish, and she wails harder still.

FUMI (*embracing Kin*): Don't cry, please! (*Shocked after looking at her face*): Mother, bring something quick! She's bleeding!

Yū hands her some tissues, then exits to the inner rooms. Pause.

ŌURA: Manabu! You too, get over here.

FUMI: That's enough now. Don't cry. It'll only make the bleeding worse. (*To Kunio*): Help her lie down.

ŌURA: Did you hear what Kin said? You're just the same, getting all heated up about some skirt! Who do you think made it possible for you to go to school? Who do you owe your life to? You'd be nothing without your mother and me! You're so smart, you've always got some goddam excuse, but you act like some damned cat in heat! Kunio was your student. The teacher's an ungrateful bastard, so how can you expect the student to be any better? He said he'd kill me. Well, first thing tomorrow morning, I'm reporting you to the chairman of the school board and see to it that you're fired! You can go to Kobe or Osaka or anywhere you damn well please! The likes of you has no business teaching in the first place!

Kunio rises suddenly and goes to the kitchen. Yū returns with some cotton. Zombielike, Kunio reappears with a kitchen knife in his right hand.

YŪ: No! Somebody, come quick!

Kin immediately tries to stop Kunio by throwing herself at his legs. But Kunio brushes her aside and continues toward Ōura.

KIN: Mr. Manabu! Stop him!

Manabu and Mōri restrain the struggling Kunio. Ōura jumps into the garden and runs off. Manabu twists the knife from Kunio's hand.

MANABU: Kunio! (*He and Kunio glare at each other.*) How many times have I told you! There's nothing more sacred than a human life! (*Pause.*) Why can't you go to high school? Why? What's stopping you? The man who resorts to violence is the real weakling! If you're going to kill someone, you'll have to do it over my dead body! (*He holds out the knife.*) Kill me first! Go ahead! Kunio!

Kunio grabs the knife and glares at Manabu. Pause.

KUNIO: You'll never understand! (*He throws the knife into the garden and exits through the kitchen.*)

KIN: Kunio! Kunio! (*She continues to stare, as if following Kunio's retreating figure with her eyes.*)

The remaining four characters are breathless. Kin looks at Manabu, as do Yū, Fumi, and Mōri.

Curtain.

ACT THREE

Early March the following year. The day of the Kiyomori Festival.
Overcast. The home of Kurihara Manabu. In the room at stage right, a
magnificent table has been installed, set with plates, thimblelike sake
cups, and layered boxes filled with food. Kin sits in the kotatsu *at*
stage left while Yū treats her with moxa on her bare back. Firecrackers.
The clock strikes four.

YŪ: I wonder when it will be low tide?

KIN: Five fifteen.

YŪ: A little more than an hour from now. I just hope the rain
holds off until the procession's made it across the beach. And
I wish Manabu'd get back here. What's he up to, anyway?

KIN: Wish I knew where that fool Kunio had gotten himself and
what he was up to.

YŪ: He hasn't been back since the night we had that trouble
here. That was last May. It's been five, six . . . ten months!
You think he's been in Hiroshima all this time?

KIN: Mizz Kurihara, why do we suffer like this? Ever since I was
a child, I never went to school like other kids, just worked and
worked for my parents. I never did anything wrong to deserve suffering like this. If there are really gods and Buddhas
in the world, you'd think we'd be the first to be saved!

Yū does not answer.

KIN: "I wonder if someone wouldn't pay us for Mitsuko?"
Sometimes in the middle of the night, I get these thoughts
about my fifteen-year-old. Gods help me, I've got the heart of
a demon! Clasp my hands and pray Shichi to forgive me I do:
No matter how poor I get, I'll never do like Yajima and turn
our daughter into a whore. What good could come of that?

YŪ: You're right. It's times like those you've got to pray. Buddha knows all. All the sufferings of his world are our just
deserts for deeds committed in our previous lives. We have to
pray for the strength to resign ourselves to our fate.

KIN: That's right, but there are times when you just can't
accept . . . .

YŪ: Like the preacher says: we're born into this world full of
sin. From the moment of birth we have the horns of demons

sprouting from our head. All we can hope for is the strength to persevere. If we feel like complaining, the six syllables of the nembutsu will save us. When you think of the suffering of the Buddha Amida, our troubles are just so much dust in the wind.

KIN: Even so, you know what they say: money softens even the winds of hell.

YŪ: See, that's why you're punished: because you think and talk like that!

KIN: But it's too unfair: the rich get richer and the poor get poorer. Does that mean that the poor are lazy? Not on your life. (*Pause.*) Isn't that enough?

YŪ: Oh! (*Laughing*): You see what I mean, that's your punishment! You said those sinful things, and I forgot how many I started.

KIN (*laughing*): This woman's too much! Everything's my fault, isn't it!

YŪ: Well, I counted up to thirty-three. I suppose a few more won't hurt.

KIN: Easy for you to say, it's my back! You're the one who'll end up in hell for inflicting so much pain in the world!

YŪ: Wouldn't be surprised!

They both laugh. Yū puts away the can containing the moxa.

KIN: Is the fire still lit? I feel so cold. (*She sticks her head into the* kotatsu *and stirs the charcoal.*) "Pine resin's good for the liver, take it as often as you can," they say, but who can drink that awful stuff?

YŪ: They say it really works, though.

KIN: Are people who say Wakamatsu works for stomach pain,* but my problems began after the baby was born last year if you ask me. Haven't stopped bleeding since. Supposed to be a good gynecologist on Etajima, but add in the boat fare, and it'd cost more than 500 yen to see him.

YŪ: You're just exhausted, that's all. If you'd stay in bed and rest, you'd feel better in no time.

KIN: Never used to get chills like this.

---

*Wakamatsu is a patent stomach remedy.

YŪ: The stew's ready. Come over here and have a taste.

KIN: I really don't feel hungry. (*So saying, she goes to the room at stage right. She is wearing a sleeveless padded jacket and a man's muffler.*)

Yū pours the tea. Kin does not touch the food but only sips the warm liquid.

YŪ (*taking a photo album from the alcove*): Look at this. Here's one of Shichi carrying little Tsutomu and giving him a ride on a horse.

KIN: Look how cute Tsutomu is! Was me made him up for this picture.

YŪ: Shichi was such a good, quiet man . . . .

KIN: Shichi, you fool! Up and dying like that. . . . He was a kind man. Raise my voice, you know, and he'd say, "Take it easy, will you?" and laugh. Take the wind right out of my sails. (*Pause.*) Your father, old Mr. Ōura, wasn't feeling well when this was taken, either, was he?

YŪ: The night before, he'd told the young men in the New Land Association to "drink to their heart's content," and together they'd polished off twenty gallons of sake!

KIN: That's right! Now I remember. I danced and your father gave me a bouquet of flowers. Really liked me best he did. Never forget. Eleven I was. Quit school and was going out with the fishermen to work the nets off the coast of Korea for the first time. Soon as we'd got past Shimonoseki, my belly began to ache. "Might be cholera," he said and turned the boat back to Hakata before we reached the open sea. Owe him my life. When I got pregnant with Haruko, rest her soul, he didn't say a word to me but told my parents to let me marry Shichirō. Even gave us his blessing at the ceremony. Then there was the time he was in bed with the palsy. Shichi'd been drafted and wasn't there. Looked after him, I did, day and night. "Kin," he said, "I don't know what I'd do without you." Squeezed my hand . . . . (*She sniffs back the tears.*) He really died with dignity.

Firecrackers.

KIN: Bet he and Shichi are together right now. "Cold sake really hits the spot, right Shichi!" he'll be saying. (*She laughs but*

there is something forlorn in her voice.) Can't shake these chills.
I'm going to get back in the *kotatsu.*
Ōura enters from the garden. He is wearing a suit.
ŌURA: Hello!
YŪ: How's the work going?
ŌURA: Slowly. It's coming along. (*To Kin*): Still not feeling
   well, eh?
KIN: Don't think I'm long for this world.
ŌURA (*laughing*): Your kind doesn't die so easy. If you'd rest,
   you'd be better in no time.
YŪ: Come in and have a drink.
ŌURA: Tea's fine. (*He takes a thousand-yen note from his pocket. To
   Kin*): I wish I could do more, but I'm still a little strapped.
   (*Yū takes the money and gives it to Kin.*) Stop worrying. Just
   concentrate on getting well. When you're back on your feet,
   you can work in my kitchen, and I'll take Mitsuko on as a
   maid. (*Pause. He accepts a cup of tea. To Yū*): Economy's a
   mess, so the parade's more like a funeral procession.
YŪ: The fishing's not good either.
ŌURA: In the old days . . . . (*He indicates the sea with his chin.*)
   Just take a look. Not a single boat out there flying streamers
   to boast a good catch. In the old days, the town'd be upside
   down with the ruckus . . . . By the way, I gave three thousand
   to the New Land Association.
YŪ: That was good of you. They seem to be having a hard time
   getting contributions.
ŌURA: How are people going to get along? We're in one hell of
   a mess.
YŪ: Can't something be done?
ŌURA: Too many damned fools around, that's all. They're only
   looking out for number one. Put them in office, and the first
   thing they do is raise the taxes of the people who elected
   them! Why, I was just over in Kure today, raising hell at the
   tax office . . . .
SHIMIZU (*from the garden*): Hello!
YŪ: Toku! Welcome back! (*To Ōura*): Maybe you don't recognize him. It's Shimizu Tokumatsu's boy. He went to grade
   school with Manabu. He's in Tokyo these days.

ŌURA: Tokumatsu? He died awful young, didn't he?

YŪ: Tokuichi was raised by his granny.

ŌURA: So Tokumatsu had a fine boy like this, did he? Well, how are things in Tokyo?

SHIMIZU (*laughing*): Nothing to boast about.

YŪ: We're so proud of you. You lost both parents so young, nobody'd have been surprised if you'd turned out bad.

ŌURA: Took real guts. Speaking of guts, whatever became of Kunio? Doesn't anybody know what became of him?

YŪ: As a matter of fact, the police were here yesterday . . . .

ŌURA: I was afraid of that.

YŪ: They didn't say he was in any trouble, just that they had him in the Hiroshima East precinct and we should come and get him. So this morning Manabu went to pick him up.

ŌURA: Why didn't you tell me? I'd have gone.

YŪ: Manabu said he had to drop in the bookstore in Hiroshima anyway. He should be back any time now.

ŌURA (*to Kin*): Life hasn't been easy, has it? This time make sure to tell him. When you're in a jam, let me know. I can always let you have five hundred or a thousand yen to tide you over. Take care of yourself. (*To Yū*): I'll try to drop by again tonight. (*Exits.*)

YŪ: Toku, come on in.

SHIMIZU (*going to the* kotatsu, *to Kin*): Not feeling well, are you?

KIN: Been better. Been in and out of bed since last summer. Haven't been able to work a stitch.

SHIMIZU: You lost your husband in that incident with the torpedo. Things really have been rough.

KIN: Like being cast into hell. At the end of last year, sent a blood sample to the Red Cross Hospital in Hiroshima. Said I had leukemia.

SHIMIZU (*shocked*): Leukemia?

KIN: Some kind of mistake.

SHIMIZU: You think the radiation you got when you went looking for your sister did it?

KIN: Don't see why I should get sick now, after eight years. What do you think? Could radiation do it? Ever hear of anything like this in Tokyo?

SHIMIZU (*pausing*): Manabu'd be the one to ask.

KIN: "Never been anything like this before, so it's hard to tell," he says.

SHIMIZU: Don't they say moxa helps?

KIN: If it were the bomb, then moxa should help, but it doesn't, so it must be something else.

SHIMIZU: I hope you're right.

KIN: Maybe there's some good medicine I could take in Tokyo?

YŪ: You can't expect to see yourself get better overnight. It's the same with any disease. You have to treat the source of the problem.

KIN: But I haven't worked for more than six months!

YŪ: Where could Manabu be?

KIN: Kunio ran away from home last year. Got mad when I said I wouldn't let him go to high school and ran off. Been hoping after he graduated you'd be able to help him find a job in Tokyo . . . . Couldn't find anything just out of junior high like this, could he?

SHIMIZU: That is a problem . . . .

KIN: Be much obliged for anything you could do. (*Hands on the floor, she bows deeply.*)

Shimizu is silent. Fumi, dressed in a kimono, returns.

YŪ: Let's worry about that after Kunio gets back, shall we?

SHIMIZU: Let me discuss the matter with Manabu. (*He seats himself at the table.*)

YŪ: Where's the procession now?

FUMI: Oh, it's still got a long way to go—it's still down by the school. (*To Shimizu*): Welcome home!

YŪ: Fumi, pour Toku some sake.

SHIMIZU: If I wait by Kiyomori's Tomb, I'll be able to see the whole thing, won't I?

FUMI: It's already crowded there.

YŪ: Why not stay here? They're going to carry the shrine right past here this year.

KIN: But to really appreciate the festival, you have to watch the procession when it goes along the beach. That's the part city folk like best.

SHIMIZU (*laughing*): Hey, don't forget I was born and raised on this island!

YŪ: That's right!

KIN: Sorry, Fumi, a cup of tea?

YŪ: Wouldn't you be better off going home to bed?

KIN: I'll wait for Kunio.

SHIMIZU: You sure have had your troubles. (*He is staring at Kin.*) *Kin just wipes away her tears.*

FUMI: Here's your tea.

KIN: Thanks.

Fumi places a flask of sake on a tray. Then she pours a cup for Shimizu.

SHIMIZU: Thank you.

KIN: Anybody'd mistake them for a happily married couple. Not married yet are you?

SHIMIZU (*concealing his embarrassment with a laugh*): Maybe I should take Fumi here back with me.

KIN: See, that's the way city folk go about things.

SHIMIZU: Have some. (*He hands his cup to Fumi.*)

FUMI: I don't drink.

KIN: Don't say that. It's not good manners.

YŪ (*watching as Fumi accepts the cup*): Well!

KIN: Fumi, get him to take you to Tokyo.

FUMI: I'm just having fun, Mother. (*She returns the cup empty.*)

KIN (*laughing weakly*): Almost never served my husband sake. "Here you are," I said once. Handed him his cup, and he just stared at me and said, "What's wrong?" But he sure looked happy as he drank. "Tastes different," he said. "Kin, let's work hard as we can," he said. "Our children are our treasure." (*Tears cloud her voice. Pause.*) Sorry. I'm spoiling your sake. Just habit, I guess, complaining like this.

YŪ: A little home cooking must taste good. Have dinner with us once before you leave, all right? We missed our chance the last time you were here.

Fumi pours sake for Shimizu.

SHIMIZU (*drinking and offering the cup to Fumi*): One more cup.

FUMI: This'll be all for me. (*Drinks.*) I must be red as a beet. My face feels hot.

KIKUO (*dressed for the festival enters from the garden*): Mother, is Kunio back yet?

YŪ: Not yet.

FUMI: Where's the procession now?

KIKUO: Over by the fish mousse shop. Mother, come on. I'll give you a ride on my back. You can sit over in Maruichi's living room and watch from there.

KIN: No thanks. Can't go looking like this.

KIKUO: You can't see the girls in the palanquins from here. Come on. They're really something to see.

KIN: Kunio'll be disappointed if I'm not here when he gets back.

FUMI: Have some. (*She hands Kikuo the sake cup.*)

YŪ: He's the spitting image of Shichi when he was young!

Shintani enters. He is dressed like Kikuo but carries a ceremonial box tied to a pole over his shoulder.

SHINTANI: Kikuo, there you are! (*Referring to the sake*): I'll have mine in a big cup if you don't mind. Cold'd be fine. Toku, go up on the hill and take a look. You'll be surprised how big the pines have gotten. Hey, this is great, having somebody whose hands smell like powder pour your sake! Taira Kiyomori, here's looking at you! (*He empties the cup in one gulp.*)

FUMI: Tadashi!

KIKUO: What do you expect? Poor man's drinking all by himself!

SHIMIZU: Don't overdo it. You won't be able to walk a straight line, and you'll be the laughingstock of the parade! (*He laughs.*)

SHINTANI: Don't worry! We're the famous duo from the NBC, right, Kikuo? Let's show them a little teamwork, what d'you say? Come on, let's go! Come on!

Kin crawls out of the kotatsu. *Shintani and Kikuo toss the box back and forth in a traditional display of agility and strength.*

SHINTANI: How's that? Okay, let's give 'em an encore. Once more, come on!

KIKUO: Hey, take it easy!

KIN: Go ahead, one more time.

They repeat their performance, but this time Shintani fumbles.

SHIMIZU: Watch it!

SHINTANI: Not enough sake!

KIKUO: See what I mean? The man's dedicated to making my life difficult!

SHINTANI: Talk, talk! Toku, believe it or not, you're looking at the vice-chairman of the Young Men's Society.

SHIMIZU: Hey, really?

KIKUO: Corrupt to the core he is, too!

SHINTANI: You idiot! (*Sonorously*): "We of the Young Men's Society, working toward the creation of a peaceful Japan and for the happiness of the workers . . . ." See, Toku?

Shimizu is laughing.

KIN: Tadashi, sing him a song, why don't you? Such a fine voice you've got.

SHINTANI: Fumi, give me something to wet my whistle. (*He drinks and sings.*) "Well, here's a song of the Seto Sea!"

KIKUO (*chiming in*): "Seto Sea, the Seto Sea!"

SHINTANI:

"This the tomb of Kiyomori?
Fell in love, or so they say."

KIKUO: "Fell in love! He fell in love!"

SHINTANI:

"Pined away, or so they say,
His love comes to meet him every day!"

(He begins to clap his hands.)

"Three hundred leagues to Edo town!
Let's go and take a look around.
No shoes on our feet, how far'll we get?
Who cares? A journey starts with a single step!
No wine in our craw, how far'll we get?
Ah, the road so long, we'll make it yet!"

Shouting this refrain, he prances as if carrying and rocking the portable shrine and exits at a run.

KIKUO: Hey, wait for me! (*In a rush, he picks up the pole-box and chases after his friend.*)

YŪ: He really does have a fine voice!

Firecrackers.

YŪ: Looks like it's going to rain.

KIN: Can't stand these chills. Going to bed. Shivering something awful. (*Exits to the kitchen.*)

YŪ: Bundle up and stay in bed. Fumi, pour some more sake for Toku.

SHIMIZU: I still have some, thanks. She seems awfully weak.

YŪ: They say once you get leukemia, it's all over. Excuse me, I'll go look in on her.

After a moment's thought, she exits.

SHIMIZU: Let me have some tea, will you?

FUMI: You haven't finished your sake. (*She pours.*)

SHIMIZU: Fumi . . . what are you going to do about marriage?

FUMI: Nobody'd want someone like me. I never even finished high school.

SHIMIZU (*pausing*): You still working for the Occupation?

FUMI: We all got fired the end of last year. Maybe I should ask you to help me find a job in Tokyo too! (*She laughs.*)

SHIMIZU: Is that a promise? (*Laughs.*) Will you really come?

FUMI: You're kidding, aren't you?

SHIMIZU: I . . . . Fumi, what would you say if I asked you to marry me?

Fumi looks at him astonished.

SHIMIZU: I mean it.

FUMI: What would you want with a country girl like me?

SHIMIZU: What are you talking about? (*Pause. Feeling rejected*): Oh, never mind. Let's have another drink. (*Pouring for himself, he downs several thimbles of sake in rapid succession.*)

Fumi takes the empty flask to the kitchen.

SHIMIZU: Could I have a glass of water?

He watches her figure disappear. Then he consumes the water she brings him in a single gulp.

SHIMIZU (*after a pause*): Anyway, give it some thought. (*He leaves through the garden.*)

Fumi just sits and watches Shimizu leave. Pause. Mōri enters, sketch-book in hand. Fumi goes to the kitchen.

FUMI (*carrying a full flask of sake*): Have a drink, Mr. Mōri. (*She pours for him.*) I think I'll join you! (*She laughs vivaciously.*)

MŌRI: What's the occasion?

FUMI: Well, it's my first Kiyomori Festival as an adult, after all. Come on, now, drink up! (*She bursts into laughter.*)

MŌRI: What's got into you?

FUMI: Come on, bottoms up!

MŌRI: Hold your horses. Not on an empty stomach! (*He eats greedily.*)

FUMI: Here. (*She pours.*) What do you think? Would I make a good wife?

MŌRI: What? Whose, mine? You're going to spoil my appetite! (*He stares at Fumi.*)

YŪ (*returning through the kitchen*): Kin's got the chills and can't stop shaking. Maybe I should call the doctor . . . . (*Pause.*) Her bedding's completely worn out, and the stuffing's all over the place. It's a regular pigsty in there.

FUMI: I'm going to have a look at the parade. (*Exits.*)

YŪ: How do you like it, the festival, I mean? Actually, it's usually livelier than this. Here, have some more. (*She fills his cup.*) It really looks like rain. (*Pause.*) Have you heard anything more about Manabu and Reiko?

MŌRI: Not really.

YŪ: What about that job at the bank?

MŌRI: I haven't seen Kido for a while either. I really don't know.

YŪ: Mr. Mōri, you're a good friend. Watch out for Manabu, will you?

MŌRI (*laughing after a pause*): Of course I will. That's one thing you don't have to worry about.

YŪ: He's just plain unlucky. If it hadn't been for the bomb! . . . (*She weeps.*)

Kin enters from the darkening recesses of the kitchen. Her face is swollen and even paler than before. Her hair is dishelved, and the padded vested she wears is full of holes. Racked with fever, her gait is unsteady.

KIN (*weakly*): Mizz Kurihara . . . I . . . think I'm dying . . . .

YŪ (*shocked*): Kin!

KIN: Going to die . . . .

YŪ: You will if you don't lie down.

KIN: I . . . just can't die now! . . . (*Her voice is filled with tears, but her eyes are dry.*)

YŪ: You're not going to die. Don't worry!

KIN: Shichi's come for me. But I can't die now. Can't leave so many debts . . . my children . . . .

YŪ: You're not going to die! Hey! You're burning up with fever! (*At a loss, she stands stupefied.*)

KIN (*taking her hand*): Please . . . please. . . . (*She cries weakly.*) My children . . . the children . . . . (*Exhausted, she collapses in tears.*) Water . . . water . . . water . . . .

Mōri flies to the kitchen.

YŪ: Kin! (*She takes the cup Mōri brings and holds it to Kin's lips.*) Help her back to her room, will you?

Mōri helps Kin to her feet. Manabu returns with Kunio. Kunio has matured visibly. Yū looks at them, speechless.

MANABU: What happened!

KIN: Kuni. . . . (*Just barely standing*): Kunio . . . Kunio! (*She longs to hold him close.*) Kunio, you're just in time. Not going to . . . . (*She collapses.*)

YŪ (*regaining control*): Mr. Mōri, take her, quick!

Mōri picks her up and moves to the kitchen.

YŪ: Kunio, get the doctor! Dr. Tsuda! And on the way back, find Kikuo and Fumi and tell them to get back here. Tell them your mother's dying!

Kunio exits at a run.

YŪ (*looking at the clock*): Thirty minutes till the tide turns. I hope she can last . . . . (*Hastily, she runs to Kin's house.*)

Manabu is left standing alone and confused. Firecrackers. Manabu goes to his desk and sits staring into space. He is exhausted. Pause. Reiko appears in the garden dressed in a kimono. Partly because of the gaiety of her costume and partly because she has been ill and is thinner, she appears a full-grown woman. Pause.

MANABU: What's wrong?

REIKO: I'm so sorry. (*They have not seen each other in some time, and partially for that reason, her voice is already tearful.*)

MANABU: You've lost weight.

A little more at ease. Reiko sits down near Manabu.

REIKO (*sweetly*): Have you been well?

MANABU: Thanks.

Pause.

REIKO: Are you mad at me?

Manabu is silent.

REIKO: I've been sick. (*Pause.*) What's wrong? It's your health, isn't it?

Manabu does not answer.
REIKO: I've been suffering, too, you know.
MANABU: And?
REIKO: And? . . .
Manabu is silent.
REIKO: I don't know what to think anymore.
MANABU: Marry him.
Reiko stares at Manabu. Pause.
REIKO (*playfully*): You don't mind if I get married?
Manabu's eyes are fixed on her.
REIKO (*laughing, uncomfortable under his gaze*): Don't be such a child! Show a little spunk!
MANABU (*trying to return her smile*): Shall we go see the procession?
REIKO: We ought to stay here, don't you think?
MANABU: How about some sake?
REIKO: You mustn't! (*Pause.*) You're not any better, are you?
MANABU: I am! What do you mean? (*Pause.*) Reiko, if . . . what if I had to go in the hospital? Are you sure you could handle it?
REIKO: Are you going in the hospital?
MANABU: Just supposing.
REIKO: Aren't you feeling well?
MANABU (*forcing a smile*): I thought I was asking the questions.
REIKO: Is it true what they say, that with A-bomb disease there's no telling when you might die?
MANABU (*laughing*): Why do you ask all of a sudden?
REIKO: Is is true that your days are numbered?
MANABU: Maybe.
REIKO (*with a steady gaze on Manabu*): Then it's true?
MANABU: What is this all of a sudden?
There is the sound of a motor boat making its way through the Inland Sea.
MANABU: If you don't go see the procession soon, it'll be over.
REIKO (*after a pause*): When I was in bed with my cold, Mother said, "Let's suppose you married Manabu. If you got sick like you are now, who'd take care of him?" She said as far as she's concerned, I could do what I pleased and she didn't care what anybody said. But then you know what? (*Pause. She looks at*

Manabu.) She said, "The saddest thing in life is when a woman's husband dies before she does," and when I looked at her, she was crying.

Manabu is silent.

REIKO: Mother says she likes you a lot, and Father says he has nothing but respect for you. And they say it's really awful about what happened. But they also say there's no reason why I should take the curse of the bomb on myself.

MANABU: Curse of the bomb?

REIKO: Yes. They say there's nothing we can do for the victims now . . . . Why did you have to go and get bombed like that! (*Pause.*) Please, help me! Tell me what to do! (*She clings to Manabu.*)

Pause. Manabu is silent.

REIKO (*looking into Manabu's face*): Please, tell me what I should do!

MANABU: Reiko! (*He embraces her. Pause.*)

In the distance, the song of the men carrying the portable shrine can be heard.

REIKO: Father's gone and invited the branch manager of that bank and his family to come to our house today. I ran out to come here. (*Manabu has loosened his embrace.*) What's wrong? (*Forcing a smile.*) I don't care. You're my teacher after all.

Manabu gazes into Reiko's eyes. Fumi hastens in from the kitchen. She runs to the inner room, reemerges with an apron and a cord to tie up the sleeves of her kimono, and runs off again.

MANABU (*after a pause*): Reiko, go ahead and marry him.

Reiko looks at him, speechless.

MANABU: Maybe your father's right. Maybe I should be the only one sacrificed to the bomb.

REIKO: I don't care. I don't care!

MANABU: Reiko!

REIKO: Honestly! (*She takes his hand.*) I don't care! I don't care!

MANABU: Reiko!

REIKO: I don't care what my father says. I'll show him! You'll see!

MANABU: Reiko! (*He is about to embrace her but stops.*) Reiko! (*He forces himself to shake his head.*)

Reiko stares at him.

MANABU: Reiko, marry him . . . for me.

REIKO: No!

MANABU: Reiko, I'm done for. There's no hope for me.

REIKO: No! I won't! I won't!

MANABU (*struggling to remain rational*): Listen, I'm thinking only of myself here. I really couldn't care less about whether you're happy or not. That's right. There's no reason why you should have to take the wreckage of war on yourself. Reiko, you'll have to think of your own future.

REIKO: What are you saying!

MANABU: Don't be too angry with me. I know I've hurt you.

REIKO: Please, don't give up on me now!

MANABU (*hesitating*): Reiko, please, for my sake! Leave me alone, please. I want to be alone!

REIKO (*staring at him, then pushing away the hand she has been holding*): Weakling! I hate you and the bomb! I hate you! I hate you!

She glares at him. Her eyes are overflowing with tears. Manabu is silent. He can only return her stare.

Large drops of rain begin to fall from the dark sky. The song of the men carrying the shrine can be heard. It is a continuation of the song Shintani sang earlier.

"Kumosuke carried the shrine, you bet!
Up to the clouds and around he went!
In nothing but a loincloth yet!
Kumosuke carried the shrine, you bet!"

Firecrackers. Suddenly, Manabu pulls Reiko to him and embraces her ferociously. He covers her face with kisses and cries, "Reiko! Reiko!" as if he has lost his mind. It is as if he is trying to exhaust in a single instant all the youthful passion that has been pent up within him. The rain falls still harder. Straining for breath. Reiko gently pulls her face away and, taking Manabu's face in her hands, says, "Don't die, all right? Please don't die!" Then she pulls his face toward her. Reiko's words brings Manabu back to his senses, and he pushes her away. Reiko, her heart about to burst, stares at Manabu. Yū enters from the door to the kitchen.

YŪ (*walking slowly toward the altar, half mad with grief*): Kin was burning up with fever . . . she died vomiting bright red blood. She died . . . .
She opens the altar, kindles the lamp inside, and intones the nembutsu.
YŪ: She died babbling about her children. . . . (*Nembutsu.*) Now the Buddha will take you in . . . . There was blood flowing from her nose and mouth . . . .
Reiko is standing and staring at Yū's back at the altar and at Manabu, who is still seated at his desk. Pause. The only sound is Yū's prayer. The rain lets up a bit.
REIKO (*softly*): Manabu . . . .
Manabu does not respond. Quietly, Reiko exits. Manabu follows her with his eyes, wordlessly. Yū intones the nembutsu as if it were a weapon to beat back her grief. After a few moments, Mōri, also dumb with grief, enters from the kitchen. He seats himself before the altar. The portable shrine passes, leaving a wake of vigorous song. Firecrackers. Pause. Yū's prayers continue, but they are no longer prayers of grief. They are urgent pleas for Kin's salvation.
YŪ: You worked and worked . . . from the day you were born till the day you died. Your life was nothing but suffering and pain, wasn't it, Kin?
Pause. Unconsciously, in the same manner as Yū, Mōri has slowly clasped his hands before him and is also praying for Kin.
FUMI (*from the kitchen*): Mother! What are you doing? We'll boil the water to wash the body here, all right?
YŪ: Go ahead.
The light from the newly kindled hearth flickers in the dark kitchen.
MANABU: I'm next.
YŪ (*looking at him sternly*): Manabu! Don't talk like that! (*Pause.*) You have to keep your spirits up and live!
FUMI: Mother, somebody has to stay with Kin. (*She has acquired the strength to direct even her mother's actions.*)
YŪ (*rising*): Manabu, don't give up!
FUMI (*urgently*): Mother!
Yū exits through the kitchen. Manabu and Mōri both remain silent. A long pause.
MŌRI (*still looking at the altar*): She was a regular workhorse . . . had hands like a man . . . biggest damned knuckles . . . . (*He*

is staring at his own hands.) Her life . . . she worked her whole life . . . .
Manabu slams the altar shut.

MANABU (*almost as if speaking to himself*): I dropped in at the Red Cross Hospital in Hiroshima today. They said my white cell count is way up.
Pause. Shimizu enters.

MŌRI (*glancing at Manabu for an instant*): Those hands were alive! (*He picks up his sketchbook and exits.*)

FUMI (*to Kunio, who has returned through the kitchen*): What's wrong with you? Don't just leave your mother like that.

KUNIO: She's dead. What do you want me to do?
Pause.

MANABU (*intensely anguished*): Why did she have to die? Why? Why?
Shocked, Kunio cannot move. Pause.

KUNIO (*kneeling before Manabu and bowing*): Forgive me.
Manabu is silent. The rain stops, and the clouds in the western sky begin to disperse.

SHIMIZU: Hey, Kunio! You want to go back with me?
Kunio does not respond.

SHIMIZU: Manabu, you mind if I take him back to Tokyo with me? His mother wanted me to find him a job so badly. (*To Kunio*) Come on, Kunio, I'll take you!

KUNIO: May I?
Manabu's eyes are fixed on Kunio. Rays of the setting sun pour through the clouds.

MANABU: Kunio, you and Toku go up on the hill. The evening sun's beautiful after a rain. The pines should have new greenery, too.

SHIMIZU: Good idea. Come on, let's go. (*Exits.*)

KUNIO: Sir, I . . . .

MANABU (*looking at Kunio hard*): Take care of yourself. You have to work for your mother as well as yourself.

KUNIO: Thanks. You won't have to worry about me. (*Exits.*)
Manabu watches him go. "A human being is born!" In the western sky the sun appears between the clouds and bathes the room in a crimson light. Manabu gazes into the western sky. He looks at his shadow and experiments moving it. He looks at his hands. Pause. He has re-

discovered, "I'm alive!" Gazing into space, he seems to have said something. Was it, "Mother!"? Tears are running down his cheeks. Pause. It is more likely he has sworn, "Damn it! I'm going to live!" Staring into the sun, he clenches his fists. Firecrackers. After the rain, the sun in the pellucid evening sky is beautiful.
Curtain.

The Island (act 1, scene 1)

Photographs of the original 1957 production of *The Island* by the Mingei Company are provided courtesy of Hotta Kiyomi.

The Island (act 3)

The Island (act 3)

The Island (act 3)

The Head of Mary (act 2, scene 2)

Photographs of the 1980 production of *The Head of Mary* by the Haiyūza Company are provided courtesy of Haiyūza.

The Head of Mary (act 4)

The Elephant (act 2)
Photographs of the 1970 production of *The Elephant* by Seinenza are provided courtesy of Seinenza.

The Elephant (act 2)

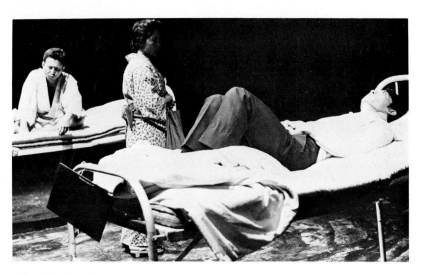

The Elephant (act 2)

Nezumi Kozō: The Rat (one)

Nezumi Kozō: The Rat (six)

Nezumi Kozō: The Rat (three)

Nezumi Kozō: The Rat (seven)

THE HEAD OF MARY

The Head of Mary: Nagasaki as Theophany

Nagasaki presents a unique dilemma. Here was the most Christian city in Japan obliterated by an atomic bomb. How could this have happened? How could God have allowed the faithful to be destroyed?

A CATHOLIC RESPONSE

The classic answer to this question was formulated by Nagai Takashi, a Catholic physician who experienced the bomb and published a moving memoir before his death in 1951 from radiation aftereffects. The Nagasaki bomb had been aimed at the Mitsubishi Munitions factory but had been diverted by wind and had exploded over the Urakami district of the city where a major cathedral dedicated to the Virgin Mary stood. Nagai interpreted this as a sign of divine providence, and he saw those Christians who had perished as the elect, the chosen few who would redeem the sins of Japan and indeed of all mankind.

Is there not a profound relationship between the destruction of Nagasaki and the end of the war? Nagasaki, the only holy place in all Japan—was it not chosen as a victim, a pure lamb, to be slaughtered and burned on the altar of sacrifice to expiate the sins committed by humanity in the Second World War? . . .

How noble, how splendid was that holocaust of August 9, when flames soared up from the cathedral, dispelling the darkness of war and bringing the light of peace! In the very depth of our grief we reverently saw here something beautiful, something pure, something sublime. Eight thousand [Christians], together with their priests, burning with pure smoke, entered into eternal life. All without exception were good people whom we deeply mourn. . . .

Why did we not die with them on that day, at that time, in [the Urakami Cathedral]? Why must we alone continue this miserable existence? It is because we are sinners. Ah! Now indeed we are forced to see the enormity of our sins! It is because I have not made expiation for my sins that I am left behind. Those are left who were so deeply rooted in sin that they were not worthy to be offered to God.[1]

Tanaka Chikao's 1958 play *The Head of Mary* elaborates on these themes. It does not simply recapitulate them but explores the problematic aspects of a Christian interpretation of Nagasaki and reformulates that interpretation in a uniquely Japanese idiom.

TANAKA CHIKAO AND THE IMPORTANCE OF STYLE

An elder statesmen of Japanese modern theater, Tanaka was born in Nagasaki in 1905. He began his career in the theater in the late 1920s under the influence of Kishida Kunio, the leading dramatist in the "literary" school of playwriting, and he has remained faithful to Kishida's legacy, teaching and writing widely on the literary aspects of dramatic composition. His plays reveal an emphasis on language and style that distinguishes them from the more prosaic works of most shingeki dramatists, where the function of language is principally to communicate ideas. In Tanaka's work language takes precedence over ideas; and ideas frequently originate and are amplified in an assiduously crafted style.[2]

Although he has never been baptized, Tanaka considers himself a Christian and has had his family baptized in the Catholic Church.[3] He was not in Nagasaki on August 9, 1945, but as a native of the city and as a Christian, the questions raised by the bombing and by its theological implications clearly troubled him. In general, Tanaka seems to accept Nagai's interpretation, but as a dramatist acutely concerned with language, he could not accept Nagai's overtly Christian rhetoric. To what extent could notions of divine providence, sin, and expiation be truly meaningful in Japan's non-Christian culture? In *The Head of Mary*, Tanaka employs his unique gifts as a stylist to recast the Christian interpretation of Nagasaki in an original, Japanese idiom.

The names of the characters in *The Head of Mary* are significant. Jigorō is, for example, a gigolo: a small-time hood and lecher. Yabari is a college student who has returned to his native Nagasaki to urge the survivors to stand up and be counted for the cause of peace. His name is written with the same characters as the word *yahari*, "as one might have expected," and he is in fact filled with precisely the kind of passionate but sophomoric ideas one would expect of a college student in his twenties. A third character with a significant name is Shinobu, "to endure." The significance of her name is revealed in her opening soliloquy, one of the most famous speeches in modern Japanese drama and a passage that typifies the unique poetic and theological idiom of Tanaka's play.

> Again tonight I am standing.
> Like a dedicated servant girl
> Carved voluptuously into the cold stone pillar,
> The polished white marble,
> The imposing marble edifice of a bank.
> But,
> Beneath my skirt, a dagger sheathed in white,
> This borrowed dagger,
> A dagger to be returned,
> Returned to its rightful owner.
> Shinobu—"Endurance"—
> That is my name.
> When I see him, I will approach him in silence,
> And with a single thrust, return his dagger!
> Ohhhh! (*As a deep sigh.*)
> At that moment, Shinobu, unperturbed . . . .
> Hah-hah-hah-hah! (*She laughs captivatingly.*)
> My complexion, the hue of my eyes will be as always.
> As if to ask directions,
> I will draw near, inquire,
> Press my belly to his—
> Then thrust!
> Disengage!
> And resume my journey down the road.
> Like any pebble on that road,
> I will obliterate chance;
> Traveling the path of the infinite, the limitless, the relative,

I will expand, billow,
Disperse like the mist in my own existence.
Ah! How I long to extinguish the necessity,
The absoluteness of my being! But for him!
But for that man who encumbered me,
Who left me with this something,
Who left it unbidden then vanished—
I hate that man!
That is why
I must kill him,
Extinguish him!
Because I am a woman who knows not how to give love,
I must take life
From the one who left me with this dagger,
Who taught me a necessity outside myself!
I shall be my own beneficiary.
I must cool this warm dagger,
Warmed by the blood coursing through my belly,
In the heat of my opponent's blood.
To the frigidity of fire!
My heart will shudder with delight,
My hand will grip the blade!

A CATHOLIC DRAMA COUCHED IN BUDDHIST TERMS

The Head of Mary is a Catholic drama. The main story line concerns a conspiracy by a group of Catholic believers to abscond with the pieces of an imposing statue of the Virgin Mary that had stood in front of the Urakami Cathedral at the time of the Nagasaki bombing.[4] They want to reassemble the neglected icon in their hideaway as their unique object of veneration. The group identifies with this Mary because like them she is a *hibakusha* scarred by the atomic blast. They believe that she alone can understand their suffering and their pain, because she has experienced it herself. Their prayers are heard, and in the final scene, the statue of Mary actually speaks to the group in their own Nagasaki dialect. Try as they might, however, they are unable to budge her head, the last piece of the statue that remains.

Although *The Head of Mary* is thoroughly Catholic in conception, it may seem foreign to Catholic readers. This is because Tanaka avoids the familiar tropes of Nagai's formulation and couches the play instead in native Japanese—principally Buddhist—terms.

Shinobu is the long-suffering, enduring woman. Her husband Momozono is bedridden with severe anemia that may or may not have been caused by the bomb, and she nurtures him and their child even as she struggles to fill the vacuum of meaning within herself. She dreams of killing Jigorō, whom she met in the ruins after the bombing. Jigorō had stolen Shinobu's ring, her last memento of her mother, and left a dagger in its place; but as her soliloquy reveals, that is not her real reason for wanting him dead. She dreams of killing him because she blames him for "teaching her a necessity outside herself," that is, for anchoring her in her own particularity, by showing her that she is defined by forces, events, circumstances beyond herself. Shinobu represents stoic endurance under this "encumbrance." She wishes to disencumber herself and "extinguish the necessity,/ The absoluteness of her being."

As it turns out, Shinobu's soliloquy is actually a poem composed by her husband, and it reflects his understanding of her situation more than her own. Shinobu herself is much more ambivalent toward Jigorō, confessing later as he lies dying that she loves him; and her love stems from her gratitude to him, not only for a certain kindness he showed her in the atomic wasteland, but more importantly for the gift of the knowledge that she lives in some relation with "absoluteness," that all is not relative. She loves Jigorō because he awoke in her the idea that all is not endurance, that there is absolute, ultimate truth, just as her experience, the experience he confirmed by witnessing it, was absolute.

There is in all this a unique mixture of Catholic and Buddhist ideas. Shinobu's desire to "expand, billow,/ Disperse like the mist in [her] own existence" closely resembles the Buddhist quest for the extinction of the self. Shinobu's resentment against Jigorō for teaching her the "absoluteness" or irreducibility of her existence and her wish to "disperse like the mist" parallel the Buddhist longing to escape *karma,* the endless cycle of birth and rebirth that results from just such absoluteness of identity, just such historical anchoredness, just such attachment as the experience of the bomb forced on Shinobu and other survivors. And her love for him derives from the same source, from her gratitude to him for teaching her that she is not alone, damned by her experience, that there is truth and salvation outside herself.

Tanaka juxtaposes to this longing for total relativity, dispersion, and salvation from karmic suffering, the conviction that there is value in experience, that rather than reject it as an encumbrance, it should be embraced as a source of meaning. However, as he indicates in his depiction of Yabari, a clear understanding of that meaning is beyond man's capacity. Only God truly understands the meaning of human suffering.

Essentially, *The Head of Mary* expresses a Catholic theology using Buddhist terms and symbols. It is a Catholic drama written in Japan, a nation with a thousand-year Buddhist tradition that has proved highly resistant to Christianity and its ideas. Perhaps for a writer like Tanaka, who wished to hold out to the survivors of Nagasaki the salvific promise of Catholicism but who could not accept the overtly Christian rhetoric of a man like Nagai, there was no alternative but to couch his argument in Buddhist or quasi-Buddhist terms.

A REMAINING CONTRADICTION

The characters in *The Head of Mary* are rife with ambiguity and individual idiosyncrasy. Shika, the chief conspirator in the plot to steal Mary's head, works as a nurse by day and a prostitute by night. Shinobu loves the man she hates. Momozono is a "survivor" with apparently no connection with the bomb; and Jigorō commits suicide to escape his fear of death. This moral ambiguity is far richer than the more schematic portrayal in *The Island,* where basically good people are compromised by an evil social system. Moreover, Tanaka goes beyond Nagai's dualistic juxtaposition of "the elect" and "the sinners" to describe a highly complex relationship between an inscrutable God and His all-too human flock.

The Head of Mary breaks with shingeki orthodoxy in important respects. Its poetic idiom distinguishes it from realistic shingeki works, and its Catholic theology differs from the general-
ized humanism and tragedy characteristic of orthodox shingeki.
Concomitantly, activism replaces resignation. The plot to steal
Mary's head is an attempt to act meaningfully in response to the
atomic bomb experience, and it is contrasted with other possible responses, from Yabari's politics to Momozono's denial.

However, despite these considerable successes (or perhaps because of them), Tanaka's play seems cramped in the inhospitable
confines of the proscenium arch. In the end, Tanaka accepts the
prescriptions of realistic *staging* even as he rejects realistic *dramaturgy,* and the play is structured to meet the demands of a traditional production. The imaginative language and conception of
the play cry out to be freed from the restraints of the proscenium stage, to be given a performance form more consistent
with their creative élan. One of the achievements of the postmodern theater movement has been to develop those forms.

THE HEAD OF MARY
A Nagasaki Fantasia

A PLAY IN FOUR ACTS

by *Tanaka Chikao*

The Head of Mary (*Maria no kubi*) was first performed by the Shinjinkai (New Man) troupe in February 1959. The production was directed by the playwright. This translation is of the text found in *Gendai nihon gikyoku taikei,* vol. 4 (Tokyo: San'ichi shobō, 1971).

CAST OF CHARACTERS

Shinobu
Shika
Shizuka
Woman I
Woman II
Woman III
Woman IV
The Head of Mary
Three Women's Voices
Jigorō
Yabari
Momozono
A Policeman
Man I (Negro seaman)
Man II (Greying elderly man)
Man III (Caped man with a peg leg)
Man IV (Bureaucrat in his prime)
Man V (Thin, young man)
Dr. Sakamoto
Statue of a Saint

ACT ONE

SCENE ONE: SECOND FLOOR OF THE COMMUNITY MARKET

A winter night.
The sound of someone gently strumming a guitar. As it reverberates through the port, surrounded by mountains, the piercing sound of a steam whistle deepens the sleep of the harbor. Shika's room.
Actually, it is nothing more than a vacant storage room (A general outline of this community market should be gathered from the information provided in the next scene, as well as that provided here.) On four sides, rough plank walls. On a shelf affixed to one of them, a small mirror and a bundle. Very likely, the picture on the calendar that has been put up to stop a draft is the only decoration. There is a makeshift bed put together from fruit crates overlaid with a mattress. There is one chair. A small electric heater stands on the floor. In one corner, a dim, naked light bulb hangs on a cord strung from outside.
A door unhinged from who knows where stands in the opposite corner, and over it has been draped a large, soiled, arabesque wrapping cloth. Shika, who has just thrown over her shoulders the kimono she uses to cover her chemise, is opening the front door and looking outside. Her makeup is so thick it is almost pure white. Perhaps there is something wrong with her left ear, for she is wearing a dirty bandage over it that extends all the way to her jaw and gives her a disturbing appearance. With her rotund face, however, she would be classified as a beautiful woman, and her dark eyes shine with a mysterious light. Appropriately, her voice, too, is deep and raspy.
SHIKA *(fulsomely)*: Come again, you hear . . . don't forget! What? Hah-hah, you lecher, you!
She closes the door with a bang. We should see a large crucifix painted crudely on the door with black ink, but for the moment it is obscured by Shika, who is leaning against the door, listening briefly to the sounds outside, and raising her arms in a yawn. The thin stripe under her arm is clearly the result of some earlier repair.
She counts the bills she grips in one hand, then puts them away in a billfold she takes from under the bed. She goes to the mirror and checks her bandage. Finally, she switches off the light, removes her robe, and crawls into bed.

SCENE TWO: ENTRANCE TO THE COMMUNITY MARKET

The same night.
The fierce sound of someone strumming a guitar.
The porticoed entrance to the community market, an aged, worn barracks on the brink of collapse. The double, plank doors on the front are closed. Pickle barrels and the like are strewn about. Separated slightly from these doors is another, narrower one with a (broken) glass window through which the stairs leading to the second floor can be seen.
A naked light bulb shines coldly over the front doors.
Separated from this structure by an alley of perhaps three feet is a public toilet. Behind it stands a wall of piled stones, and beyond the stone wall at a distance of some three hundred meters is a river that extends into the harbor. It is not so much a filthy, polluted flow as it is a stagnant pond. The smokestacks and green masts bearing signal lamps of three or four ships and yachts can be seen overlapping in the distance.
Now then.
Black-caped Shinobu stands silhouetted against a pillar of the market portico. Her face is not visible, but in fact she is not beautiful. She cuts her hair short. Like a hawker at a train station, a tray hangs suspended from her neck.
The piercing sound of a small steam whistle.
Woman I appears without a sound, leans against the wall of the toilet, and smokes a cigarette with an air of innocence. She wears sandals and a cheap overcoat.
From the opposite direction, Man I enters and stops in front of Shinobu. He peers into her tray. He is asking her something in a low voice: "Kezgi l'yas hata eh, d'lasanda d'lasanna, aouh . . . . regard a lou," but it is barely audible and cannot be clearly identified. There is a possibility that it is French. As this is taking place, Woman I discards her cigarette and, concealing herself, observes the proceedings.
Shinobu's labored reply is as follows: "Shsh, mauj'gida lit. Ka, kaimo sneglisa subes uo oh . . . ." The Negro takes four or five bills from his pocket and places them in her tray. Warily, Shinobu goes to the smaller door behind her and opens it. "Shsh, mauj'gida lit. . . ." The Negro mounts the stairs. Woman I observes this whole process, then disappears.

Shinobu resumes her original stance.
A light comes on on the second floor.
Yabari, dressed in a student uniform, enters. He is looking for some-
one and shoots a quick glance at Shinobu but exits without stopping.
SHINOBU (*her voice is beautiful*):
Again tonight I am standing.
Like a dedicated servant girl
Carved voluptuously into the cold stone pillar,
The polished white marble,
The imposing marble edifice of a bank.
But,
Beneath my skirt, a dagger sheathed in white,
This borrowed dagger,
A dagger to be returned,
Returned to its rightful owner.
Shinobu—"Endurance"—
That is my name.
When I see him, I will approach him in silence,
And with a single thrust, return his dagger!
Ohhhh! (*As a deep sigh.*)
At that moment, Shinobu, unperturbed . . . .
Hah-hah-hah-hah! (*She laughs captivatingly.*)
My complexion, the hue of my eyes will be as always.
As if to ask directions,
I will draw near, inquire,
Press my belly to his—
Then thrust!
Disengage!
And resume my journey down the road.
Like any pebble on that road,
I will obliterate chance;
Traveling the path of the infinite, the limitless, the relative,
I will expand, billow,
Disperse like the mist in my own existence.
Ah! How I long to extinguish the necessity,
The absoluteness of my being! But for him!
But for that man who encumbered me,
Who left me with this something,

Who left it unbidden then vanished—
I hate that man!
That is why
I must kill him,
Extinguish him!
Because I am a woman who knows not how to give love,
I must take life
From the one who left me with this dagger,
Who taught me a necessity outside myself!
I shall be my own beneficiary.
I must cool this warm dagger,
Warmed by the blood coursing through my belly,
In the heat of my opponents blood.
To the frigidity of fire!
My heart will shudder with delight,
My hand will grip the blade!

Man II has been listening to Shinobu and observing her in silence for some time. He is wearing black tabi and wooden clogs. His black, straight-sleeved kimono looks like the costume worn by stage hands in the kabuki theater.

He has a small towel stuck in his sash and a square lunch box under his arm. His emaciated figure is permeated with loneliness, but there is still a glint deep in his eyes.

Now he has approached and gently spoken.

MAN II: Any takers?

Shinobu stiffens.

MAN II (*smiling*): Any takers?

Shaking her head, Shinobu retreats.

MAN II (*following her*): Neither one?

Without warning, Shinobu grabs Man II by the neck and forces him under the light.

MAN II: He . . . hey! (*He does not resist.*)

SHINOBU: You're not the one. (*She pushes him away.*)

MAN II (*massaging his neck*): It's like it was burning, here.

SHINOBU: What do you want?

MAN II: What I'm after's not in those boxes. It's this book of poetry . . . (*He picks up a thin pamphlet from inside the tray.*) This one. Hey, a new collection!

SHINOBU: Who are you?

MAN II: Me? What with the orders for publicity materials from the prefectural government, printers are busy these days. It's the showdown with the union. Beside that, there are appeals for peace, appeals from mothers, calls to action in the Such-and-Such Incident. . . . Thanks to them, it's overtime every night. (*Looking at the fingertips of both hands*): At the beginning I went about my work in the grand manner, but, well, thirty-five years is a long time. These hard, gray fingertips. There's hardly a fingerprint left. A man who's frittered away his life picking up pieces of lead type, the perpetual typesetter, that's me.

The sound of footsteps slowly approaches. Man II hastily pretends to be absorbed in the pamphlet. A heavy-set Policeman walks onto the stage.

SHINOBU (*affably*): Good evening.

POLICEMAN: Good evening. You're out late tonight.

SHINOBU: Yes.

POLICEMAN: How's your husband? A little better, I hope.

SHINOBU: If only!

POLICEMAN: The baby must miss you. Why don't you call it a night (*Exiting*): You know it's not safe around here.

MAN II: A friend?

Shinobu laughs ambiguously.

MAN II: Let me see, now. Thirty yen, wasn't it?

SHINOBU: Yes.

Policeman returns.

POLICEMAN: There's a favor I meant to ask. It's those stone thieves, the ones who've been pillaging the Urakami Cathedral.

Shinobu does not respond.

POLICEMAN: If it were just a brick or two taken for educational purposes, things would be different, but . . . .

SHINOBU: Tourists, walking off with "a memento," as they say.

POLICEMAN: But there's more to it than that. It seems there's someone trying little by little to steal the entire body of that Mary that stood before the Cathedral!

SHINOBU: You don't say!

POLICEMAN: My guess is they're selling the pieces to foreigners as souvenirs. They seem to be sneaking in after dark and carrying off the pieces. It's downright malicious. If you hear anything about it, let me know, will you?

SHINOBU: Of course.

POLICEMAN (*exiting*): These are hard times even for the Jesus gods. Getting atomic bombed and all, Mary's face covered with a keloid scar, and her body cracked to pieces . . . .

MAN II (*taking money from his coin purse*): The poem I like best is "Endurance's Dagger." The one you were just reciting.

SHINOBU: Is that a fact?

MAN II: You wrote it yourself, didn't you?

Shinobu shakes her head.

MAN II: But . . . .

SHINOBU: My husband is the author.

MAN II: Ah, your husband . . . .

SHINOBU: Is there something wrong with that?

MAN II: No. (*He chuckles.*) I just took it for granted that you'd written the poem about yourself, that's all.

SHINOBU: Why?

MAN II (*looking around the portico*): Now that you mention it, these pillars aren't exactly marble, are they!

SHINOBU: No, they're just wooden posts stinking of rotten vegetable scraps and the dregs of fermented bean paste.

MAN II: But the person in the poem is you, isn't it?

SHINOBU: No, it's just a woman. A woman.

MAN II: Yes it is! Your husband must be a good poet. He understands you . . . I mean, women so well.

SHINOBU (*denying it with a gesture*): You don't understand.

MAN II: And in the bottom of his heart, he . . . .

SHINOBU: He? . . .

MAN II: And you love him, too.

Shinobu does not answer.

MAN II: Don't you?

SHINOBU (*ironically*): If he heard you say that, he wouldn't be able to stop laughing.

MAN II: You're standing out here for your husband, an unknown poet, selling his poetry, aren't you?

SHINOBU: Yes. I think he's a wonderful poet. But . . . he's confined to bed. Anemia.

MAN II: I see. The bomb, eh? Poor fellow.

SHINOBU: He says it's not the bomb.

MAN II: That's even worse. Do you have children?

Shinobu casts her eyes downward.

MAN II: I'm sorry. Being a man, I could never hope to understand.

SHINOBU: What are you going on about?

MAN II: A saint, that's what you are.

SHINOBU: Yes. I think so myself. But why do you know that poem?

MAN II: I, er . . . .

SHINOBU: I remember!

MAN II: You used to stand in front of the bank in Hamanomachi.

SHINOBU: Yes.

MAN II: You're not going to sell many copies in a lonely place like this.

SHINOBU (*chuckling*): But the contraceptive jelly won't sell in a crowd.

MAN II: I see. Of course, I don't know the first thing about poetry. I just like the book.

SHINOBU: The book?

MAN II: Yes, written with a brush on rice paper then hand-bound with twisted strips of paper and covered with red, purple, green, and gold-flecked construction paper, I like the hand-made book itself.

Shinobu says nothing.

MAN II: Is it your handwriting?

SHINOBU: Yes. I'm afraid it's hardly legible.

MAN II: On the contrary, it's a practiced hand. You don't see such beautiful brush work very often these days. In every part of the book, you can feel the warmth of the person who made it.

SHINOBU: It's as my dead mother would have liked it. Yes, you're right, the book is covered with the grime of my hands. More than a few drops of my blood went into its making.

MAN II: I'm too poor to buy a woman's sympathy. And I certainly don't expect to buy yours for thirty yen. But if I can stand close enough to hear the limpid tones of your voice, gaze into your eyes, and distinguish the downy hairs on your cheek, then thirty yen is a bargain. Please forgive this slight contact with life that has been vouchsafed me. Yes, you, proud woman, your eyes half-closed, your nose held high! I know I am being forward. But I take your tolerance less as an indulgence than as a blessing. And yet, even as these words sleave my mouth, my own baseness comes flooding in on me, and . . . .

SHINOBU: Blessing? I never blessed you.

MAN II: Of course not, of course not. Please don't take offense. My days are numbered. I'm like this market, condemned and soon to be torn down. I have no family; my children . . . both of them must have died, bathed in the light and heat from the sky that August ninth day. I haven't seen them since. I'd been drafted to dig coal and was down in the mines on Kōyakijima. As a result, I'm condemned to live with the shame of survival. I have no past nor hope for the future. It's only that, well . . . the purple mushroom cloud I saw when I looked up from that island was so beautiful! I couldn't forget it even if I tried. When the mushroom cloud disappeared, a great crowd of people gathered and began running, first to the right and then to the left, like a pack of wild dogs before their prey, feinting and howling.

SHINOBU: Yes, wild dogs. Male wild dogs.

MAN II: But even if they were bad, how can you blame them? There was no order to their lives, no peace, and of course no posterity. Anxiety became a way of life. Then I discovered you, standing there in silence. Like a black narcissus, you stood silently in the darkness. Marvelous. Your silence, I mean. For the last two weeks, I have walked past you each night. Tonight I finally found the courage to speak.

SHINOBU: The consolation of ships passing in the night, is that it?

MAN II: Don't say that. You have meant so much to me. You are a respite, a blessing, however short-lived.

SHINOBU: A blessing.

MAN II: Yes. Don't worry, I'm just as fickle as the next man. Before long I'll get tired of you and move on to someone else.

(*Laughs.*) To know oneself; to know the self that deceives the self, that alone I cannot forget. How very sad to be born human! Thank you. Thanks to you even my poor blood is showing faint signs of life, and tonight I'll be able to enjoy warm dreams in my unheated room. I'm grateful. Farewell.

SHINOBU: Wait. If you are truly grateful . . . .

MAN II: Yes?

SHINOBU: I have a secret request of you.

MAN II: Of me? Me?

SHINOBU: Yes. Listen, if we have a night when the snow falls and lingers on the ground . . . .

MAN II: Snow? But snow almost never falls here, not in Nagasaki.

SHINOBU: Even so, if we have a night when snow lingers on the ground . . . .

MAN II: Then?

SHINOBU: Then come to Urakami.

MAN II: To your place in Urakami?

SHINOBU: No, to the Cathedral.

MAN II: The Cathedral! To the Temple of Jesus?

SHINOBU: Yes, to the entrance of the Cathedral, crumbling, scorched by the whirlwind of fire, to the entrance where the Head of Mary lies.

MAN II: What for?

SHINOBU: To be with me . . . to pray.

MAN II: To pray for what?

SHINOBU: To pray for a direction to life.

MAN II: A direction to life? Whose?

SHINOBU: Mine and yours . . . women's and men's . . . everyone's.

MAN II: Ah!

SHINOBU: That is, if you are truly grateful.

MAN II: All right. Perhaps unto me, too, a dream will be born. I promise. If there should be a night when snow falls . . . .

SHINOBU: And lingers white on the ground.

MAN II: Yes. Thank you. Thank you for asking me. Farewell . . . farewell. (*As he exits*): The sky is filled with stars . . . The masts shine green . . . the masts . . . green . . . .

Man II quietly exits.
SHINOBU:
  Heh-heh . . . hah-hah-hah! . . .
  Do as you damn please!
  Some dirty old man pops out of the woodwork
  And confesses he loves me.
  Fine.
  Let him have his few drops of blood.
  Compared to the way the blood of my being
  Has been wrung from me
  And the residence of my flesh reduced to emptiness,
  What are a few drops of blood?
  Let him be my companion in search of a direction to life.

The sound of the guitar is heard continuously. Man I descends. Whistling, he taps Shinobu lightly on the shoulder from behind and looks up at the second floor. "Dadour sana, eh!" he whispers as he leaves. "Pervert!" she replies.
Yabari enters and pursues Man I but stops short. "Damn, a nigger!" He approaches Shinobu.
YABARI: Hey, you seen a woman around here?
Shinobu scrutinizes him.
YABARI: Well, have you?
SHINOBU: There are lots of women.
YABARI: The one I'm looking for's got a keloid scar on her face, from around her ear down to here.
SHINOBU: Sorry, I can't help you.
YABARI: How long have you been coming here?
SHINOBU (*examining him closely*): Who wants to know?
YABARI: Not long, I'll bet. You're a newcomer. I haven't seen you around before.
SHINOBU (*sharply*): I asked you who the hell you are!
YABARI: Hey, don't get so riled up!
Shinobu abruptly moves away from him, but Yabari, no longer interested, exits grumbling, "Where could she be?"
SHINOBU (*returning to her original position*): Back to work.
Man III enters, the cold steel of his prosthesis silent against the ground. His broad white cape bulges slightly in the back. He halts before

Shinobu. She nods to him. His prosthesis thumping on the stairs, Man III climbs to Shika's room and enters.

Shortly, Man IV will enter on the stage below, but before describing that, let's follow the action that takes place wordlessly above.

Pronouncing the password "In nomine," Man III enters, and although he turns on the light, Shika, in bed, does not react, and he goes about his business as if there were no one else in the room. He removes his cape, lowers the bundle tied to his back, and moves the door propped in the corner off to one side.

Ah! There behind the door, missing its head and one arm, stands a statue of the Virgin Mary! With long skirts flowing from her waist, the icon is a larger-than-life representation in the medieval style. This Mary has her arm extended slightly and seems about to embrace a child. Incidentally, it is apparent that the statue has been reassembled from five or six separate pieces. He unwraps his bundle. Sure enough, it is an arm of stone. He tests the arm against the shoulder of the icon. With the exception of the head, it is complete. He turns around and smiling looks questioningly at Shika, who has just propped herself up on the bed.

Shika rises slowly to her feet, approaches, embraces, and kisses the embarrassed man. He fetches a pan and some cement from behind the statue and begins to mix the adhesive.

It is at about this point that Man IV begins tangling with Shinobu below. Shika signals to Man III, who abruptly stops working and begins to clean up. Shika turns off the light. Now let us go back and describe the events that have taken place on the portico below while all this is going on. That is, after Man III mounted the stairs and Man IV, drunk, entered.

MAN IV: Whatcha doin' over there, huh? Whatcha got ina tray? *Shinobu remains silent.*

MAN IV (*approaching, he unceremoniously grabs something that looks like a box of toothpaste from the tray and holds it up to the light*): Jelly? . . . Jelly! . . . (*He starts laughing.*) I'll be damned! Hah-hah-hah!

Without warning, Shinobu grabs the man by his collars and drags him under the lamp.

MAN IV: I'll . . . I'll buy it, I'll buy it! Quit pulling on me! *Shinobu closely examines the man's face, then, disappointed, thrusts him away.*

MAN IV (*reeling and angry*): Whatcha think you're doing, eh!
Shinobu, no longer interested, stands in her place.

MAN IV (*once again approaching her*): Hey! You gotta lotta nerve
standing out in fronta people with a mug like that! Yeah!
More brazen damned women around these days'n you can
shake a stick at! Listen, you want me to buy your medicine?
Then how 'bout a little smile? Smile, like this. Cut out this
holier-'an-thou routine, will you? Let's have a little smile.
Then I'll buy your medicine. That's it, smile! What's wrong
with you, don't you know how to smile! (*He grabs both her
arms.*)

*Behind them, the door with the glass opens, and, her hands folded
under her shawl, Shika appears. To repeat, her expressionless face is
covered with a black bandage and a thick coat of dead white make-up
luminous even in the dark. Her mustard-colored knit shawl is long—
long enough to drag along the ground—and with her dark blue kasuri
kimono she wears a vivid, sky-blue sash. In short, everything about
her is out of kilter, and she cuts a foreboding figure.*

MAN IV (*truculently*): I'll teach you some charm. Smile! Smile,
dammit!

Shinobu tries to force a smile

MAN IV: A little more. 'Til I can see your pearly teeth. Pearly
teeth. Like this, see. See!

SHIKA: Hello there. (*Her voice is husky.*)

Man IV turns to look at her.

SHIKA: If it's company you're looking for . . . .

MAN IV: Hey, you scared me! (*He looks her over.*) Awright . . . .
(*Approaching her*): How much?

SHIKA (*smiling at him without a word*): Is this right?

MAN IV: Yeah. Now how much, huh?

The sound of shoes, faintly.

SHINOBU (*looking around, suddenly in a loud voice*): Jelly! Jelly!

Shika, grinning, opens the door.

MAN IV (*to Shinobu*): Now, that's a smile! Hah-hah!

Man IV climbs the stairs after Shika. A steam whistle.

SHINOBU: Jelly! Jelly for sale!

*Man V enters and stands, leaning against the wall of the toilet. He
chuckles to himself forbiddingly.*

The light on the second floor comes on.

Man V moves unsteadily in front of Shinobu and laughs again the same way.

He takes out some money and places it in Shinobu's tray.

Shinobu starts to hand him a box of jelly. Man V shakes his head. She hands him the poetry collection. Again he shakes his head.

SHINOBU: I'm trying to do business here. If you don't want anything, get out of my way.

MAN V: Kannai. Jigorō of Kannai.

SHINOBU: Jigorō!

MAN V: Jigorō.

SHINOBU (*whispering*): Go into that narrow alleyway, take the first right, and its the third house at the end. There's a rope curtain over the door. (*Handing him a box of jelly*): Show them this . . . as a sign.

MAN V: Show them this, huh? (*He starts to leave.*)

SHINOBU (*calling him back*): What kind of person is Jigorō of Kannai?

MAN V: What kind? I don't know.

SHINOBU: A kingpin?

MAN V: I guess you could say that.

SHINOBU: All right. Get going.

MAN V: Right. (*With another laugh, he disappears into the alley.*)

Shinobu hums sadly in a low voice. The tune is "By the Waters of Minnetonka." While she is occupied in this way, Woman III and Woman IV enter led by Woman I, and giggling noisily they sneak up on Shinobu.*

They are in Western clothes, but some of them wear only a coat over a slip. They say nothing but grinning surround Shinobu.

WOMAN II: Sister.

WOMAN III: Business looks good!

WOMAN IV: Sister.

WOMAN II: You work so hard!

WOMAN I: Say something!

SHINOBU: What do you want?

---

*"By the Waters of Minnetonka" (1914), words by J. M. Cavanass, music by Thurlow Lieurance, may be found in Denes Agay, *Best Loved Songs of the American People* (New York: Doubleday, 1975).

WOMAN III: What do *we* want?

WOMAN IV: Who told you you could work here?

WOMAN I: Night after night out here, pimping.

WOMAN II: Without permission.

WOMAN I: What have you got to say for yourself? Not mute are you?

SHINOBU: I don't know what you're talking about.

WOMAN III: What's that?

WOMAN II (*intervening*): Now, now. If that's the way you feel, let's take a little walk.

WOMAN III: Yeah, let's have a little talk, shall we?

SHINOBU: What for?

WOMAN IV: It'll only take a minute.

SHINOBU: I'd rather . . . . Hey! What are you doing!

Without warning Woman I has yanked Shinobu's tray. Pulled forward by the cord around her neck, Shinobu is grabbed from both sides.

SHINOBU: What are you doing!

WOMAN I: Heh-heh, just keep quiet and come along.

Shinobu flees toward the alley but there is no escape. She resists. Her cape falls from her shoulders. No longer concerned about being detected, the Women pummel her and knock her to the ground, then make her a prisoner in her own skirt by pulling it over her head.

Shinobu gives up and submits to her captors. Two of them drag her corpse-like form under the lamp. Her white slip has rolled up, and her thighs appear painfully vulnerable.

WOMAN II: She's become awfully quiet all of a sudden.

WOMAN III: Hey! Quit playing possum!

WOMAN IV: Listen up now and listen good! You probably think you can do any damn thing you want, that you're free. But is there any such thing as freedom in this world? No, no! It's a dream! We've got to teach people like you who stand around, your head up high, not afraid of anything, the error of your ways. Loneliness! That's right. Loneliness is your source of strength!

WOMAN I: The freedom that comes with loneliness! Hah!

WOMAN II: The loneliness that comes with freedom! Hah!

WOMAN III: You'd better think twice before you take that subversive spirit into your head.

WOMAN IV: Those who seek that kind of freedom are always punished. Because we humans aren't allowed that kind of freedom!

WOMAN II (*crouching down*): We better not catch you standing out here by yourself again, understand? It's the sin of pride. A transgression.

WOMAN III: Apologize and join us!

WOMAN I: Your take will increase, and you'll be able to come to us in times of trouble.

WOMAN IV: You've got such nice skin, too.

WOMAN II (*suddenly*): Hey! She's got a knife stuck in her waist!

WOMEN: What? She's right! Strange place to conceal a strange item!

Woman II removes the white-sheathed dagger from Shinobu's undergarments and shows it to Woman IV, who pulls it from its scabbard.

WOMAN III: Is it for luck?

WOMAN I: Isn't it just wood wrapped in silver foil?

WOMAN IV: No. (*She pulls a hair from the head of Woman I.*)

WOMAN I: Ouch!

WOMAN IV (*slicing the hair*): It's the real thing.

WOMAN II: Then maybe we should give her a shave! A bowl cut! Just to test the blade!

Women burst into laughter.

WOMAN IV: Shhh!!!

SCENE THREE: SECOND FLOOR OF THE COMMUNITY MARKET

Shika's room again.

The unfinished Statue of Mary is hidden in its former place, and Man III is nowhere to be seen. In fact it is still dark, however. The voice that we hear from among the shadows belongs to Man IV: "Sounds like the ladies are really going at it. You don't mind if I turn on the light, do you? It'll improve the mood." The light goes on. Man IV is standing beneath the bulb. He is a shabby, unshaven man. He sits backwards on the chair where he has hung his coat and faces Shika, who is lying on the bed. He takes out a cigarette and lights it.

MAN IV: From Shimabara, huh?* In other words, your old lady must have been a Karayuki.†

SHIKA: A Karayuki . . . yes . . . .

MAN IV: In the old days, if you were from places in Kyushu like Shimabara or Amakusa and wanted to be free, you became a Christian; in modern times you became a Karayuki and followed the army to the continent or the South Pacific.

SHIKA: Light me one, too.

MAN IV: Sure. (*Taking out a cigarette, handing it to her, and lighting it*): So how about *après guerre?*

SHIKA: I suppose I'm a common slut.

MAN IV: Hah-hah! You know, I've never been with anyone with as much class as you before. If there's something wrong with your ear, I know a good doctor . . . .

SHIKA: Doctor? Hah!

MAN IV (*edging his chair closer*): Listen, how would you like to be my steady?

Shika looks at him questioningly.

MAN IV: You know, I'll be your only customer. In exchange . . . .

SHIKA: I'm expensive.

MAN IV: How about 4,000 yen?

Shika exhales the smoke.

MAN IV: Five thousand, then.

SHIKA: What's your monthly salary?

MAN IV: Salary? Listen, I may not look it, but by April I'll make section chief. I can handle a few thousand a month.

---

*Early Christian missionaries were particularly successful in the area around Nagasaki in Kyushu, where both Shimabara and Amakusa are located. In 1637 and 1638, Christian converts from Shimabara and Amakusa revolted unsuccessfully against the Tokugawa regime's ban on Christianity; and "secret Christians" (*kakure kirishitan*) in the area continued surreptitiously to practice their proscribed religion until it was once again recognized by the state in 1873.

†*Karayuki* refers to the camp followers, particularly prostitutes from the islands of Amakusa, who accompanied Japanese forces on their foreign adventures beginning in the late nineteenth century. For a novelist's description, see Tomoko Yamazaki, "Sandakan No. 8 Brothel," Tomoko Moore and Steffan Richards, trs., *Bulletin of Concerned Asian Scholars,* (October–December 1975).

SHIKA: With the company's money? You going to pull the same tricks as that crook Takujima or whatever his name was?

MAN IV: I don't work for any company.

SHIKA: What then, city hall? The prefectural government? Or the courts maybe?

MAN IV: Hah-hah, what do I look like?

SHIKA: Let me see . . . a city councilman. I'm right, aren't I?

MAN IV: The secret affair of a city councilman, is that it? Hah-hah!

SHIKA: In any case, you're the one sitting way in the back with an air of self-importance, bored with the whole business.

MAN IV: Hah-hah! The voice of the people speaks! Hah-hah-hah!

SHIKA: Listen, what's going on in the city council these days?

MAN IV: Which city council?

SHIKA: Which? You mean you don't know?

MAN IV: Hey, what is this? You a voter or something?

SHIKA: Don't steadies have the right to vote?

MAN IV: Hah-hah! You'll have to have a steady address first. What party do you belong to? The Communists?

SHIKA: Not the Party, but the original idea of communal property's all right—way back, I mean.

MAN IV: You're right, there really is something wrong with our present marriage system, that's a fact.

SHIKA (*laughing under her breath at his incomprehension*): So tell me, what's going on in the city council?

MAN IV: That's what I mean, what about the city council?

SHIKA: The cathedral. The issue of the Urakami Cathedral.

MAN IV: Cathedral? Oh, the A-bomb cathedral, the red brick one.

SHIKA: Are they going to preserve it or tear it down? If you're a city councilman . . . one of the "righteous," . . .

MAN IV: One of the "righteous," huh?

SHIKA: Come on, tell me. What are they going to do?

MAN IV: If I'm not mistaken, the council has already passed a resolution to preserve it.

SHIKA: They say they'll preserve it, but nobody has the slightest idea how, and they're not doing anything!

MAN IV: The people of Nagasaki are united in their desire to preserve it forever as a reminder of what happened, so the council is hardly going to oppose the idea. The problem is with the Catholic Church. They're not so keen on preserving it, because they say if they want to rebuild the cathedral, those brick walls will get in the way.*

SHIKA: Of course the Church feels that way. So instead of passing resolutions, why doesn't the city come up with the money to find them an alternate site or something?

MAN IV: Hey, take it easy. Chewing me out isn't going to do any good. Hah-hah. Listen, the council will do something eventually, don't worry.

SHIKA: Eventually! Eventually it's going to get torn down! Eventually the head of Mary's going to get lost somewhere, that's what! And then every trace of what happened will disappear, and the city will revert to its peacetime appearance. A memorial park will be established, the peace statue will sit with its legs crossed, pointing up at the sky,† and the view from Urakami will become just another high-class tourist attraction. But even if thousands of people, tens of thousands of people come, they'll never be able to touch the true soul of Urakami.

MAN IV: You're a Christian, aren't you?

SHIKA: Okay, your time was up a long while ago. Your wife must be worried about you.

MAN IV: I want an answer to my question.

SHIKA: Quit while you're ahead. Save your displays of male pride for executive board meetings, the city council, or the prefectural assembly—don't waste them on frail womenfolk.

---

*The attempt to preserve remnants of the atomic destruction as a memorial was met in both Nagasaki and Hiroshima with ambivalence. As indicated here, controversy in Nagasaki centered upon the remains of Urakami Cathedral; in Hiroshima, advocates were successful in having the dome of an industrial exhibition hall (known today as the A-Bomb or Peace Dome) retained as a monument. For a description of the dynamics of this ambivalence, refer to Robert Jay Lifton, *Death in Life: Survivors of Hiroshima* (New York: Random House, 1967), pp. 275–280.

†A statue of this description actually stands in Nagasaki's Peace Park.

MAN IV (*suddenly falling to his knees beside the bed and taking one of her hands*): I've never met anyone like you before. I'm not acting. I'm in love with you!

SHIKA (*pushing him away*): Don't be disgusting.

MAN IV: I . . . I want to crawl inside you. What is it about you? What is it that makes you so special?

SHIKA: I'm going to have to charge you overtime if you keep this up. You want to stay the night? It'll be five times my hourly rate. In advance.

MAN IV (*meekly*): All right, let's get married. I'll divorce my wife, you'll see.

SHIKA (*girlishly*): Really? I'm so thrilled!

MAN IV: Then you'll be mine alone?

SHIKA (*putting her arms around his neck*): How much will you give me?

MAN IV: How much?

SHIKA: I want money. I've never met a prospect like you before, either. Take good care of me, all right?

Man IV kisses her.

SHIKA: You're really passionate, you know that?

MAN IV: You, too.

SHIKA: I can't go on like this forever, and I've been wanting to go straight. Give me two hundred thousand. Then I'll become your wife. A good wife.

MAN IV (*pulling her arms from his neck*): Two hundred thousand! You must be up to your neck in debt!

SHIKA: No.

MAN IV: Then? . . .

SHIKA: Is there something wrong with putting a price on love?

Man IV puts on his suit jacket and then his topcoat.

SHIKA (*reclining*): Why do men go cold the minute you bring up the subject of money? There are any number of women who've worked their fingers to the bone to pay off a man's debts.

MAN IV: This isn't the age of primitive communism! Sorry! (*Exits.*)

SHIKA (*to his retreating figure, with charm*): Come again, now, Mr. City Councilman!

Her pose is the same as the one she held at the beginning of Scene One.

SCENE FOUR: ONCE AGAIN IN FRONT OF THE COMMUNITY MARKET

Shinobu is crouching down, her cape over her head. When the sound of footsteps has faded into the distance, she removes the cape, leans her head against the center door, and slumps down, her legs splayed to one side. The light on the second floor is out.

SHINOBU:
Inside the bag they drew over my head,
I no longer resisted.
I felt just as I did in the air raid shelter among the ruins,
Just as I did then!
Tears welled up;
Below my waist, beneath the skin grown cold to the touch,
Flames of shame and rage and self-hatred burned;
And on the sand, black seaweed dried and scattered.
Yes, this is all I have to depend on!
My life's blood!
Sisters!
Can you claim your skin,
Like the skin of this dagger,
Is more beautiful
Than this pure, unblemished skin of mine?
Now is the time to look!
Examine
Your rough flesh
And know the shame of your mottled, ruined hide.

Isn't there anybody here?
The starry sky has spread over Mount Inasa,
Its infinite expanse
The sole witness to my loneliness.
My abdomen tingles with pain.
I laugh out loud:
Hah-hah . . . .
Oh, you wandering barbers,
Barbers who painted me
As the women of Greece and Sparta,
Thank you!
Like those women of old,

Healthy, fertile, pure,
And above all free,
I grow large with courage.
So, rise, Shinobu!

Shinobu attempts to rise but loses her balance and has to support herself against one of the posts. Yabari once again passes. Shinobu covers her face with her cape. Yabari approaches and forcibly pulls the cape away. "Damn!" he exclaims, then leaps away and runs off.

Shinobu slumps back onto the floor. She raises her head, eyes half-closed, and for a moment the upper half of her body, her underwear ripped exposing her breast, appears to convulse with terror before noiselessly collapsing. The fierce sound of the guitar has come to an abrupt halt.

His prosthesis thumping against the stairs, Man III descends to the stage. He collects the props scattered about her, then hoists Shinobu onto his shoulder and carries her off. The sound of a steam whistle. Curtain.

ACT TWO

SCENE ONE: SAKAMOTO CLINIC

A second floor sickroom in the Sakamoto Clinic at the foot of Ura-kami. It is a Japanese-style room with floors of tatami matting. A framed inscription in Chinese, "Medicine is the Art of Compassion," hangs from the wall. It is signed, "To Dr. Sakamoto, From Chen Shun-cheng."

It is a clear morning.

Yabari is lying in bedding spread on the floor.

Shizuka, a heavy set, middle-aged nurse wearing colored socks over her white stockings, sits reading a newspaper beside his pillow. The sound of a passing train.

YABARI: It's a freight train. It's easy to tell in the morning.

SHIZUKA: Things have really heated up in the city council. It looks like they're going to tear it down after all. No matter how much the "righteous" councilmen oppose it, mayor's made up his mind, it seems.

YABARI: They've got the same problem in Hiroshima: whether or not to preserve the skeleton of that dome. There are those who say that it should be left as a permanent reminder, and others who say that it's no use living in the past and the whole experience ought to be forgotten.

SHIZUKA: You mean there was something left standing to remind people of the bomb in Hiroshima too?

YABARI: Right near the river.

SHIZUKA: But Urakami's a real attraction in its own right. They ought to leave it alone. Why, all the tour buses stop for a look.

YABARI: Yeah, but how many people who look at it really feel the horror of the atomic bomb? They're just a bunch of ambulance chasers: so long as it wasn't their house that burned down, they don't really give a damn. The minute it becomes an "attraction," the place loses its meaning. I'd rather see them tear it down.

SHIZUKA: You only say that because you're an outsider. When the bomb fell, my cousin was inside the cathedral and was turned to ashes with the priests.

YABARI: I see. Then you must be a Christian, too . . . from Urakami?

SHIZUKA (*looking up*): All right, that should be enough . . . . In any case, they ought to do something about poor Mary's head, lying out there in the open like the severed head of some criminal.

Yabari removes the thermometer he has had under his arm through the front of his pajamas. His hand remains on his chest.

SHIZUKA (*reading the thermometer*): You see, it's gone up. Thirty-seven point eight. (*Taking his pulse*): Where were you last night anyway? You ran around enough to tear all the stitches out of that belly the doctor worked so hard to sew up! It was after one by the time you got back. Hah-hah! There's no use hiding it. I know where you went. For a little "companion-ship," right? You couldn't even control yourself for a week, could you? You were in Maruyama . . . or maybe Shianbashi . . . or maybe you stooped as low as Kannai? (*As she speaks, she writes his temperature on the chart that rests beside his pillow. She yawns.*) Well, I guess I'll get some sleep. Today I'll sleep till noon, then go see Kinnosuke.*

YABARI (*grinning*): Who with?

SHIZUKA: By myself.

YABARI: Really?

SHIZUKA: Look who's talking!

YABARI: I wanted to go with you.

SHIZUKA: Hah! Don't say it if you don't mean it.

YABARI: But I do!

SHIZUKA: Shika's the one you want to go out with. I can see right through you.

YABARI: Very observant. But it's a bum rap. (*He puts his hand on her knee.*)

SHIZUKA: You're disgusting!

YABARI: What's disgusting?

SHIZUKA: The other day you had your appendix out, right?

YABARI: Yeah, otherwise why would I be lying here like this?

SHIZUKA: Well, I'm the one who shaved you before the opera-tion.

---

*Nakamura (presently Yorozuya) Kinnosuke, is a handsome *kabuki* actor who also appears frequently on television and in films.

YABARI: Yeah, you did a better job than a barber. You must've had some experience.

SHIZUKA: I'm also the one who gave you your enema before that.

YABARI: Yeah.

SHIZUKA: Is that all you have to say?

YABARI: What is this, the third-degree? So what?

SHIZUKA: Well, when a doctor's been around as long as the head of this clinic, he can tell without looking if a woman's a virgin. If the patient's a man. . . .

YABARI: Whether he's ever been with a woman? How convenient!

SHIZUKA: That's right. He can tell at a glance. And so can I.

YABARI: Is that anything to get so upset about? Humanity will never progress if you insist on getting hung up on details like that. Actually, it's for your own good as a woman that I say this. The worship of virgins has always been the basis of male-dominated societies.

SHIZUKA: Wait just a minute. I know as well as anybody that this is supposed to be a new age. But "male-dominated"? Really! If you ask me, that's just a conceit of you and your male friends! From the days of creation, men have . . . .

YABARI: Creation?

SHIZUKA: Yes, creation, the days of Adam and Eve. From creation, men have always been the enemy of women.

YABARI: Is that so. I don't recall having heard a declaration of war.

SHIZUKA: Listen, I'm speaking the truth here. All right? I've been at this game for thirteen years. Nothing escapes me, hah-hah . . . . What I'm trying to tell you is that a person's tools are more important than his face. That's the truth, a scientific, physiological truth. Young people like you ought to remember that.

YABARI: Wow! This is one hell of a hospital I've got myself into!

SHIZUKA: Most people go up to the university hospital on the hill, but you can search Nagasaki and you won't find a hospital more accommodating than this one.

YABARI: I don't like public hospitals either. It's always "procedure—sign this—procedure—sign that."

SHIZUKA: The proof is that we'd even admit the likes of you.

YABARI: Out of religious principle, no doubt. But listen, this "truth" you were telling me about. From a religious perspective . . . . (*Realizing*): Oh, *that* creation!

SHIZUKA: Truth. God's the only one who knows the truth. Human beings delude themselves into thinking they're the ones who know it, but . . . .

YABARI: Yes, ma'am. (*He pretends to be cowed.*)

SHIZUKA: The same thing's true of love. The kind of love that appears on the surface can't be trusted, and as time passes, it can even turn ugly. Our true form and substance is in the hands of God, Ruler of the Universe, and it remains unchanging deep within us, unchanging in a place even we ourselves don't know. That's why, even . . . .

YABARI: In other words, for all we know even a woman as heavy on form as you might be the most blessed with love, the most deeply compassionate, is that it?

SHIZUKA (*unfazed*): That's right. You seem intent on ridiculing me, but . . . . Well, be my guest. You're at an age when you only have eyes for women who are beautiful on the surface. What I'm saying will make more sense to you in the future. I'm sure of it.

YABARI: Thanks. I don't know about the future; I'm only sorry it doesn't make much sense to me now! (*Stealthily he reaches for her knee.*)

SHIZUKA (*slapping his hand*): Not again! College students these days! Shameless! I'm not like the girls these days, whose eyes change colors the minute they see a pair of pants. In the first place, I'm married, a married woman.

YABARI: Of course. How happy he must be, having the ample form of true love always at his side. Strange I haven't seen him in the week I've been here.

SHIZUKA: Because . . . he's in the country. In the country, farming.

YABARI: In the country. Of course.

The sliding doors to the room open, and another nurse appears with Yabari's meal tray. It is Shika. Now there isn't the slightest trace of the white makeup, and instead of the black bandage, her long, uncurled

*hair falls airily on both sides of her face, naturally covering her ears;
but with the slightest motion, the keloid that stretches from behind her
ear to her jaw becomes plain to view.*

YABARI: Good morning!

SHIZUKA: It's about time. Now it's your turn.

*Shika smiles a greeting, places the tray beside the patient's pillow, and
picks up his chart.*

YABARI: Where did you go last night?

Shika continues looking at the chart in silence.

SHIZUKA: It's none of your business where she went.

YABARI: I'm not asking you. Well?

SHIZUKA: You're the last person to be asking questions! Shika,
   would you believe he didn't show up here until after one this
   morning! Prowling around like some tomcat, before his
   stitches are even out!

SHIKA (*lightly*): Is that so?

SHIZUKA: Shika, you give him a good talking to. Oh, am I
   sleepy. (*As she leaves*): No surgery today, so . . . .

*Shika goes to the charcoal brazier set in the room for heat and pours hot
water from the kettle simmering on top of it into a small teapot.*

YABARI (*trying to prop himself up*): Ouch!

SHIKA: You're going to pull out the stitches like that.

YABARI: I've already pulled them out. I just want to get a good
   look at you.

SHIKA: Eat before it gets cold.

YABARI: Listen, I . . . you snuck out last night, didn't you,
   around nine o'clock?

Shika does not answer.

YABARI: I followed you, on the same train.

SHIKA: Were you spying on me?

YABARI: I'm sure you looked over at me once.

Shika turns away.

YABARI: It was the Hamanomachi train. You got off at Senba-
   chō.

*Shika stands and goes to the window, where she gazes out through the
glass.*

YABARI: That's where I lost you. You either went to Ōura or cut
   back toward Tsuki-machi. Hah-hah, I really searched for

you, too. I asked everyone I met if they'd seen a woman with a keloid scar.

SHIKA (*without changing her position*): There must be hundreds of women with keloids in Nagasaki. (*Her hand goes up to the area beneath her ear.*)

YABARI: Yeah, that weird woman standing in front of the market said the same thing. So I never did find you. But I know when you got back. It was after two.

SHIKA: Your porridge is getting cold.

YABARI: Thanks to you I can hardly keep my eyes open this morning. (*Lying face up*): Porridge again?

Pause. Rain falls lightly.

The sound of a bell.

With a rapid motion, Shika makes the sign of the cross.

YABARI: What's so interesting to see out there? The rain!

Shika does not answer.

YABARI: The peace statue, then? That monstrosity.

Again Shika does not respond.

YABARI: Then it must be the cathedral, with its red brick walls falling down.

The gentle sound of a guitar, like a hymn.

SHIKA:

Mary! My Mary!

I want your head!

YABARI:

Whose head?

SHIKA:

Oh, Mary!

You are my love, love unto eternity.

YABARI:

A love you will never meet, a love you will never know?

SHIKA:

While I was still in my mother's womb

In that sea of darkly tainted blood,

Choking on the animal smell and the smell of albumen,

Just when I was certain I would drown,

The window of my mother's naval opened,

And from out of the warm vapor,
As if billowing clouds were clearing,
Mary! Selfless Mary!
You looked in upon me.
Woman that you are, you were there.
You, a woman and only a woman!
I survived, but
Mother died.
When women die in sin as we,
When women live in sin as we,
Only you, who have escaped sin,
Can see into the reaches of our soul.
Only you know us!
That is why before you alone
I would be truly me!

YABARI:

But we know you not.
You are nothing and no one to us. At most
Our neighbor in chance.

SHIKA:

Yet there is nothing
As pregnant with existence, impregnating existence
As chance.
Of the terror, the ferocity of chance, people are ignorant.
Not knowing when chance may transform into absolute,
They cannot know there is something determining the chaos
That lies between the two.
The emptiness, the richness of that chaos terrifies me!
Within its nothingness there is life,
There is becoming.
There I may find the truth of my being.
And you, Mary,
Unsullied you!

YABARI:

You're wasting your time on bootless fears and expectations.
There is neither nothingness nor becoming in this world.
All there is is your present, living form: you just as you are.

And that is sufficient! That determines all!
Becoming is an illusion,
The dream of greedy souls.

SHIKA:

Perhaps for you.
Existence may be all there is for you.
You may not be conscious of anything before or after being.
But is your life truly so destitute?

YABARI:

So be it.
At least being acts.
The whole body acts.
Not just the head, as you would have it.

SHIKA:

Hah-hah.
This head of mine,
This face, bloated and twisted in ugliness—
It indeed is my glorious purpose,
The sign of my sacred freedom!
This, my friend, is human existence.
Far transcending evil and good,
The sum total of all existence,
It signifies the freedom of being alive!

YABARI:

No, there you are wrong:
It only signifies the sum total of all politics!

SHIKA:

Ah!
Sign of all blessings lost!
Sign of grace!

YABARI:

Sign of all justice lost!

SHIKA:

Justice!
Justice cannot restore my face!

YABARI:

Justice itself can be restored,
And the scalpel of science
Can change the skin of your face.

SHIKA:

And if my face were to be restored,
Then the grocer who told me
That the onions would rot if I stood before his stall,
And the mistress of the bath who warned
That the water would be polluted if I got into the tub;
And the lovers who laughed under their breath
As they fled from the park bench when I sat down—
They would all welcome me with smiles, no doubt.
But
The two hundred thousand souls dispatched in Hiroshima,
The seventy thousand who perished in Nagasaki
Would not return.

YABARI:

That's right.
With that sadness and rage you fight.

SHIKA:

Fight?
Against what?

YABARI:

Against the heat and light of the atom,
Against the politics that treats it as a toy.

SHIKA:

Politics
Is either right or wrong,
Always one or the other.
And those who pass on its rectitude
Are one or the other, too.
Be it time or place,
Inscrutable powers rule.
Absolute justice cannot be found in politics.
Nor in existence;
Nor absolute freedom either.

YABARI:

Politics moves forward:
For that we struggle.

SHIKA:

Then struggle.
I will struggle with myself.

I reserve the right even to wreak vengeance on myself.
That is
My struggle with the heat and light of the atom.
Therein lies my justice!
It is because of my greedy soul
That I will be able to survive myself.

YABARI (*propping himself up*): An egotist, an awful egotist, that's what you are. You mustn't trust in the power of the individual. It's limited. Forget the individual!

SHIKA:
I too want to forget. Yes, to forget.
In a direction different from you.
But . . . oh, Mary!
I want your head!

YABARI: I'll give you Mary's head or anything else you want, just come over here. Listen, Shika, reconsider. If you would just stand before us, it would be worth a hundred speeches, a thousand placards. You wouldn't have to say anything, just stand there in silence. You don't have to worry about money or anything.

SHIKA: I would be your placard, right?

YABARI: In a word, yes.

SHIKA: I would be a placard . . . and you a sandwich man. A sandwich man selling "politics." Or do you see yourself as head of the sandwich man's union?

YABARI: Go ahead, say what you like. I'd do anything, no matter how thankless, to see you realize your potential!

SHIKA: Why do you pay so much attention to me? Do I have some special value you think's worth exploiting, that justifies spying on me and following me around, even at night? Forget the individual, you just said so yourself.

YABARI: Don't throw a person's words back at him. All right, I take back what I said. I didn't mean it. Ah, why am I so clumsy with words?

SHIKA: What you said before or what you said just now?

YABARI: Take your pick, I don't care. You'll see how sincere I am before long. I just want to do something for people, you and people like you, don't you understand?

SHIKA: What's in it for you? Is that how you get your kicks?

YABARI: Hah-hah! You surprise me. Go ahead, say anything you like. I'll just have to be patient. In the mean time, I guess I'll eat my breakfast. I really worked up an appetite.

SHIKA (*having scrutinized him closely*): Tell me the truth.

YABARI: About what?

SHIKA: Your real intentions. What college are you from anyway? Or maybe I should ask, are you really a student, or . . . .

YABARI: Or?

SHIKA: From the Party? If not, then a police . . . .

YABARI: Spy? Hah-hah! You're giving me too much credit.

SHIKA: Then what did you come all the way to Nagasaki for?

YABARI: You want me to answer that question again?

SHIKA: Yes.

YABARI: I told you before: I'm from Nagasaki originally. I even have a Nagasaki accent.

SHIKA: Yes, you told me.

YABARI: I don't mean to make a big thing out of it, but I wasn't just born in Nagasaki; I was born in the women's cell block at Katafuchi Prison. In the words of the song, "It was more than nostalgia/ That brought me home again!" Hah-Hah! Nagasaki's not the same, though, really; it's a different place from the town where I was born. The Nagasaki I knew was burned to the ground, and today you can ride all the way to the top of Kazagashira and Inasa without getting out of the car! Katafuchi Prison's gone—its just another residential neighborhood—and my dream of diapers flapping in the prison yard has just evaporated. Hah-hah . . . . I've had my share of troubles because of my birth, don't be fooled by appearances. I can play the clarinet and speak American like a native. But never mind. While I'm at it though, I might as well tell you what's really on my mind. Don't be surprised. I want to take you to America, right smack-dab to the middle. I've got it all worked out.

SHIKA: The Council Against Atomic and Hydrogen Bombs* has even held its world conference in Russia. But in America?

---

*The Council Against Atomic and Hydrogen Bombs (*Gensuikyō*), an organization closely affiliated with the Japanese Communist Party, became embroiled in a controversy during the years around 1960 because of its con-

YABARI: America will never sponsor such a conference. That's why it'd be worth taking you there.

SHIKA: You should take it up with the Council Against Atomic and Hydrogen Bombs, then.

YABARI: There's nothing wrong with relying on an organization like that, but I'm going to try a more kamikaze approach. I want to achieve the same goals as the Council, but in America. See, we'd go over there under the pretense of studying or something, and once we were there we'd spring into action. We'd ask them how they'd feel if ashes of death rained on their country? But it wouldn't be convincing for them just to hear about it. That's why you'd stand on every corner. Stand and stand until they got the point. I'd be your escort and bodyguard.

SHIKA: If you're thinking about something like the Hiroshima Maidens,* Americans are used to that sort of thing. And anyway, I'm not interested in having this keloid fixed.

YABARI: Plastic surgery hasn't always been successful, so you have every reason to feel that way. I guess you wouldn't have to have surgery if you didn't want to. In any case, wouldn't you meet a certain American for me? I say American, but actually he's a second-generation Japanese-American. A doctor, from Washington.

SHIKA (*sharply, to the outside*): Who's there?

The sliding doors have opened. Man III is standing there.

SHIKA: Oh, it's you. (*Getting to her feet*): It's raining.

MAN III: Ex . . . ex . . . excuse . . . .

SHIKA: This is a patient's room. Let's talk downstairs.

---

demnation of U.S. atomic testing and its advocacy of Soviet testing as "peaceful." In 1964 the organization split over this issue into *Gensuikyō* and *Gensuikin*.

*The Hiroshima Maidens—also known as A-Bomb Maidens—were a group of young women with keloids and severe burn scars who were brought to the United States in the 1950s for plastic surgery in an effort organized by Norman Cousins. See Lifton, *Death in Life*, pp. 337–338, for a description of the problems faced and issues raised by their visit to the United States.

YABARI: Don't mind me. I'm not really sick anymore anyway. Hah-hah.

MAN III: It's been de . . . decided, Shika. (*He has a slight speech impediment.*)

SHIKA: What?

MAN III: I just met the father.

SHIKA: And?

MAN III: It's been decided, Shika.

SHIKA: They're going to tear it down after all.

MAN III: Ye . . . yes.

Shika goes to the window. Man III follows her. From below, the voice of Dr. Sakamoto: "Shika! Shika!" Shika responds, "Coming!"

Man V appears hurriedly, says, "Downstairs, the doctor . . . ." and leaves.

Shika whispers to Man III, "Then perhaps tonight!" and exits. His eyes shining, Man III responds, "Yes!" and once again looks out the window. Then he moves to leave.

YABARI (*his attitude changing*): Hey. Haven't you got any manners?

MAN III (*smiling sheepishly*): O . . . oh, sorry. I'm a little worried about something. How've you been?

YABARI: You were wandering around the waterfront at Ōura last night, too, weren't you?

MAN III: Uh . . . Yes. I had something I had to work out.

YABARI: What are you to her anyway?

MAN III: Who?

YABARI: Don't play dumb. Shika, of course.

MAN III: She . . . she's a believer. And I'm a believer, too.

YABARI: You're really a suspicious character. What do you have to go around making a spectacle of yourself still dressed up like that for?

MAN III: I don't mean to make a spectacle of myself. I just naturally look this way.

YABARI: Why can't you put on a pair of trousers and some shoes like everybody else?

MAN III: The next time I see you, I'll try my best to dress that way. Please forgive me.

YABARI: What a creep! Don't be so hypocritical. The world's

just filled with people you can't make out these days. Shika
leads the pack, then you . . . .

MAN III: Don't forget yourself.

*From below the voice of someone screaming, "That hurts. It hurts, you
damned quack!"*

YABARI: What's going on?

MAN III: The doctor here's not known for his gentleness.

YABARI: I thought there wasn't supposed to be any surgery
today.

MAN III: You never know what's going to come up. But you'd
better forget about other people and start worrying about
yourself.

YABARI: If I wasn't in this condition I'd rip that cape off you,
pull out your third leg and teach you some manners.

MAN III: There's nothing concealed in my leg, Mr. Narcotics
Agent, sir. If you like, I'll take it off and show you. But, if
you'll excuse me for asking . . . .

YABARI: What are you talking about all of a sudden?

MAN III: What are you to Shika? Or perhaps I should ask what
you'd like to be.

YABARI: Now you're talking. I'm no inspector, but your rival?
Maybe.

MAN III: It would be an hon . . . honor.

YABARI: Are you trying to tell me you've had that shining steel
leg of yours between her thighs then?

MAN III: Heaven forbid! I thought I wouldn't have to mention
it, but I've got shrapnel bristling sharply in my body like
needles—thirty or forty pieces in number—that migrate silently around my body as they suck my blood. If I were to
embrace her, blood would gush from thirty or forty places on
her white skin. I could never do that. It would remind me of
the war.

YABARI: If you really loved her, so what? What I wouldn't give
to make her blood gush! Damn!

MAN III: If I were you . . . if I were you, I'd be satisfied just to
live in her shadow and secretly enjoy her happiness as my
own. Please, don't hang around her or get in her way. If you
really love her, please.

YABARI: You mean her work?

MAN III: Yes. I beg you.

YABARI: I don't have to listen to you.

MAN III: No, of course not. But, Mr. Yabari, I . . . .

Again the sound of shouting from below. "Hey, can't you get it out yet, you quack! I should've known better than to come to a dump like this!"

MAN III: Just so you know, I've crushed the shins of more men than I care to count with this steel leg of mine. (*As he is leaving*): If it would only snow!

As he opens the sliding doors, a person appears outside. It is Shinobu. Over her Western-style clothes she wears an oversized quilted jacket to warm herself and the one-year-old baby on her back.

MAN III: What? . . .

SHINOBU: Is Shika here?

MAN III: She just went downstairs. (*He whispers something to her.*)

SHINOBU (*joyfully*): Really!

MAN III: Shhh!

They exit. The sound of a train.

YABARI: I've seen that woman somewhere before.

SCENE TWO: THE OPERATING ROOM

The operating room on the first floor.

On the operating table lies Jigorō, exhausted, his eyes shut, wrapped in a bandage from his shoulder over his chest.

Dr. Sakamoto, a slight, vulgar old man with white hair, is washing his hands. Shizuka and Shika are putting away the instruments.

Man V enters stealthily.

SHIZUKA (*spying him*): You again! You can't come in here wearing slippers!

MAN V: Oh. . . . (*Changing into the clogs prepared for use in the operating room*): Hasn't the anesthetic worn off yet? Has he been talking about the nigger?

Doctor wipes his hands and sits in a chair. He is preparing to smoke a cigarette.

MAN V (*worrying*): He's not going to die without waking up, is he?

DOCTOR: Don't worry, the coward made it sound worse than it was.

JIGORŌ (*without opening his eyes*): Twenty thousand's a hell of a price to pay to be treated like a side of beef!

DOCTOR: Hear that? The bandage isn't free either, friend. (*To Shika*): How long did it take?

Shika looks at her watch.

MAN V: It took forever. I broke into a cold sweat.

DOCTOR: Worried the cops were coming, eh?

MAN V: They, uh . . . went after the nigger, see. He said so himself, right?

SHIKA: Nineteen minutes, Doctor.

SHIZUKA: Last time it only took seven.

DOCTOR: Put up one hell of a fight, this one. Made everything that much more trouble. What's this about a nigger?

Man V offers an embarrassed laugh but no explanation.

At Jigorō's bedside, Man V removes a drug-filled capsule from his mouth and shows it to Jigorō. "How 'bout settling for 500,000?" he whispers.

JIGORŌ (*opening his eyes*): Liar! You couldn't find the damned slug, that's why it took so long. What do you care about another man's skin, right? So you just went slicing and tearing away. Ugh . . . it feels like blood's collecting in my lungs . . . .

MAN V: Hey, you awright?

JIGORŌ: This ain't nothing. It's that nigger you ought to be worried about.

DOCTOR: Who shot first?

JIGORŌ: Hey, I wouldn't do a thing like that.

DOCTOR (*taking a pistol from his pocket*): You don't see a piece like this around much anymore.

JIGORŌ: Hey, that's my . . . .

DOCTOR (*putting it back in his trousers' pocket*): You'll get it back when I get the other half of my fee.

JIGORŌ: You old coot!

DOCTOR: Just to be sure . . . .

SHIZUKA: Doctor, may I get some rest now?

DOCTOR: Of course, go ahead.

SHIKA: I'll wake you at twelve.

SHIZUKA (*to Jigorō*): I'll collect my overtime from you, buster.

DOCTOR: That's the spirit!

JIGORŌ: Regular Amazon, that one. Strong as an ox, too.

Stopping Shizuka on her way out, Man V entreats her about something.

DOCTOR: Just to be sure, you do know what "illegal possession of firearms" is, don't you?

JIGORŌ: Heh-heh . . . Yeah, and did I ask you about "harboring a fugitive"?

DOCTOR: You may be smart, but if you think I'm going to shut up and not report this to the police, you've got another think coming. Of course, I'm not going to trouble them about a couple of kids who get their kicks setting off firecrackers first thing in the morning if that's all it was.

SHIZUKA: You can't be serious! Doctor, he wants me to take drugs or something.

MAN V: No, I was just, uh . . . .

SHIZUKA: Shika, make sure to keep an eye on the pharmacy while he's around. Doctor, there are two or three patients waiting. Are you dropping ashes on the floor again! Here's an ashtray. (*Looking around for an emesis basin*): Where's that tray I just put the bullet in? Ah, there it is. Try to have a little manners, will you. (*Exits.*)

In the interim, Shika has also left.

MAN V (*picking up the extracted bullet from the tray*): Hmm? So that's it. Something obscene about it, you know.

DOCTOR: Hah-hah, you want to take it along as a souvenir?

MAN V: No thanks! (*He returns it to the tray.*)

DOCTOR: Are you a friend of his?

MAN V: Friend? Not me. Absolutely not.

DOCTOR: You must at least know his name.

MAN V: No, I, er . . . .

DOCTOR: It'd better if you told the truth. Then I'll release him to you right away.

MAN V: Release him? Heh-heh . . . you sound just like the cops. You think I'm going to fall for that one?

DOCTOR: Your fingerprints are on that ash tray and all over the room. I could have them trace you, but I'd rather not take the trouble. Come on, let's have it.

MAN V: Okay, I'm . . . .

DOCTOR: I'm not asking about you. What about him? He's worn out and asleep now, so it's all right. I won't tell him you told me.

MAN V: He's gonna stay in the hospital, isn't he?

DOCTOR: He ought to stay in the hospital, but I'd just be wasting my breath if I tried to tell him that. He'd walk out first chance he got. Where does he live, by the way?

MAN V: I don't know where he lives. Just that it's in Kannai.

DOCTOR: What about his name, then? What's his name?

MAN V: Jigorō.

DOCTOR: Is that supposed to be Japanese?

MAN V: It's, uh. . . . (*He has a sudden thought and glances at Jigorō's face.*) Now that you mention it, he looks a little like a Frenchman, you know.

DOCTOR: French Indochina, huh?

MAN V: There's somebody that looks like him in the movies. What was that actor's name?

DOCTOR (*standing*): In any case, it's my duty to collect the other ten thousand yen. Why don't you go and call a cab for him?

MAN V (*on his way out*): Doc, you wouldn't report him while I'm gone, would you?

DOCTOR: It's my policy not to reveal the secrets of my patients.

MAN V (*whispering*): Doc, Jigorō tried to kill himself. He was trying to scare the other guy, but he aimed the gun at himself. Maybe he couldn't stand himself anymore. He just made up that bit about the nigger. Well, look after him. (*Exits.*)

Doctor picks the bullet out of the emesis basin and fits it into the magazine of the pistol he has taken from his pocket.

DOCTOR: Fits. Looks like I'm out ten thousand yen. (*Exits.*)

Shinobu enters humming a hymn as she comforts the baby on her back.* She wears a green shawl over the padded jacket. She paces back and forth.

---

*The hymn used here is "Hear Thy Children, Gentlest Mother" from *The St. Gregory and Catholic Choir Book,* Nicola A. Montani, ed. (Philadelphia: St. Gregory Guild, 1920), p. 115. It communicates essentially the same message as the hymn Tanaka uses in the original (Catholic hymn [Kōkyō seika] number 311), which I have been unable to locate in English.

SHINOBU: You're sleeping so soundly. (*She sings in a low voice.*)
Hear, sweet Mother, hear the weary,
Borne upon life's troubled sea;
Gentle guiding Star of Ocean,
Lead thy children home to thee.
Still watch o'er us, dearest Mother,
From thy beauteous throne above;
Guard us from all harm and danger,
'Neath thy shelt'ring wings of love.

Jigorō slowly props himself up.

JIGORŌ (*without looking in her direction*): Hey, woman.

SHINOBU: I'm sorry. I've wakened you.

JIGORŌ: Forget it. Listen, how'd you like to make some money?

SHINOBU: What do you mean?

JIGORŌ: Come here.

Shinobu draws a little closer to him.

JIGORŌ (*pulling a wad of bills unceremoniously from his pocket and trying to force them into Shinobu's hand*): Run away with me. You only have to stick with me for a day. All you have to do is pretend I'm your husband for two hours, from here to Sasebo. I'll carry the diaper bag, see. How about it?

His eyes fix on Shinobu's green shawl. A guitar begins to play. Trying to keep his balance Jigorō starts to walk.

JIGORŌ:
A distant dream:
Layers of green enfold
A spring, small but deep;
The water, green-dyed, is mute,
And though it tries to cry out . . . it cannot.
It can see the white clouds flowing over Mt. Hiko,
But they won't come to its rescue.
They are the school principal's white gloves,
The white roll of a diploma, a green table cloth, green mast!
    White scabbard!
Ahhh, no one's there.
I am alone . . . alone . . . .
Something's missing, missing.
A white scabbard without a dagger . . . .

SHINOBU: White scabbard!
JIGORŌ:
The dagger, pulled from its scabbard.
I will die.
And when I do, green blood will pour from my eyes.

Shinobu's eyes, which have been following Jigorō's movements, take on a strange glint, and now she stands in front of him, blocking his way. For a moment, the antagonists stand in silence; then Shinobu inches Jigorō back toward the operating table.

SHINOBU: Do you know me?
JIGORŌ: All I know is you're a woman. Listen, come with me as far as Sasebo. I'll give you as much money as you want.
SHINOBU: Mother, this is the man . . . Now I shall return Shinobu's dagger to its rightful owner!
All at once, Jigorō wails, grips his belly, and drops to his knees.
SHINOBU (*taken by surprise*): What's wrong?
JIGORŌ (*getting to his feet*): The green mast has broken through! (*He collapses on the operating table.*)
SHINOBU (*without emotion, as if stabbing him*): Umph!! Umph!!
JIGORŌ: You've come at last, eh? From far away. . . . (*Crawling into an upright position*): Woman, come here. Let me see your face.
As he says this, he grabs Shinobu by the hair, which comes out in a wad in his hand.
SHINOBU: Go ahead, take a good look!
JIGORŌ: That baby . . . is it mine? It is, isn't it?
SHINOBU (*joyfully*): Oh, Mother!
JIGORŌ: It is, isn't it?
SHINOBU: No, no!
JIGORŌ: Oh. I wish it had been. Then I could have been happy. Like normal people.
SHINOBU: Don't give me that. Who in the world would give you the satisfaction, huh? You're nothing but an animal. This child's father's more than that.
JIGORŌ: An animal, am I? What words to hear on my deathbed! Is that all you have to say, woman?
SHINOBU: A stud, that's all you are. A donkey stud! How many

women have lost their minds because of you? How many women have rotted!

JIGORŌ: I've lost count of the women, the dozens of women who've shown up claiming their brats were mine. Women are just cunts, that's all. Hah-hah-hah . . . .

SHINOBU: Don't laugh!

JIBORŌ: Hah-hah . . . hey, don't get so angry. You're beautiful when you're angry, you know. Hah-hah-hah . . . .

SHINOBU: So what? Those women loved of their own free choice, but you men don't know, you don't understand how much suffering their love cost them.

JIGORŌ: Suffering? Don't make me laugh. They were as free as they come. They're misfits because they're free.

SHINOBU: No! . . .

JIGORŌ: Once you've tasted freedom, you're spoiled for good. Because what's the point of behaving responsibly once you realize the world's nothing but a way station? And where there's no responsibility, there can be no true freedom—that's obvious.

SHINOBU: Big talk! You should have been a school teacher. You talk like the prize punk and pimp that you are!

JIGORŌ: If freedom's not what I say, then what is it? Bluffing?

SHINOBU: You wouldn't understand even if I told you. It'd be like casting pearls before swine.

JIGORŌ: Pearls, eh? I'd like to take a look at those "pearls." Next you're going to tell me they're tucked safe away in your heart! Come here, I said. You're not afraid of me, are you—a dying man?

SHINOBU: If you saw them, you'd be afraid.

JIGORŌ: Just shut up and come over here.

Shinobu approaches. They stare at each other.

JIGORŌ (*gripping Shinobu's arm*): Heh-heh, now here's a woman fit to be the mother of my child. (*He embraces her over her thick, padded jacket.*)

Shinobu stops resisting.

JIGORŌ (*suddenly breaking out into a high-pitched laugh*): Well, whadya know! Whadya know! This is what I lost! What I've been missing!

He is brandishing Shinobu's dagger.

SHINOBU: Then you remember, don't you? What did you do with my ring?

JIGORŌ: Now let me see . . . .

SHINOBU: It's yours all right. I'm returning it to its rightful owner.

JIGORŌ: Where did you find it?

SHINOBU: Try to remember. Thirteen years ago, you forced it on me.

JIGORŌ: Yeah?

SHINOBU: Remember!

JIGORŌ: No, it was stolen. Stolen!

SHINOBU: Who stole it, then? Who?

JIGORŌ: Who knows? Hah-hah, dozens, hundreds of women have wept in these strong arms. I ain't bragging, but I never forced anyone!

SHINOBU: Is that so? Well, I'm not giving it back without getting something in return.

JIGORŌ: What exactly do you want? Money? With interest?

SHINOBU: Die! It's your punishment for stealing my freedom. Die! Ah, at last I will be free! Free!

JIGORŌ: You're not making any sense. You keep shouting about death and freedom—what exactly am I to you anyway?

Shinobu suddenly wrests the dagger from Jigorō and tries to stab him.

JIGORŌ (*spreading his arms wide*): Is this your answer?

But Shinobu cannot. She throws the dagger away and sinks, clinging to his knees.

SHINOBU: Then kill me . . . kill me!

JIGORŌ: If I could free you by dying, I'd die anytime. Come on, now, stand up. But is being free so important? Is it? Would it make you that happy? What sort of satisfaction would you enjoy all by yourself, huh? Look at you, there's the proof: you're falling apart. As long as you had the dagger, you had life.

SHINOBU (*desperately*): I'll transcend life, transcend life!

JIGORŌ: Nobody can transcend life. The freedom you talk about is the freedom of life, not the freedom of the soul.

SHINOBU: Ahhhh!

JIGORŌ: The freedom of loneliness, loneliness, that's all it is.

SHINOBU (*already defeated*): That's exactly what I want!

JIGORŌ: Heresy!

SHINOBU: Hah-hah! . . . Heresy? Thank you. I haven't heard the Christian word in ages. You're right. I walk with my head held high. Nothing's going to get in my way.

JIGORŌ: Don't pretend. The only thing that can fill the vacuum you leave in your life is the same sense of sin you've felt all along.

SHINOBU: I'll worry about my own sensibilities.

JIGORŌ: Be my guest. But let me tell you something, real freedom—are you listening?—real freedom lies further on.

SHINOBU (*smiling*): Is that so? What is this "further on," then, huh?

JIGORŌ: I'm nothing but an animal, so I don't know any better than to tell the truth. You know, there was a time when the thought of death sent a chill up my spine. But now that it's a reality, I finally seem to have . . . . But there's no way to explain it—you have to experience this feeling to understand it.

SHINOBU: If you can't explain it, I can't understand. (*She spreads a white quilt over him.*) I'm finished with you. Send me a message from hell . . . . Good-bye.

JIGORŌ: Wait. I need someone to hear my last words. Otherwise, how can I die? My murder won't be complete. Hey, don't you want to see your old enemy breathe his last?

SHINOBU: I'll leave you to hell's tender mercies.

JIGORŌ: Maybe I'll start to remember who you are . . . .

Shinobu stops in her tracks.

JIGORŌ: It's been more than ten years, and my hair's still falling out. On August ninth I was at the Ōmura factory. Starting in the evening and on into the night, trucks and trains began arriving filled with the freight of half-dead human beings. I rode into Nagasaki on the bed of one of those trucks, slippery with a sticky foul-smelling pus, my white-sheathed dagger stuck in my belt. I wandered around in that burnt-over hell, giving people water and carrying them to first aid stations. No special reason. I just wanted to do it, that's all.

SHINOBU: In the ruins. And then?

The sound of a siren approaching.

JIGORŌ: Now finally those days have come back to haunt me. My red blood count . . . the count . . . I've dished out my share of villainy, and taken my share, too. I guess it's time to settle the accounts.

SHINOBU: There's nothing special about your story. But where exactly in the ruins were you?

JIGORŌ: I don't have the slightest recollection where or how I met you, but . . . even now it's not too late. (*His breathing becomes labored.*)

SHINOBU: Even now?

JIGORŌ: Tell me. I really want to know: I've gone around and done whatever I pleased, but who am I? Who is Jigorō?

Shinobu does not answer.

JIGORŌ: Please, something, anything . . . . No, huh? That's what I was afraid of—nothing to tell. All right, so be it. I'm just another human being. So be it. Then I'll die as a cinder or vanish like an insect like everybody else. Fine! But is that all there is to it? Is that really all there is to life? Is that really all? Will everything be reduced to nothingness?

SHINOBU: What do you have to regret?

JIGORŌ: Ah, more terrifying than death!

SHINOBU: Then, Jigorō, if it will make you feel any better: Just as you said yourself, further on. You have to go further on!

SHINOBU: Yes, of course! Thank you.

SHINOBU: Jigorō, get a grip on yourself! You can't die now!

JIGORŌ: You want me to give you back the dagger so we can go at it one more time? Hah-hah-hah!

Dr. Sakamoto looks in. He carries a pair of chopsticks and appears to be in the middle of a meal.

DOCTOR: How's he doing? Seems energetic enough. Your pal's gone to call a cab for you.

JIGORŌ: Yeah, thanks. I'm feeling a lot better.

DOCTOR: Good. You've got a whole pack of pretty visitors, too. But they've just brought in an accident case, so I'll have to ask you to make room for him right away. Brrr, it's cold! (*Exits.*)

JIGORŌ: Maggot!
Women I, II, III, and IV burst into the room, laughing raucously, each carrying a large bouquet of flowers. Shinobu places the dagger on Jigorō's chest and, concealing her face, tries to run out of the room.
JIGORŌ (*to Shinobu's retreating figure*): Farewell, be seeing you. I'll go on ahead.
SHINOBU (*looking back*): Jigorō, I . . . love you. (*Exits.*)
The Women giggle about the events of the previous night as they whisper among themselves. "That's the dagger . . . ." " 'I love you'!" etc.
JIGORŌ: News travels fast.
WOMAN I: That skinny know-it-all told us.
WOMAN II: Wow, look at this bandage, how white it is!
WOMAN III: I'll bet it hurt, didn't it?
WOMAN IV: We've brought you some flowers.
The Women arrange the flowers around Jigorō's body.
WOMAN II: These are the only times we get to show our appreciation.
WOMAN III: How come you felt like killing yourself?
WOMAN I: A man like you, Jigorō, a real hero?
Pause.
JIGORŌ: They're so beautiful! (*He crushes one of the bouquets to his chest.*)
WOMAN II: Flowers for weddings.
WOMEN III: And flowers for funerals.
WOMAN IV: Shhh!
Woman III sticks out her tongue.
JIGORŌ: I was wandering around in the ruins of hell.
WOMAN IV: What? Hell?
JIGORŌ: In the dark of that air raid shelter, her ring shone green, green . . . .
WOMAN I: What ring?
JIGORŌ: Instead of calling "Water! Water!" like everybody else, that girl—she couldn't have been more than fifteen or sixteen at the time—asked if I had anything to eat. Lucky girl, she'd come through without a scratch. I gave her my last bit of rice and the last water from my canteen, and then I asked her . . . for her ring. "I can't," she said. "It's all my mother left me. I

can't." I don't remember what happened then. Anyway, in place of the dagger that had found its way into my hand, there was this diamond shining green. I used it to get started in the black market. (*Suddenly raising himself from the bed*): Murderers! Everywhere, murderers! They're wiping their chops and pretending nothing happened. Worse, they act holier-than-thou and go around yapping at others. And . . . and I'm the one who has to die! . . . Murderers! Murderers!

Repeating "Murderers . . . murderers" under his breath, Doctor rushes in.

DOCTOR: Hey, pipe down, will you! You scared me half to death.

Women laugh.

DOCTOR: Well, you can see my point, can't you? What a pain in the neck! How many people do you think make it through life with a clear conscience, with a perfectly clear conscience? How pathetic!

JIGORŌ: Pathetic! That's me all right! And so I have to die! Die!

DOCTOR: Idle threats! (*He takes his pulse.*) Mmm, it is a little . . . .

JIGORŌ: A small, deep pond . . . .

DOCTOR: Shhh!

Jigorō waves Doctor away.

DOCTOR: Shika! Shika! (*He exits in some haste.*)

JIGORŌ:
Layers of green enfold
A spring, small but deep;
The water, green-dyed, is mute . . . .

Man V rushes in.

MAN V: Hey, I've got the cab. Come on, what are you waiting for? And you girls, don't just stand there . . . .

Women continue staring at Jigorō.

JIGORŌ: White clouds . . . over Mt. Hiko . . . .

Shika hurries in with a large hypodermic needle on a tray. Dr. Sakamoto follows her.

Woman III suddenly breaks into silent tears.

JIGORŌ: White clouds . . . over Mt. Hiko . . . . They can't be expected to come to the rescue . . . .

Shika passes the tray to Doctor, then silently draws near the operating table, and takes Jigorō's hand.

SHIKA: Further on . . . further on . . . .

Curtain.

ACT THREE

SCENE ONE: A CONVERTED STABLE

A room in a boardinghouse which, in addition to being a remodeled horse stable, is also ramshackle from years of neglect. Among the kitchen utensils, toys, magazines, dirty bedding, and canvases strewn around the room lies Momozono, pale from anemia. Next to him Man III sits, helping with the paper kites that he makes for extra money. Five or six finished kites hang from the wooden walls. The patterns are abstract designs Momozono has painted himself.

(Author's note: In Nagasaki, kites are called "flags," and their colors and patterns are traditional.)

In one corner are the appurtenances of Shinobu's trade. Diapers are drying in the corridor.

It is dusk and dark. Somewhere, a baby is crying.

MAN III: Really, sometime I'd like to take you up to the top of Mount Kazagashira . . . . It's a good thing we lost the war. If Nagasaki were still a fortress, they couldn't have driven trucks up there and built a lookout so you could see from the town, to the port, to Mount Inasa.

There doesn't seem to be a fire in the brazier, and as Man III works, he occasionally warms his hands with his breath.

MAN III: You'd better hurry and get well. As soon as it's spring, we've got to go out and fly these things. (*He taps the kites.*) We'll make a paste out of ground glass, see, spread it on the string, and let it dry. That way, when you wrap the string around your opponent's flag, you can cut the string. The defeated flag sails off into the distance, sort of laughing like. When we were kids, we used to chase that flag as it drifted down through the sky. We'd run and run, and the one who got there first . . . .

MOMOZONO: Hey.

MAN III: Huh?

MOMOZONO: Why do you keep chattering today? Have you lost control of your tongue?

MAN III: I, uh, I . . . .

MOMOZONO: Now all of a sudden you're stuttering.

MAN III: I'm almost d-done with number three.

MOMOZONO: Are you waiting for Shinobu?

MAN III: When your heart's filled with anticipation, you just naturally run off at the mouth, I guess.

MOMOZONO: Then Christians must always be running off at the mouth, eh?

MAN III: Maybe so, hah-hah-hah!

MOMOZONO: What's that sound? Don't tell me it's snowing!

MAN III: It is! It's snow!

MOMOZONO: Don't you think you'd better go home before it begins to accumulate?

MAN III: I suppose you're right. You can compose poetry better on your own, anyway. W-well . . . . (*Leaving*): Listen, when Shinobu gets back, tell her that tonight snow is falling, and if it lingers on the ground . . . .

MOMOZONO: If it lingers on the ground?

MAN III: That's enough. She'll understand. Well, I'll be going then. Take care of yourself. (*Exits.*)

Man III's voice can be heard saying, "No, I haven't seen him."
Policeman enters slowly.

POLICEMAN: Good evening! May I come in? How have you been? You haven't seen a suspicious looking character around here, have you? A young man in a rain coat.

MOMOZONO: Nope. What's going on?

POLICEMAN: The kingpin of a drug ring's been killed. We arrested everyone at his wake, but this one got away. Well, look at this! Begun making flags, have you? Spring won't be long now!

MOMOZONO: What was his name, this kingpin?

POLICEMAN: They called him Jigorō.

MOMOZONO: Jigorō!

POLICEMAN: Old men like me can't take these late nights. You get an emergency call, though, and you don't have any choice. Listen, you know how to make the glass paste for the string? There's a secret way to do it . . . .

MOMOZONO: Were there any women?

POLICEMAN: As a matter of fact, there were five or six. All of them ladies of the night. Well, sorry for interrupting . . . .

MOMOZONO: Do you know who killed him? Was it one of the women?

POLICEMAN: Are you kidding? Some people say it was suicide, but frankly, I don't think scum like that have it in them. The Mrs. gone out already?

MOMOZONO: Yes, she, er . . . .

POLICEMAN: Where could that punk have gotten to? Well, sorry to bother you. I'll drop by again soon and show you how to make that glass paste. Brrrr, and on top of everything else, it's got to snow!

The window slides open and two hands appear, one carrying a basket of fruit and the other a pair of shoes. The hands place the objects in the room. Before you know it, Man V has invaded the room, glancing around as he does so. He is wearing a rain coat.

MAN V: Mr. Momozono?

MOMOZONO (*still face up in bed*): Who is it?

MAN V (*crouching down beside him*): Your wife asked me to bring you these. She said she'd be back soon.

There is a black ribbon on the basket.

MAN V: There's a lot of nourishment in fruit after all. (*He helps himself to an orange.*)

MOMOZONO: She said she'd be right back?

MAN V: Yeah.

MOMOZONO: This Jigorō, what was he like? How old was he?

MAN V: About your age, I guess.

MOMOZONO: And he already had his own gang?

MAN V: Yeah, but he couldn't take it. (*Softly*): He killed himself.

MOMOZONO: Killed himself? Why?

MAN V: His hair was falling out, and he was sure he was a goner. He was still young, too. (*Hearing something, he is suddenly on guard.*)

Woman's voice: "What? Oh, Mr. Momozono? He's in the room at the end of the hall."

Man's voice: "Thanks."

Woman's voice: "Watch your step, that board's loose."

MAN V: It's not your wife. I'll be back. (*He exits through the window.*)

Yabari enters, wearing a student uniform and a blue rain coat and carrying a notebook.

YABARI: Good evening. May I come in?

MOMOZONO: Yes?

YABARI: You must be Mr. Momozono.

MOMOZONO: If you're here about the electric bill, I'm sorry, but you'll have to wait a little . . . .

YABARI (*forcing a smile*): You're not the first one to mistake me for a bill collector. I'm making a survey of survivors of the atomic bomb. (*Looking around the room*): Improving the quality of the survivors' lives is, of course, . . . (*He refers to his notes.*) Let me see, you have severe anemia. Cancer of the bone marrow, I suppose. How are you feeling? Do you have headaches?

MOMOZONO: No. I don't, no.

YABARI: No headaches. Swelling of the lower extremities?

MOMOZONO: Absolutely not.

YABARI: No? Your complexion is rather. . . . Um, I don't mean to pry, but you haven't applied for medical care. You haven't registered as a survivor, either.* Aren't you aware that there are laws that entitle you to care?

MOMOZONO: I know.

YABARI: There are people who aren't aware, you see. If there's anything else bothering you, please don't hesitate to tell me. It won't be any trouble at all, I promise. I'll take care of everything for you. To begin with I'll see to your application for medical care.

MOMOZONO: I am not a survivor.

YABARI: Yes, but, the very fact that you've been confined to bed for so long is a clear sign of A-bomb disease.

MOMOZONO: Hah-hah . . . you're still young. You're bound to jump to conclusions.

YABARI (*pouting*): You're not so old yourself.

---

*Beginning in 1957, it became possible for survivors of Hiroshima and Nagasaki (*hibakusha*) to register with the government and receive medical treatment. Those eligible included those (1) who had been in Nagasaki or Hiroshima when the bomb was dropped, (2) who entered the center of the city within fourteen days, (3) who handled the dead or the wounded, (4) or who were *in utero* and whose mothers fit into these categories. For a description of the psychological conflicts and controversies surrounding medical welfare for survivors, see Lifton, *Death in Life,* pp. 145–148.

MOMOZONO: Are you a doctor?

YABARI: No. The real problems are the ones doctors can't treat. The more fundamental ones.

MOMOZONO: I wish they'd at least solve the medical problems.

YABARI: It takes money to solve medical problems. Transfusions and more transfusions. How can people afford it? No individual can afford those bills. That's why so many survivors are suffering. That's why I . . . .

MOMOZONO: Listen, son, they don't know what's causing my condition. It's not hookworm, and it's not hereditary; it could be aplastic anemia. Or it could be cancer of the bone marrow like you said.

YABARI: It's your marrow. That . . . that's got to be the cause.

MOMOZONO: No, it's only the result. Look, I may not know what sort of anemia I have, but I do know that it wasn't caused by the bomb. I'm sorry to disappoint you. Now, please leave me alone.

YABARI: But if you have the same symptoms as A-bomb disease, why not say that it's A-bomb disease? You'd certainly benefit, and what have you got to lose? Tell me, what have you got to lose? Nothing, right? You have no right to sacrifice yourself and waste away in resignation. You have no right at all.

MOMOZONO: You want me to have A-bomb disease no matter what, don't you? A student like you ought to have his nose buried in books, not in other people's business. It's for your own good.

YABARI: Leave my studies to me. I'm not sacrificing myself to do some irrelevant project, as you seem to think.

MOMOZONO: Then I'd like you to leave my problems to me, too. Eventually you're going to be looking for a job. Getting involved with survivors of the bomb is only going to hurt your prospects.

YABARI: I didn't come here to argue with you, so I won't. I'm just trying to conduct a national survey of atomic bomb survivors that's all.

MOMOZONO: And I've been trying to tell you I'm not a survivor.

YABARI: Why do you have to be so stubborn? Mr. Momozono, I want to be a spokesman for all of you survivors. I believe that definitions that say a survivor's white blood count has to be twice that of a healthy person or otherwise less than half, or that you have to have entered a contaminated area within two weeks of the bombings are nothing but bureaucratic constructs and that to make people sign a contract swearing that they're survivors is the height of absurdity. That's why when I meet someone like yourself who refuses to admit he's a survivor . . . .

MOMOZONO: You're wrong. Wrong, I said. I'm not trying to be difficult or anything of the sort. I was still in Korea that summer. It was October before I was repatriated and landed at Senzaki in Yamaguchi prefecture. So what happened in Hiroshima and Nagasaki hasn't got anything to do with me. I haven't even had an X-ray taken. I clearly don't qualify as a survivor, and I'm not in the least unhappy about it. I appreciate your concern, but it seems I won't be able to satisfy your passion. As a matter of fact, it's not easy for me to talk to you like this. If you're really concerned about me, the first thing to do is to leave me alone. Now please get out.

YABARI: But you're not confined to bed for no reason. If you're not a victim of the bomb, then what are you a victim of? What does the fact that you have a blood count of 1,100,500 mean?* Please tell me. Explain it to me so I'll be convinced.

MOMOZONO: Who told you about me anyway? How did you get those figures? Oh . . . Shinobu . . . my wife . . . .

YABARI: I've never met your wife.

MOMOZONO: I wonder if it's going to melt right away, the snow . . . the snow . . . .

Pause.

YABARI (*suddenly, in a loud voice*): I've got it! You were in a particular place in Japan, and you were there within a particular period of time. Just after the atomic experiments on Hiroshima and Nagasaki, they were saying in America that no

---

*A normal red blood count is in the neighborhood of 5,000,000.

plants or animals would grow there for seventy years. There must be a place like that somewhere, contaminated by radioactivity—and you were there!

MOMOZONO: Listen, this is a rooming house. I have enough trouble holding my head up around here already without you shouting.

YABARI: It's crazy, the idea that you had to be at the site of the bombings within two weeks!

MOMOZONO: That's enough, now, please leave.

YABARI: Mr. Momozono, that "particular place" is all of Japan. Since 1954, the United States and Russia have carried out more than a dozen tests of atomic and hydrogen weapons. Which country has its coast washed by the Japan Current? Against the mountains of which country do the north winds blow out of Siberia? And to make matters worse, the bones of the Japanese, who eat rice as their staple, are particularly sensitive to radiation. The fact is that there have already been two instances when intense radiation was absorbed at particular places at particular times in Japan, and who can say categorically that it will never happen again? Every time there is a test, that possibility is rekindled. Even if they are not direct victims of the bomb, there must be dozens, no hundreds of indirect, extremely indirect victims like yourself, who have sacrificed their lives.

MOMOZONO: Hah-hah . . . . If what you say is true, then everyone in Japan is doomed to die from anemia or leukemia.

YABARI: That's exactly right. And it's no laughing matter! It's not just you. Everyone's so damned nonchalant! Disaster strikes when you've forgotten about it. And everyone's forgotten. Forgotten!

MOMOZONO: They're trying to forget. And your getting all hot and bothered isn't going to change things.

YABARI: Are you saying people should go on with their day-to-day lives and push everything else out of their minds?

MOMOZONO (*quietly*): What exactly did you come to see me for?

YABARI: I'm sorry. I guess I just don't express myself well enough.

MOMOZONO: Hardly.

YABARI: I'll get back to the point. All I really need to do is collect material on the damage caused by the bomb; it's not my mission to get involved in your feelings. But if there is a person who, even though he has a right to happiness, is either unaware that he has such a right or does not know the legitimate way to exercise that right, then I believe that it is both my right and my obligation as a human being to open his eyes, to brighten his horizons, and to show him the way to happiness. There is nothing more detrimental to human progress than a lack of awareness. Look, since the war, aren't the peoples of the underdeveloped countries of Southeast Asia and Africa becoming free precisely because they have escaped their own lack of awareness? The same thing could happen to you!

MOMOZONO: You mean I should awake to my lack of awareness and be happy? That's precious!

YABARI: Set an example. Please. Don't let your sacrifice be for nothing.

MOMOZONO: I've told you again and again that I'm not qualified to accept that honor. As a matter of fact, despite appearances, I used to be a painter by profession. The abstracts on those flags are just a bit of extravagance to make them sell; my paintings were rather run-of-the-mill, actually. Even so, I've had a love of truth and freedom after my own fashion. It's been insignificant and nothing to be proud of, but . . . .

YABARI: Hah-hah, so you're an artist! I never could seem to relate to artists.

MOMOZONO: Hah-hah, neither can I! In my case, art may be what's standing between me and true freedom.

YABARI: How can you say that? Oh, boy! The essence of art is to express yourself, to express yourself with freedom and originality. I've always thought that everyone wanted to be an artist.

MOMOZONO: I used to think so too.

YABARI: But first your art has to be exceptional.

MOMOZONO: Hah-hah, you're absolutely right. You've struck at the painful truth. That's the first time you've made sense since you walked in here. Well, that ought to be enough. I'll sign your petition or whatever.

YABARI: You will? Well, then, sign here, please. (*He takes a petition from his pocket and hands it to Momozono along with a fountain pen.*) Print your name in Roman letters, too, please.

Momozono signs without really reading the petition.

YABARI (*while Momozono is signing*): I'm confident that our little talk has stimulated you in meaningful ways.

MOMOZONO: In Roman letters, too?

YABARI: Yes, please.

Shinobu, a shawl over her head, returned a few minutes ago, but realizing her husband had a visitor, she has stayed inconspicuously in the corridor.

MOMOZONO: As you say, I don't have much talent. But as a human being I still have other dreams. And those dreams are probably quite different from yours. (*He returns the petition and pen.*) The question is how those dreams will echo in my talent. That's what I have to look forward to in the short life remaining to me.

YABARI: I wish you luck. Even if our dreams are different now, I'm sure that eventually they'll coincide. Sorry for the interruption. He's getting old, but I'll introduce you to a good doctor I know. Well, take care of yourself. (*Exits.*)

The sharp sound of a ship's steam whistle.

Momozono picks up the notebook beside his pillow.

MOMOZONO:

And resume my journey down the road.

Like any pebble on that road,

I will obliterate chance;

Traveling the path of the infinite, the limitless, the relative,

I will expand, billow,

Disperse like the mist in my own existence.

Ah! How I long to extinguish the necessity,

The absoluteness of my being! But for him!

But for that man who encumbered me,

Who left me with this something,

Who left it unbidden then vanished—

I hate that man!

Shinobu once again shows herself. She is listening.

MOMOZONO:

Do I hate him,

Or do I love him so much I hate him?
What do I mean by "this something"?
Now, I must solve this riddle. (*He is referring to himself.*)
What is "this something"?
The soul?
The flesh?
Or perhaps . . . the self?
. . . .
Then, Shinobu, unperturbed . . . .
SHINOBU: Then Shinobu was greatly perturbed!
MOMOZONO (*still lying face up in bed*): So you finally met him.
SHINOBU: I met him. Finally.
MOMOZONO: What about the dagger, Shinobu's dagger?
SHINOBU: I returned it.
MOMOZONO: Did he take it?
SHINOBU: He took it.
MOMOZONO: At last! Now you are truly free!
SHINOBU: No. I thought I would be, but . . . I was wrong.
MOMOZONO: Even though you achieved what you had so
longed for? Why? Why?
SHINOBU: You . . . . (*Lowering the baby from her back and giving it
her breast*): He died. He died all by himself. Even so, it's as if I
killed him. Yes, it's as if I killed him with my own hands. My
sin, my inborn sin killed him.
MOMOZONO: Because you had to kill him. That was your life.
SHINOBU: Then why haven't I killed you?
MOMOZONO: Because you haven't loved me.
SHINOBU: If we knew that, why did we marry? Why have we
stayed married?
MOMOZONO: Perhaps in order to free ourselves of sin.
SHINOBU: To free ourselves, and then what? What lies beyond
freedom?
MOMOZONO: Freedom is limitless, infinite, relative . . . .
SHINOBU: Ah! What empty joy!
MOMOZONO: With courage, you are a woman who grows large
with courage, transcending both the relative and the absolute.
SHINOBU: Yes, like the women of old.
MOMOZONO: Healthy, fertile, pure . . . .
SHINOBU: That . . . that is your love.

MOMOZONO: Yes. Now, grow large. Swell with your freedom!

SHINOBU: You are like the devil, watching me and licking his chops.

MOMOZONO: We are both devils, coconspirators.

SHINOBU: Though I see through you, I'm no longer surprised. (*She lays the baby in bed beside Momozono and pulls the fruit basket toward her.*) What will you choose from this basket of fruit bound with its black ribbon of mourning? A banana? An orange? An apple?

MOMOZONO: It goes without saying: Woman always gives man. . . .

SHINOBU (*sitting*): An apple. (*Wiping it with her hand, she bites off a piece and hands it to Momozono.*)

MOMOZONO: It looks like our diabolical game is at an end. There's nothing left in me to tempt.

SHINOBU: Oh! Is that so? (*She takes a bite herself.*)

MOMOZONO: It's delicious! Now I'm ready to die.

SHINOBU (*laughing*): After only one bite of the apple? You're easy to please!

MOMOZONO: Yes, after only one bite. The beauty of the white skin, the firmness of the flesh engraved with your teeth-marks—that is enough to make the life of this creature overflow with the purity, the power of life. One bite? Even that much outweighs the value of my life!

SHINOBU (*gently*): You really want to live, like this bit of fruit.

MOMOZONO: Listen, the snake is whispering . . . whispering.

SHINOBU: Tell me, who is trying to shorten your life? Please, tell me? I want to know. Please. You know who it is, don't you? Please!

MOMOZONO: I don't understand very well myself, why I have to die. What sins have I committed? A certain pride, I suppose, and the fact that I dragged you into poverty. No, I admit it. But that's about all. When you come right down to it, they're the sins of any meek, ordinary man. But what use is such self-consciousness of one's humanity? A man as good as sinless is killed, and people say, "How sad!" People call the atomic bomb, the hydrogen bomb terrible. But, what good is it to recognize the terror? Isn't it more important to do away with war than to agree not to use nuclear weapons? Evil exists, sin exists within man himself. And when men clothe themselves in "justice" or in "freedom," it becomes impossible to tell what's bad, what's good, what's just. And we're adrift amidst it all, buffeted by the waves.

SHINOBU: Then where is our salvation? You can lie there and talk as if you've graduated from life and achieved enlightenment. But how am I, how are the baby and I supposed to go on?

MOMOZONO: Why so faint hearted? You've just achieved your freedom. What are you worried about when you haven't even tested your new happiness?

SHINOBU: I'm not the strong woman you think I am. I'm not!

MOMOZONO: You must grow healthy, strong, sturdy for the sake of the child as well as yourself.

SHINOBU: You're a cruel man. How can you be so cruel! (*She weeps.*)

MOMOZONO: Your friend dropped by tonight. He asked me to tell you, "If the snow lingers on the ground . . . ."

SHINOBU: Snow? . . . (*She stands and goes to the window.*) Snow!

MOMOZONO: I guess you won't be working tonight.

SHINOBU: Who was it that told me? Further on? Where exactly is "further on"? Please! Won't someone tell me? Please!

Momozono is lulling the baby to sleep.

SCENE TWO: THE TYPESETTING ROOM OF A PRINT SHOP

Sloping walls lined with numberless large, shallow boxes containing pieces of lead type, and the narrow valley between them.*
Night. Snow is falling.

With a manuscript and small box in his left hand, Man II is walking back and forth picking up pieces of type.

From no place in particular the easily distinguishable voices of several middle-aged women can be heard, repeatedly imploring, "Please!" "Please!" low and far away. They are the voices of the manuscript he carries in his hand.

---

*Because of the thousands of different characters in Japanese, fonts of type are arranged vertically like this to allow easy access as the typesetter walks between them.

WOMAN'S VOICE: We now share our grief and our joy with you in the hope that we may truly say from the bottom of our hearts, "We are glad to have survived," and with a plea for peace and our children's happiness, we pray . . . .

Pause.

SECOND WOMAN'S VOICE: The single wish of those of us who survived the baptism of the atomic bomb is that our martyred families might rest in peace, safe in the knowledge that the same catastrophe will not befall humankind again . . . .

Man II sits down on a chair and reads the contents of his now-full box as he warms himself beside a charcoal brazier.

THIRD WOMAN'S VOICE: As one project to promote our peace movement, we mothers seek to build in Nagasaki, site of the atomic bombing, a Nagasaki International Culture Center, in the fervent hope of the people of Nagasaki that "Out of Nagasaki shall come peace!" . . .

MAN II (*reading the type in his box*): Moreover, comma, we must live on . . . the *n*'s missing . . . . (*He gets up, retrieves the letter* n, *places it in his box, and sits down again.*) . . . live on, comma, overcoming whatever suffering, comma, so that we may raise our children to be strong, upright human beings, period. New paragraph. Even though we each suffered alone, comma, as we look back now on the futile past, comma, we . . . (*He inserts a character.*) . . . we now share our sadness and our joy with you so that we may truly say from the bottom of our hearts, comma, quotation marks, we are glad to have survived . . . . (*He raises his head.*) If they were alive today, how old would they be?!

Again the voices: "Please!"

MAN II: You can hear the pleading voices ever so faintly . . . . Those voices have to sink into each human being's heart . . . each person must . . . .

The bell of the cathedral begins to ring.

MAN II (*rising and looking through the window*): The snow . . . the snow . . . . It's lingering on the ground!

(Author's Note: The foregoing scene is written in standard Japanese, but the voices of the women should have a distinct regional flavor.)

Curtain.

ACT FOUR

THE RUINED ENTRANCE OF THE URAKAMI CATHEDRAL

(Author's Note: The following setting does not necessarily correspond to the actual site it purports to represent.)

In addition to the arch, parts of the blackened red-brick walls are still standing. Embedded in a recess in the wall, the Statue of a Saint with a long beard stands, but part of its shoulders have been blown away. Beneath the arch, the entrance to the cathedral consists of a broad floor at the top of three steps piled with debris. The Head of Mary rests on the floor, and if one were to brush away the snow that conceals it, one would find that the face is the face of a mother of the long-suffering common people, and one would also see that the profile has been burned black. The entire site is roped off, but it is only for appearance' sake, and anyone could enter the premises. It would therefore be easy to go in and stand leaning against the wall opposite the image of the saint.

There is already one person there. Partially covered with snow, the figure is sitting with its legs splayed to one side, frantically clutching a rosary to its chest. It is Shika.

Illuminated by the reflected light of the snow against the background of Urakami Hill, these eerie ruins, standing abandoned in the open plaza, have been beautified by a light powdering of snow. But now the snow has stopped.

SHIKA *(murmuring)*:
Mary!
Only you, who have escaped sin,
Can see into the reaches of our soul.
Only you know us!
That is why before you alone
I would be truly me!
. . . .
Aaaah, it's no good! No good!

HEAD OF MARY *(speaking with a heavy Nagasaki accent)*: Why's it no good, Shika, dear, why?

SAINT *(similarly)*: You were just reciting a long prayer, after all.

SHIKA: But I'm just not worthy of your blessing. Unloved by the world, I wrought vengeance on myself. And out of the ecstasy of that faithless path I loved you. Then my vengeance spread to the world. To implement my vengeance on the world, I assembled a group to abduct you. Tonight is the night, tonight as the snow falls. Please, Holy Mother of God, aid us unworthy sinners to achieve our goal. I beg you!

SAINT: Hah-hah-hah . . . Mary?

HEAD OF MARY: Yes?

SAINT: It looks like it's finally time for us to say so long.

HEAD OF MARY: Yes, but it's about time I was reunited with my arms and body and legs!

SAINT: The troubles you've seen aren't like anything you've experienced since that trouble with young Jesus down in Egypt! Hah-hah-hah!

HEAD OF MARY: Hah-hah . . . by this time my breasts must be aching, filled with milk.

SAINT: Hah-hah-hah!

HEAD OF MARY: I want to go and see, and let my children suckle at my breast.

SAINT: Children?

HEAD OF MARY: There's one right in front of you. How forlorn she is!

SAINT: Yes . . . . Look, more children are coming.

Shinobu and Man III enter, running from stage right.

SHINOBU: Oh dear! Shika's not there yet.

MAN III: She'll be here soon. You must be cold!

SHINOBU: I'm trembling all over but not cold at all.

MAN III: It's the anticipation. After all, your prayers are about to be fulfilled.

SHINOBU: When this is over, you're going to marry Shika, aren't you?

MAN III: Heavens no!

SHINOBU: Why not?

MAN III: Because as far as she's concerned, she's Mary.

SHINOBU: Oh!

MAN III (*looking off stage right*): Somebody's coming. Is it her?

SHINOBU: No, it's a man.

MAN III: A man? Let's hide!

SHINOBU: Don't worry. I know him. He's one of us. A new member of our congregation.

Man II enters from stage right.

MAN II: Good evening. It snowed tonight, so as we agreed . . . .

SHINOBU: Welcome.

MAN III: First off, let me explain the nature of our prayer. The Church got fed up with the foot-dragging city council and finally decided to remove this image of blood and death and hate from this real and eternal place. We sacrificial victims of war must repossess her, the eternal witness of our suffering.

SHINOBU: We must recapture the keloid Madonna.

MAN III: And bring her near us.

MAN II: Yes! I see!

MAN III: We are only four, including you.

MAN II: Who is the fourth?

MAN III: She'll be here soon. But, we who possess Mary are as if we had a million allies.

SHINOBU: One day, after we have moved her to our secret hiding place, Mary will reappear to us. Until that day!

MAN II: When will that be?

SHIKA: It will be the day . . . .

TOGETHER (*turning around*): Ah?!

SHINOBU: Shika!

SHIKA (*in a raspy voice*): It will be the day when the weak, passing their days in unertainty, are once again being led into war.

MAN II: Yes!

SHIKA (*making the sign of the cross*): Mother Mary, I know that I am not qualified to cross myself and pray to you like this. I know. But we need you, keloid Madonna, eternal witness to the holocaust of August ninth. We ask you to move to our hiding place, there to feed the flames of our hatred, to keep alive the eternal flame in our hearts. We beg of you!

MAN III: Yes!

MAN II: Yes!

SHINOBU: But, Shika, what were you doing there all this time?

MAN III: Shika?!

SHIKA: I'm praying. Now the three of you, quickly, before somebody comes . . . .

SHINOBU: Let's begin!

MAN III: Yes, let's begin!

They all climb to the top of the steps.

MAN III (*to Shika*): Aren't you cold?

SHIKA: Don't worry about me. Hurry!

The three people lay their hands on The Head of Mary. Snow begins to fall.

SHINOBU: It won't move!

MAN III: It's heavy!

MAN II: Umph!

SHINOBU: Don't be ridiculous, come on! . . . (*To Man II*) Don't just stand there, heave!

MAN II: Okay, but, she's beautiful, isn't she?

Saint laughs.

SHINOBU: Heave!

MAN III: Wait! (*He takes out the wrapping cloth he used in Act One and spreads it on the ground.*) Roll her onto this.

The three of them try rolling the Head together.

TOGETHER: One . . . two . . .

HEAD OF MARY: Three!

TOGETHER: One . . . two . . .

SHIKA: Three!

The three people look at each other and signal with their eyes.

TOGETHER (*concentrating*): One . . . two . . . (*They all look quickly at Shika.*)

SHIKA: Three!

Relieved, the three believers glance at each other as they take their hands off The Head of Mary.

HEAD OF MARY: Three!

Again the three conspirators are filled with foreboding. Simultaneously, Shika's arms extend before her. She falls forward. Her three comrades run to her.

SHIKA: Yes, Mary, . . . yes!

HEAD OF MARY: Hurry, take me quickly!

Releasing a faint cry, Man II and Shinobu rush confusedly to the base of the steps and hide; Man III props Shika up as he kneels down in an effort to protect her.

SHINOBU: Yes, I hear you! I hear you!

HEAD OF MARY: I'll let you suckle at my breast, I'll let you drink to your hearts' content. My milk is sweet, oh so sweet! First drink, then I'll listen to your prayers. So come, come!

A low, quiet song flows in out of nowhere.
  Hear, sweet Mother, hear the weary,
  Borne upon life's troubled sea;
  Gentle guiding Star of Ocean,
  Lead thy children home to thee.
  Still watch o'er us, dearest Mother,
  From thy beauteous throne above;
  Guard us from all harm and danger,
  'Neath thy shelt'ring wings of love.
At intervals during this song, a voice can be heard shouting, "Hey!
Hey!" It is safe to assume it is Yabari.
The snow continues to fall.
  But, hesitantly Shinobu has risen, flung herself on The Head of
Mary, and begun with all her might to try to lift it.
Curtain.

THE ELEPHANT

The Elephant: The Absurdity of the Real

Although it was not necessarily obvious at the time, the production of Betsuyaku Minoru's *The Elephant* in April 1962 was one of the first of Japan's postmodern theater.[1] The play was produced by a new generation of theater practitioners and was written in a style that broke decisively with shingeki orthodoxy. The play is today a classic of the post-shingeki theater because, while it accurately and concretely depicts the unique experience of Hiroshima survivors, it also transforms that experience into a universal allegory for the human condition in the nuclear age.

THE WRITER AND THE TROUPE

The Elephant was produced by the Free Stage company (*Jiyū butai*), a group of recent graduates of Waseda University led by Suzuki Tadashi. In 1966, the Free Stage changed its name to the Waseda Little Theatre (*Waseda shōgekijō*), and it has since established itself as one of the most innovative theaters in the world.[2] Betsuyaku (1937–) was the troupe's principal writer until August 1969. In 1968 he became the first playwright of his generation to receive the Kishida Prize for Playwriting, and he has remained a prolific writer, publishing more than a dozen volumes of plays, essays, and short stories.[3]

THE INVALID: WITNESS TO THE REAL

The Elephant takes place in and around a Hiroshima hospital populated by survivors of the bomb. The atmosphere of the play is surrealistic. A dreamlike or even nightmarish quality is established immediately and maintained throughout. Characters appear and disappear without warning on a stage virtually devoid of props; the dialogue is intentionally elliptical; and little distinction is made between the real and the imagined.

The one exception to this general aura of unreality is the hospital room where the central character, an invalid suffering from the aftereffects of radiation exposure, is confined. Reality seems to emanate from this room and to grow increasingly tenebrous as one moves away. This is not an arbitrary device. The invalid is a witness to the characterizing event of the nuclear age, the event that defines reality for everyone living in the post-Hiroshima world.

The invalid was in Hiroshima when the bomb was dropped. After his initial recovery, he had made his living by publicly displaying the keloid scar his burns had left on his back. At first, people reacted with a combination of fascination and horror. He was even asked to appear at ban-the-bomb rallies as living proof of what had happened. But soon the novelty wore off, and he was forgotten.

Lying in his hospital room, the invalid dreams of returning to Hiroshima to recapture his days of glory. He cannot accept the idea that people might be indifferent to him and his experience. He rationalizes their former reaction by attributing it to his own lack of concentration. "When you come right down to it, they were skeptical, that's it. And I didn't go about my work with enough confidence either," he says.

The invalid insists that his experience is meaningful. His keloid is the outward sign of that experience and is therefore also significant. In his mind, people should be interested in him and his keloid because of what they represent: the experience of Hiroshima. He refuses to die as a cipher, to be dismissed as just one more nameless victim of a senseless holocaust. His life—and his death—are significant, *must* be significant.

The invalid's conviction of the significance of his experience and his desire to die his own personal, meaningful death lead him to fantasize that he will be murdered. Not only is his keloid meaningful, he believes, but it is also provocative—so provocative, in fact, that it will incite someone to murder.

The invalid thus represents the struggle for meaning in the face of absurd, meaningless death. Ironically, so enormous is that absurdity that *he* is the one who appears absurd.

THE NEPHEW: TO BE OR NOT TO BE

The invalid's obstinate insistence on the significance of his experience and on the general meaningfulness of life makes him seem almost demented at times. In contrast, his nephew (called simply "Man" in the play), who is also a *hibakusha*, has a firm grip on "reality." He recognizes that life is absurd and that any attempt to deny that fundamental reality is futile. The conflict between the invalid and his nephew and between their diametrically opposed views of life is the central issue of the play.

The Elephant is the nephew's explanation of how this conflict developed and how it was ultimately resolved. Structurally, the play is an extended flashback. As the lights come up, the nephew starts to relate what happened: "It was a pitch-black night," he says. "Rain was falling. It was a driving rain. A regular torrent. Gradually it grew closer." Then we are transported back to the time when he first visited his uncle in the hospital.

In his opening monologue, the nephew claims to have been "unaffected" by his atomic bomb experience. Nevertheless, he has always been haunted by the specter of death lurking within him. "I am already in its grasp," he says. And indeed, as the play progresses, he gradually develops the symptoms of A-bomb disease that eventually incapacitate him. The reason he went to visit his uncle was for guidance, to get some words of advice to help him deal with his anxiety.

His uncle's advice—to accept the anxiety and go on with the business of life—only exacerbated his fears. Relations between the two men deteriorated, and when the nephew was finally hospitalized, he begged the doctor not to put him in the same room with his uncle. The hospital was full, however, and there was nowhere else to go.

The invalid's reaction to his nephew's hospitalization was just what his nephew had dreaded: he assailed his nephew for allowing himself to be brought to the hospital without a fight. "If I were you, I'd have run away before they had a chance to bring me here. . . . I wouldn't have been as stupid as you, getting carted in here on a stretcher. You can bet on that." These words of welcome only made matters worse, and the friction between the two men increased.

A certain synergy developed as the two men talked. Each become more convinced than ever of the absolute ineluctability of his mode of action (or inaction). The invalid would risk anything to return to "that town" and reaffirm the significance of his life and of his impending death; his nephew would stop at nothing to protect himself from the threat his uncle posed, the threat of compounding absurdity through action. Convinced that his only hope lay in accepting the essential meaninglessness of the human condition, the nephew had finally been driven to murder his uncle. The invalid had been right: his existence had provoked someone to murder.

This is the nephew's story, and once it is told, the scene returns to the beginning. The nephew had successfully defended "reality" against his uncle's "absurdity," but that has put him in a terrible bind, for the reality he has embraced is itself absurd. His uncle, for all his obstreperous posturing, had been anchored in experience, and without him, the nephew is lost. He feels himself becoming lighter and lighter, about to float away. The very physical substance of his body is threatened by the encroaching absurdity of his world. As the play concludes, the nephew wails at the moon for exposing the nakedness of his suffering. It is so bright, he complains, "it might as well be broad daylight."

AN EVOCATION OF HIBAKUSHA PSYCHOLOGY

The Elephant is above all an acute evocation of *hibakusha* psychology. A comparison of the psychological traits of the characters in *The Elephant* with the *habikusha* mentality described by Robert Lifton should make this clear. Three examples will suffice.

The nephew's gnawing sense of guilt, the seemingly inexplicable feeling that he "has no excuse," for instance, relates to the stigmatization of survivors. *Hibakusha* have been subject to discrimination, particularly in employment and marriage, and there has been a tendency for them to internalize the negative evaluations of others. Lifton notes, "The internalization of this low status has been ironically summed up by one commentator as an attitude of 'I apologize for having been exposed to the atomic bomb.' Vicious circles of rejection, anticipated rejection, and self-created rejection can occur."[4] This is precisely what has taken place in the mind of the nephew.

A sense of being permanently and indelibly tainted by death is one of the primary characteristics of *hibakusha* psychology that Lifton documents. Marrying someone who was not exposed to the bomb and giving birth to healthy offspring is one way to remove this indelible taint, which survivors fear might be transmitted genetically to their children, resulting in limitless impairment.

In *The Elephant,* the nurse poignantly evokes this facet of survivor psychology. Herself a *hibakusha,* she dreams of marrying a supremely healthy farmer and bearing his child. She hopes to deny and transcend her survivor identity through marriage. "A major expression of denial-transcendence conflict," Lifton writes, "is the *hibakusha*'s marriage preference, the urge we have noted in some to marry non*hibakusha.*"[5]

Finally, the invalid himself is an archetypal *hibakusha.* In the first place, as Lifton points out, "the keloid, or whitish-yellow area of overgrown scar tissue which can disfigure hands and particularly faces, has come to symbolize the *hibakusha* identity."[6] With his keloid, therefore, the invalid is in a sense the survivor *par excellence.* But the invalid is an individual as well as an archetype. His character was modeled after a real survivor who styled himself "A-Bomb Victim Number One."[7] Lifton describes this man:

He was known . . . on occasion to take off his shirt and demonstrate the extensive keloids on his chest. . . . Because of the severity and prototypical nature of his injuries, he was frequently singled out for demonstration to visiting Japanese and American medical dignitaries, to which he seemed to react with mixed feelings of resentment and pride.[8]

INFLUENCE, STYLE, AND SUBJECT

On the stage even more than on the page, *The Elephant* is a disturbingly powerful evocation of the major features of *hibakusha* psychology. This is all the more reason to wonder at the fact that Betsuyaku had never visited Hiroshima and had no personal contact with survivors at the time he wrote the play. He had seen pictures of "A-Bomb Victim Number One" in a collection by photographer Domon Ken, but that was the extent of his direct knowledge.[9] How then could he have formulated such a precise image of the survivor mentality?

In writing *The Elephant,* Betsuyaku was influenced by the work of Eugene Ionesco and Samuel Beckett. Nowhere is this influence more apparent than in the conversations between the invalid and his wife, which closely resemble the dialogue in plays like Ionesco's *The Bald Soprano.* In these conversations, the most mundane subject—the proper way to eat rice balls (*onigiri*) and radishes (*takuan*), for instance—takes on unparalleled, indeed absurd, importance.

It would be a mistake to overemphasize the significance of European influence and concur with the critic who believes *The Elephant* to be "an almost totally derivative work," however.[10] Betsuyaku acknowledges the influence of Ionesco and Beckett, but he maintains that that influence has been primarily in the realm of style: he has admired their way of writing dialogue.[11] The fact that European influence has been restricted primarily to the area of style and that the overall conception of Betsuyaku's plays is his own is also clear in the conversations between the invalid and his wife, for although the dialogue echoes Ionesco, the function of these conversations—to illustrate the invalid's picayune insistence on the significance of all human actions, for example—is pure Betsuyaku.

Betsuyaku did not create *The Elephant* out of direct experience with *hibakusha* or by mimicking European Absurdist playwrights. The play was born out of his own experience of the 1960 demonstrations. As critic Tsuno Kaitarō has written,

It isn't the experience of Hiroshima alone that is eroded by the obliterating currents of time. I am convinced that the experiential impoverishment hinted at [in *The Elephant*] as our own debilitating disease is an event that preceded the publication of this play in 1962 by two years, that is, the anti–United States-Japan Mutual Security Treaty struggle. For better or for worse, there can be no doubt that we are rapidly losing the ability to take an experience, even the tragic death of a young girl at the very height of that struggle, and give it a strong and solid form impervious to the passage of time.[12]

In *The Elephant,* Betsuyaku applied insights from his own experience to his depiction of the psychology of Hiroshima survivors. The central issue of the play—whether to accept or reject the devaluation of experience—comes directly from the 1960 demonstrations and has specific political implications. Should one continue to struggle in the knowledge that to do so would be futile and even absurd? Or would it be wiser (or at least less painful) to accept defeat and resign oneself to a life of passive resignation? These were the questions young Japanese like Betsuyaku were left with after 1960, and because they were crystallized most clearly in the experience of the *hibakusha,* Betsuyaku invested these conflicts in them.[13]

Betsuyaku recognized that the *hibakusha* experience crystallized the dilemma of human survival in the nuclear age, an age in which the threat of imminent mass death makes a mockery of all human action. The play achieves universal significance because it derives from a universal source: the images of extinction and the presentiment of the end of the world Betsuyaku knew from his 1960 experience and that we all share in the post-Hiroshima age.[14]

SHINGEKI AND "THE ELEPHANT"

It is no coincidence that the play that helped launch the postmodern theater movement concerned the atomic bomb experience. Betsuyaku understood that Hiroshima had made the basic tragic, humanistic conception of shingeki unsatisfying, if not completely untenable. The shingeki notion so clearly evinced in *The Island,* that individual sacrifice will be redeemed through a glorious human future, is rejected as incredible in *The Elephant.* What human future? the play asks. It rejects the attitude of passive resignation mandatory in orthodox shingeki and replaces it with a call to action. The object and method of that action is by no means clear—it remained for Satoh and other postmodern playwrights, including Betsuyaku himself, to make it so—but *The Elephant*'s call is nonetheless unequivocal: act or be condemned to madness and death.

But why title such a play "The Elephant"? Betsuyaku suggests that the invalid's keloid reminded him of the skin of an elephant. Suzuki Tadashi, director of the original production, recalls that Prime Minister Nehru of India had brought an elephant as a gift to Japan about the time the play was written. Elephants remind him and his peers of extinction, Suzuki says, of a strong, lovable beast destined for oblivion.[15]

Both of these interpretations take the invalid to be the elephant of the title. It might also be possible to interpret the atomic bomb experience itself as the elephant. The Japanese, too, have the parable of the blindmen who encounter an elephant: *Gunmō zō o nazu,* they say. Each man thinks he knows what he is experiencing—the leg is a tree, the tail a broom, the belly a wall—but they cannot identify it as a whole. The atomic bomb experience may be similar. We can deal with it piecemeal, but to understand it in its totality is nearly impossible. In this respect, we are all a little like blindmen. Betsuyaku helps open our eyes in this play.

THE ELEPHANT
A PLAY IN THREE ACTS

by Betsuyaku Minoru

The Elephant (Zō) was first performed by the Jiyū butai (Free Stage) troupe in April 1962, directed by Suzuki Tadashi. The text for this translation is included in *Matchi-uri no shōjo/Zō* (Tokyo: San'ichi shobō, 1969).

CAST OF CHARACTERS

Man
Invalid
Invalid's Wife
Doctor
Nurse
Man in White 1
Man in White 2
Passerby 1
Passerby 2
The Wagon Man

ACT ONE

SCENE ONE

It is dark.

A few moments pass after the curtain rises, and then a solitary figure carrying a black umbrella appears vaguely.

The point is, not everyone necessarily aspires to higher things, nor do all survivors of calamity necessarily inspire pity. For the most part people remain unaffected.

Man slowly comes to a halt. At least he appears to come to a halt. Of course he has come to a halt, but . . . .

For a moment he seems to be testing his weight, then almost as if that were his conclusion, he sinks under it. Then surprisingly his mouth opens to speak.

MAN: Good evening, everyone. I am, if you will, the moon. In the sky, round and full.

He lowers the umbrella and gazes up into the sky.

MAN: Or . . . or a fish. A lonely fish, if you will. For example, I shed many tears. They seem almost endless. That is, from my point of view, it is all but unthinkable that in times of grief I should not weep. My tears are like fine white threads, flowing somewhere deep and dark, somewhere that turns me upside down. That's why, for all I know, I might be a fish hanging by my tears.

He takes two or three steps.

MAN: It is a good moonlit night. The kind that makes you want to take a long, leisurely piss . . . or fall to some faraway place. . . . It is not too warm, but, then again, it is not cold either. . . . The wind is blowing. Of course, it is nothing more than a breeze at best.

He places his index finger in his mouth and, after wetting it thoroughly, thrusts it into the air.

MAN: It is blowing. But, this is a delicate problem. It might be better to say that it is not blowing. It may just be moving very slowly, that's all. In any event, I have the feeling that it is going from here to here. From here to here . . . .

He thinks for a moment.

MAN: At the same time, bit by bit, it's changing its direction,

from here to here. . . . That is, the situation is rather complex. For instance . . . .
*He folds up the umbrella and places it on the stage as if to show the
direction of the wind.*
MAN: The wind is flowing from here to here. Slowly, that is. At
the same time, that direction is changing, bit by bit, to here.
Then . . . I am here; the moon is there. . . . Ah, how very
unexpected. I am here, the moon there. And the wind is
blowing. I understand! I mean, well, I did understand. I have
now, probably, begun to face in yet another direction. That's
the way it's always been. In yet another direction. In the direction my tears flow . . . . To somewhere deep and dark . . . .
If I am a fish hanging by my tears, then I must be upside
down from that direction.
Man squats down.
*On the stage there is a simple, steel-frame bed with Invalid in it.
Next to him sits his Wife, who is slowly consuming rice balls. Invalid
is watching her intently.*
*Man's monologue continues, flowing over the two figures, who re-
main wordless throughout.*
MAN: It was a pitch-black night. Rain was falling. It was a
driving rain. A regular torrent. Gradually it grew closer. (*He
rises.*) Shhh! Please be quiet! Please! I'd like you to be quiet! I
must be pretty tired. My nerves are on edge. Please, I beg of
you, be quiet for just a few moments. I only want to sit idly in
the darkness here. That's all I'm asking. If, if only you'd be so
kind as to leave me alone in peace. . . . I'm not telling you to
do this or do that. I don't want anything. If everyone, when
they meet me on the street, would just pass me by, paying me
no attention, everything would be fine. I don't want people
saying, "Is something wrong?" or "Are you in pain?" or "Has
anything happened?" or "Are you all right?" or "How very
unfortunate," or "Please do take care of yourself," or "Can I
lend you a hand?" I want people to leave me alone. And what
I'd like instead is for people to forget I exist. Nobody knows
anything. That's right. You don't know anything. For instance, when I listen intently to something, I can hear a whole
range of sounds. Pumped out by my heart, my blood goes

groaning to every corner of my body. I bend a finger, and every nerve in my body creaks. My stomach constantly vomits up melancholic humors in a hoarse and whispering voice. And my intestines, coiled like a great snake below it, set up a hysterical howl so obscene that at times I cannot stand to listen. I am sitting here, in the darkness of many things; and I am waiting. From beyond this translucent vapor, it has already identified me; I am already in its grasp. And sometimes I wonder, about the day it begins to run wild within me—whether I'll be able to laugh.

Two Men in White slowly cross upstage carrying a stretcher bearing a corpse. Doctor accompanies them. Invalid and Wife remain silent and motionless.

MAN IN WHITE: Where shall we take him?

DOCTOR: To autopsy.

Very slowly Wife gathers her things and rises.

INVALID: You going?

WIFE: Yes.

Wife, her eyes downcast, slowly exits. Nurse appears out of nowhere. She whispers to Man.

NURSE: Go straight ahead and you'll come to the end of the corridor. Turn right. On the left you'll find a staircase. Climb the stairs, and the third room on the right is his. He might already be asleep, so I'll have to ask you to be as quiet as possible. And please be quiet in the corridors, too. And, even if one of the patients should call out, please refrain from answering.

MAN: Call out?

NURSE: He will have heard your footsteps. They try to pick up the slightest sound.

MAN: Pick up the slightest sound?

NURSE: They're listening.

MAN: What for?

NURSE: Good-bye. Please give him my best regards.

MAN: But, what are they listening for?

NURSE: Good-bye. I am going to rest. Tomorrow is another busy day.

Nurse exits.

But then, with the stealth that is the hallmark of hospital nurses, she reappears and races up to Man again.

NURSE (*speaking quickly*): Go straight ahead and you'll come to the end of the corridor. Turn right. On the left you'll find a staircase. Climb the stairs, and the third room on the right is his. He might already be asleep, so I'll have to ask you to be as quiet as possible. And please be quiet in the corridors, too. And, even if one of the patients should call out, please refrain from answering. He will have heard your footsteps. They try to pick up the slightest sound. Goodbye. Please give him my best regards. I am going to rest. Tomorrow is another busy day.

Nurse exits, her eyes fixed on the ground.

MAN: That was the day. It was raining that day too. I turned the corner, and a man in white was just standing there. When I looked back, there behind me too . . . .

Man walks downstage.

NURSE (*just her voice, from upstage left*): To the right, you understand, you turn to the right.

MAN: Yes, I understand. I understand!

NURSE (*voice only*): My best regards. Please give him my best regards.

Man exits stage left.

Lights come up on the sickroom. Invalid is laughing to himself, his laughter rippling through his entire body. His half-swallowed laughter continues.

Man enters.

MAN: Uncle?

INVALID: Shhh! Be quiet!

MAN: What's wrong?

INVALID: Be quiet. Just sit over there. That's right.

Man lowers himself into a chair.

INVALID (*chuckling*): Well?

MAN: What?

INVALID: You can hear her, can't you? My wife. Sniveling.

MAN: Aunty is?

INVALID: That's right. You can hear her, can't you?

MAN: But, why should she be crying?

INVALID: Overweight! That's what's got her scared. Think about it: your body swelling up bigger and bigger. Pretty frightening, if you ask me. She's always lying around, rubbing her swollen belly. In the little nine-by-twelve room there, off the pantry. She won't even turn on a light. Sometimes she gets to feeling sad and starts crying, just with her face. I mean, just with her eyes and mouth, crying. Her belly doesn't mind; it'll just go on getting fatter and fatter.

Invalid tries to suppress the urge to burst out laughing, but, an occasional giggle escapes, sending spasms through his body.

INVALID: She still laughs, though. Occasionally. Last night was one of those times. When night comes, you know how it gets dark around you? Well, she got to feeling peaceful and laughed. Heh-heh, she got to feeling happy. She relaxed, you see. You know what I mean—in the darkness, lying down like this, you get to feeling like you're your own possession, down to each downy hair. You get to feeling like, like you could move every hair on your body if you wanted to, every downy little hair, heh-heh-heh. You're happy, you get to feeling happy.

MAN: Has Aunty been coming around lately?

INVALID: Mm?

MAN: Aunty, has she come recently?

INVALID: No. No, she doesn't come. Not at all. What's she doing, I wonder. At home, I mean. Do you know?

MAN: Sorry. I haven't seen her, not recently, anyway.

INVALID: Is that so? Doesn't come around, not her. She's always off in some corner, sitting and sulking. Puts that sour look on her face and . . . .

MAN: I went by once, quite a while ago. I went by the house. Aunty was lying down. In the little nine-by-twelve room there off the kitchen. "Dark, isn't it?" she says. So I said, "Should I turn on the light?" And she says, "Quit it, it's bad for my skin!"

INVALID: What did you come for?

MAN: Huh?

INVALID: How're you feeling?

MAN: I'm all right.

INVALID: You don't get dizzy?

MAN: No.

INVALID: I'll bet your gums bleed.

MAN: No, they don't.

INVALID: Your nose?

MAN: My nose doesn't bleed either.

INVALID: Don't you feel sluggish all over?

MAN: Not at all.

INVALID: You've lost weight. You're deathly pale.

MAN: I haven't lost any weight; and there's nothing wrong with my color. You just worry too much. I'm all right.

INVALID: Is that so? If that's the case, things couldn't be better.

MAN: Just one thing, a little strange I'll admit. In the evening, when I open the door, there's always a big red moon right out front. Then, from a long way off, a little man comes running. He comes running and shouting, "A red moon a red moon a red moon a red moon." He's waving his arms and shouting, "A red moon a red moon a red moon!"

INVALID: Can't be helped.

MAN: It's as if his life depended upon it . . . he comes running as if his life depended on it.

INVALID: Can't be helped. You just have to steel yourself and be patient.

MAN: It's just that I, I feel awfully sorry. I feel like I haven't got any excuse.

INVALID: Then why don't you do it too? Why don't you run?

MAN: Run? Where?

INVALID: Where? Don't be silly. You just run. As if your life depended on it.

MAN: Uncle, how about you? Are you all right?

INVALID: It's the same with me. There's a sea, a pitch-black sea. It . . . it doesn't make a sound. The surface of the water, it rises up there before my eyes; and then, like it's washing through the pit of my stomach, it ebbs and goes away. It's big and black as pitch. It just approaches without a sound, and then ebbs and goes away. You understand? Nobody's there. I just steel myself and be patient. I just grab this bed, this railing here, and hold on.

Several Men in White appear slowly from stage right, pass upstage, and disappear.

MAN: Don't you think you'd just like to die quietly?

INVALID: Not at all! As a matter of fact, I think I'd like to be murdered before I had a chance to die.

MAN: Why?

INVALID: No idea. I just want to live passionately!

MAN: I know how you got up on the platform at that ban-the-bomb rally and showed everybody the keloid on your back.

INVALID: A lot of foolishness. I was full of passion, all right, up until I got up there on the platform and flung off my shirt, until I took off my shirt and threw it down on the floor. Listen, you were there. How come nobody clapped? I figured there'd be a terrific ovation . . . you know, that's what I expected. But the audience just sat there. A black wave ebbed and vanished before my eyes. I thought I'd be sucked up in it and carried away, but I just clenched my fist and stood there. Beads of sweat rolled down my body . . . and when I looked around, the audience was gone, down to the last man. They'd all disappeared, every one of them. When I climbed up to the dais, that big hall was overflowing. Everyone dressed in white, you know. They seemed to glisten. Then, when I started to undo the buttons on my shirt, they all held their breath. The place was packed. It was ready to explode!

MAN: It was packed, all right. It was really ready to explode.

INVALID: There was no one there. There wasn't anybody there at all, not a man.

MAN: But listen, Uncle. You used to strip down and show off your keloid in the streets, didn't you? I remember those days. Your back, it shone.

INVALID: Out there, the road was kind of dusty. When evening fell and I got ready to pack up and go home, the mat I'd spread on the road would be covered with sand. And it was hot, too. The passersby seemed to reel with the heat. No, I really didn't mind that work at first. The sightseers would come by, and I'd tell them about Hiroshima and what it had been like. I'd tell them a bit of a joke that would really get 'em where it hurts. And I'd think up new poses for their cameras. I'd take off my shirt, and then, all at once, a gasp of shock and surprise would rise from the crowd. That wasn't bad. And then, I sort of liked the gentle click-click sound of the shut-

ters. I'd move the muscles on my back just a bit, and click-
click, click-click, the shutters would all be going at once.
Actually, it was . . . what do I want to say . . . it felt so right.
And I remember, when was it now? Once a little girl came
with her mother to see. That kid, she said she wanted to
touch the keloid on my back, and she wouldn't listen to anything her mother said! And her mother, she did just about
everything to make that little girl forget the whole thing, but
the kid just kept saying how she wanted to touch it and
wouldn't listen. Ha-ha-ha, that was some kid, I'll tell you! I
figured that the little girl wasn't going to catch anything by
touching it, so I let her. She stretched out her hand so full of
fear and hesitation, you know, and then she touched me for
just an instant and snapped her hand back fast as you please.
She was so cute! Ha-ha-ha! Her hair cut straight across the
bottom and her bangs cut square. I wonder how old she'd be?
I'd like to see her again—that little girl, I mean. Her mother
got all excited and dragged her off. I haven't seen her since.

*Nurse appears at stage left, walking a cloth doll a yard or so tall. The
doll is unclothed and has no facial features.*

NURSE (*in a low, monotonous voice*): See how well we walk. See
   how well we walk. See how well we walk.

She slowly crosses upstage as she speaks and exits stage right.

INVALID: Somebody call me?

MAN: Huh?

INVALID: Somebody was calling me . . . far away.

MAN: Is that so?

INVALID (*darkly*): Things just haven't been the same since that
   ban-the-bomb rally. I began to realize. What those bastards
   really want to see, I mean. *It's your eyes!* My eyes! They're
   busier peering into my eyes than looking at the keloid on my
   back. I'd begin to put on my shirt, and they'd be standing
   there, searching my eyes. Do you understand me? No matter
   what funny stories I told, no matter what gay dances I did,
   the bastards wouldn't laugh. After that, I threw myself, body
   and soul, into my work. Body and soul, you see. For the first
   time in my life I decided to cut out the monkey business and
   really work at what I was doing. Every day I'd go home and

figure out new poses for the cameras, and how I'd make the sightseers laugh. I'd lie awake most of the night thinking. And in those days, even my wife was caught up in what I was doing. It was her, you know, who said how the keloid under my arm was more horrible than the one on my back, and how I should be raising my right arm to show it off better. She said, "Raise your right arm more." That's what she said. You know that pose of mine, that famous pose where I raise my right arm up high and put my left hand on my hip? My wife discovered that. Hey, didn't somebody just say something?

MAN: Somebody?

INVALID: Just now, somebody said something. The bastard laughed.

MAN: There's nobody around. Not here.

INVALID: But why do they try to look into my eyes? Why? It beats me. No matter how hard I tried, it didn't do any good. I really worked at it, but my body began to give out on me, and . . . . Like you were saying, in the old days the keloid on my back glistened. I'd stand there with my back to the sun and flex my muscles, and, you know, it was the sun that seemed to lose its balance for a moment. No kidding. It's no good any more. . . . After that, I stopped thinking about how to please the crowds. Every day I'd go out into that town, and I'd spread my mat out on the ground and just stand there daydreaming. The bastards didn't even notice. The naked keloid man's sold out his supply of charm and moved on to pathos, that's what they said. I could have real blood running out of my nose, or, like the time I collapsed and was lying flat on the ground, a young American soldier just figured it was a new pose and tripped the shutter on his precision-made German camera.

MAN: That was in the fall. By that time there was practically no one left in that town.

INVALID: No one left? They'd all died off! But I'll live a little longer. And when I'm feeling better, I'll go out to that town again and see.

MAN: What for?

INVALID: Ha-ha-ha! To work, of course. Merrily, zestfully. You

see, I've been thinking about it. When you come right down
to it, they were skeptical, that's it. And I didn't go about my
work with enough confidence, either. That's what did it. It's
got to be man-to-man. The naked truth, no holds barred.
Something authentic. Something you can count on. I'm
going to shake hands with them!

MAN: That town has changed. (*He rises.*)

INVALID: Hey, you going?

MAN: Yes, it's getting late.

INVALID: Come on, let's talk a little more. Wouldn't mind if we
talked all night. That's it, I'll tell you the story about how
your mom and dad died. You were still a tot at the time, so
you probably don't remember, but . . . .

Nurse stands absently in the doorway to the sickroom.
Invalid looks at her inquiringly.

NURSE: It's getting rather late. It's time to get some rest, so
. . . .

Invalid drops heavily into bed. Man approaches Nurse.

MAN: Is my uncle pretty bad?

NURSE: It won't be long now . . . not long.

INVALID: You said it's changed?

MAN: What?

INVALID: You said that town has changed.

MAN: Yes, quite a bit.

INVALID: Come on, won't you tell me about it?

MAN: But it's late.

INVALID: Changed?

MAN: Good night.

INVALID: Wait a minute. Do people die in their sleep sometimes?

MAN: I suppose. It certainly would be an easy way to go.

INVALID: I wouldn't go for it, not me. Listen, how about doing
me a favor and sticking around. What do you say? Then, just
in case, if it looked like I was going to die in my sleep, you
could wake me, couldn't you?

MAN: But . . . I have to get home.

INVALID (*getting up*): I see.

MAN: I'll call Aunty. I'll call her for you. She'll wake you up.

INVALID: Never mind. You don't have to worry about me. I'm fit as a fiddle. I'll take care of myself.

MAN: You'd better get some rest now. I'll tell Aunty to come as soon as she can.

INVALID: Yeah. Goodbye then.

MAN: Goodbye.

Nurse and Man leave the room.

MAN: Are you also a survivor?

NURSE: Survivor? Yes, a survivor.

MAN: Can you remember?

NURSE: Dahlias were blooming along a dusty, white road.

MAN: Ah, the dahlias were blooming.

NURSE: That's all.

MAN: No aftereffects, then?

NURSE: All my hair fell out once, but then it grew back.

MAN: Me, too. I was in Hiroshima, too. It . . . hasn't affected me.

NURSE: Haven't you noticed?

MAN: What's that?

NURSE: It smells.

MAN: Smells?

NURSE: I've worked in this hospital for some time, but I've never gotten used to it.

MAN: What sort of smell is it?

NURSE: A vile smell. In your uncle's room, here, everywhere. Do I smell, too?

MAN: I'm afraid I can't tell.

NURSE: You were talking about the red moon, weren't you?

MAN: How did you know that?

NURSE: There's an intercom in every room. It allows us to hear everything that's said in each of the sickrooms.

MAN: Then you were listening.

NURSE: It's the rule.

Pause.

NURSE: Your uncle won't sleep tonight.

MAN: No?

NURSE: He'll be awake, you can bet on it.

Blackout.

SCENE TWO

Dim lights illuminate the stage. It is too dark to tell, but Invalid and Wife seem to be in the sickroom; and as usual, Wife appears to be eating three-cornered rice balls. In any event, two people are moving about in the darknes. A half-whispered conversation is going on. It really matters very little whether the conversation is heard or not, but if it were heard, it would sound like this.

INVALID (*peering through the darkness*): Rice balls, aren't they?

WIFE: Yes.

INVALID: Good?

WIFE: They're delicious.

INVALID: Something inside?

WIFE: Pickles and tuna.

INVALID: Ah, pickles and tuna. How about it, which do you prefer, pickles or tuna?

WIFE: Well, let me see. Pickles are nice too, but you can't be eating them all the time. I guess when it comes to rice balls, tuna's the thing.

INVALID: I suppose so, tuna's the thing. How about it? How about me? Which do I prefer, pickles or tuna?

WIFE: Well, let me see. You prefer tuna, too.

INVALID: Oh. (*He seems a little disappointed.*) You guessed it. Well I'll be, radishes!

WIFE: Yes.

INVALID: Did you bring them with you? I hadn't noticed them.

WIFE: I got them as a present from the neighbors yesterday.

INVALID: How nice, radishes are so crispy. Right? They're crispy, aren't they?

WIFE: Yes, they're crispy.

INVALID: Listen, this is just a bit of talk I heard, but, you know, they say there are two kinds of radishes, the strong kind and the mild kind.

WIFE: That's right, there's a strong kind and a mild kind.

INVALID: Which are those?

WIFE: The strong kind.

INVALID: Are they strong?

WIFE: Yes, they're strong.

INVALID: I guess it's a matter of taste, isn't it? But listen, you, I guess you must prefer the strong kind.

WIFE: You guessed it.

INVALID: Hm, then how about me, I wonder?

WIFE: You prefer the strong kind, too.

INVALID: Mm, that's right, you guessed it. Hey, did you eat them all? All the radishes?

WIFE: All? There were only three.

INVALID: Even if there were only three. I mean, there's still one rice ball left, isn't there? You're going to have to eat that without any radish.

WIFE: I suppose so.

INVALID: Will you listen to me if I tell you something? You don't understand what it means to plan. I'll let you in on something. It's this way. I always go about it like this. See, when you have two rice balls you divide your radish in half, see? Then, you just make do with that portion for each rice ball. You see what I'm getting at? That way, you eliminate the problem of having to eat rice balls without any radish.

WIFE: I suppose you're right.

INVALID: Of course I'm right. And then, it may seem like I'm being picayunish, but it's the way you go about eating those rice balls. It's a bit haphazard if you ask me. All right? Now listen, you begin chomping it down from the very top, eat your way right down to the garnish in the middle, don't you? I always watch you to see what you're going to do. Like a fool you march right in there and down all the garnish in one bite. Then, a little bit at a time, like you really didn't want it, you nibble away at the rest. Go ahead, tell me I'm wrong. Now, if you ask me, that's what you call artless. Tell me I'm wrong, go ahead. I'll let you in on something, all right? You start out at the top and eat your way down. You get to the garnish. So you turn the thing over. You see what I'm getting at? This time, you eat a little bit at a time from the bottom, see? Finally, only the garnish is left. You eat it as the final morsel. That's what you call order. In other words, a plan. A strategy. That way it's fun till the very last. Am I right? That's what you can't get through your head. You're so haphazard, see, you just go running off in whatever direction you're headed.

To eat up all the garnish and then eat the rest without—I can't imagine such a thing. (*He continues, mumbling disjointedly.*) That's just the way you go about things, isn't it, like . . . without thinking, I mean . . . that's just not the way you go about . . . .

Wife hurriedly gathers her things together and rises.

INVALID: What, you leaving?

WIFE: Yes.

Wife exits slowly, her eyes downcast. Invalid emptily lies back in bed. Blackout.

Man and Nurse are standing vaguely in the distance.

MAN: When the sun sets I bolt the door. If someone came, there would surely be the sound of knocking. Knock, knock, knock. At first it would be very light, and for a while I'd keep perfectly still. Knock, knock, knock. It would grow a little louder. Knock, knock, knock. I would slowly get to my feet and open the door. "Good evening. Who are you? Where have you come from? Might you have some business with me?" And the man would laugh hollowly. Looking at my face, he'd laugh, hollowly. With his slender fingers he'd point at me and slowly his swallowed laughter would spill from his lips. But I would not know how to explain. You understand. I do not know how to explain.

NURSE: First of all, you begin to bleed from the nose. Everyone is that way. First of all, you begin to bleed from the nose . . . .

Blackout.

The sickroom. Invalid is lying in bed.

INVALID: What are you doing around the house?

WIFE: Nothing in particular.

Carrying a glass of water, Wife enters.

WIFE: Here's the water.

INVALID: Water? What for?

WIFE: You just said you wanted some, didn't you?

INVALID: Water? I didn't ask for anything. But, look how pretty it is. Water. Just like the sky. Whenever I see water like this, I remember, you know . . . .

WIFE: You didn't want a drink in the first place, did you?

INVALID: What do you mean?

WIFE: I don't care for it. Not that story.

INVALID: Of course I wanted a drink. That's why I asked for it. All of a sudden my thirst went away. That sort of thing happens, you know. And then I just happened to remember, that's all. Anyway, there's nothing wrong with that story, heart-rending and . . . .

WIFE: I don't like it.

INVALID: All right, all right. I'm not going to force you to listen to it. That's not the only story I have, anyway.

WIFE: I went out to that town.

INVALID: You went? How was it? Just as it was?

WIFE: Yes, just as it was.

INVALID: Just as it was . . . hasn't changed at all?

WIFE: Not at all.

INVALID: It must have seemed like yesterday.

WIFE: It seemed just like yesterday.

INVALID: The white, dusty road going along . . . .

WIFE: It was a dusty road, all right, with a concrete wall running along it.

INVALID: The one that's broken down here and there, right?

WIFE: Yes, it's broken down. Here and there.

INVALID: That's right, that's right! You can see inside from there. . . .

WIFE: The grass had grown up thick and high all around.

INVALID: That's right, that's the road. The grass is grown up thick and high around there. When you look through the wall, you can see the grass growing up thick and . . . . It's as if it were broad daylight. Or maybe it's evening? The grass is thick and high. It's an open field. The wind is blowing.

Blackout.

Man and Nurse appear vaguely upstage.

NURSE:
    Robin, robin, red robin,
    Why, oh, why are you so red?
    Because I ate the fruit that's red.

MAN: What's that?

NURSE: A song.

MAN: Oh.

NURSE:

Warbler, warbler, blue warbler,
Why, oh, why are you so blue?
Because I ate the fruit that's blue.
Somebody, a little child, was singing it.
Somewhere far away.

MAN: Far away? It seems so dark. I wonder why?

Invalid's low, suppressed laughter steals out and spreads across the stage.

INVALID: Ha-ha-ha-ha-ha-ha! Say, do you remember that little girl?

Man and Nurse disappear. Invalid sits alone in his sickroom.

INVALID: An empty-headed little beggar just as cute as they come. What, you've forgotten? When was it now? There was this little girl who wanted to touch the keloid on my back, remember? That's the little girl I mean. An innocent little face. I'll bet she was a kid from that town. But, you know, somehow I have the feeling that she was a real pitiful little kid, you know what I mean? How about it? I wonder if she's not sick or something. For all I know she might be lying in some hospital somewhere. Don't you think so? Somehow she gave the impression of being a very fragile child. She must be ten or so by this time. Hm? Say, where are you? Where are you? You go home? Hey! . . .

Doctor enters. He stands in place for a few moments.

INVALID (*noticing him*): What do you want?

DOCTOR: Nothing really. Did you laugh a minute ago?

INVALID: Laugh, me?

DOCTOR: I thought I heard somebody laugh. Haven't you gone to sleep yet?

INVALID: See, there was this little girl . . . and lately she's been crying all the time.

DOCTOR: That won't do.

INVALID: She's so fragile.

DOCTOR: Fragile, yes. But she'll get well. Children recover quickly.

INVALID: She calls me. I'm afraid she's lonely.

DOCTOR: But somebody must be with her.

INVALID: With her? Yes, her mother. That's right . . . but then why? She must always be alone . . . she's all alone and calling me.

DOCTOR: Her mother must be sitting there, in the shadow of the bed or somewhere. You just haven't noticed. It's unthinkable that a mother should just leave her child alone. You know that as well as I do.

INVALID: She died.

DOCTOR: What?

INVALID: She died. She just died. That's all there is to it. Poor thing. Her mother was so weak. She died and left her child alone. That's why she cries so much.

DOCTOR: Even if her mother did die, there's still her father. And even if both her parents passed away, there must be a kind aunt or somebody . . . . You hear about cases like that all the time.

INVALID: I don't like it.

DOCTOR: What?

INVALID: An aunt or somebody. It's not even funny. Some scowling old woman.

DOCTOR: She wouldn't be scowling; she'd be kind. She'd take good care of her.

INVALID: I don't want that kind of money!

DOCTOR: Money? But everybody needs money.

INVALID: No thanks! She wrapped it up in a piece of tissue in her lap so she wouldn't have to look me in the face. Why? Did I embarrass her? It's not even funny.

DOCTOR: Did you take the money?

INVALID: Hell no. I threw it away. But why didn't I shake her hand? If I'd stretched out my hand . . . . Instead she ran away.

DOCTOR: You mustn't speak ill of people. It's not as if the lady didn't do anything for you. In fact, it's because she sympathized with you that she wrapped up that money. They're all good people. They're just a little self-conscious.

INVALID: But why do they all look into my eyes?

DOCTOR: It's a sign of their love. It's strange you haven't realized that.

INVALID: They're shocked.

DOCTOR: By what?

INVALID: There must be something. How about you? Do I shock you?

DOCTOR: Not especially. Why? The only thing special about you is the keloid on your back.

INVALID: Something else. There must be. What is it? What's different about me?

DOCTOR: Nothing at all. It's not good to put it that way. It's offensive. But why didn't you try to shake hands with her that time? If you had, everything would have been all right.

INVALID: That's just it. What I regret, I mean. Why wasn't it like that?

DOCTOR: You didn't have the courage. Or maybe you just missed your chance. Even the most courageous people miss their chance sometimes. And then they live to regret it.

INVALID: Then it is a problem of courage. All right, I'll shake hands. You think I'll weep?

DOCTOR: That's the spirit! To love one's fellow man is the best thing one can do. I mean, there's nothing quite as inspiring as seeing people in love with each other. The point is, everyone is good. They're overflowing with good intentions. That's why they're kind and gentle and always smiling. They're saints, really, that's what they are. All right, now, let me take your pulse.

INVALID: What?

DOCTOR: Let me take your pulse.

INVALID: It's all right.

DOCTOR: Put out your hand.

INVALID: Maybe later.

Blackout.

Nurse and Man appear downstage.

NURSE: Was it a nosebleed?

MAN: I was bleeding through the nose. I didn't know it. When I opened the door, everyone was staring me in the face. I didn't know it. I looked down and there were little black things going drip-drop on the floor. One, two, three, I counted. That's all. Then I went home and lay down. It wouldn't do for anyone to come, so I locked the door and stayed in bed for several days.

NURSE: What are your plans for the future?

MAN: Future? Future? . . . Future? . . . .

NURSE Where will you go?

MAN: Go? Where?

NURSE: I thought perhaps you'd go somewhere. Everyone does that. Then they come back.

MAN: I'm not going anywhere. I just want to lie quietly someplace dark and warm.

NURSE: Why?

MAN: Listen, Nurse, couldn't you find the time to talk with me, just a bit?

NURSE: Talk? What sort of talk?

MAN: About all sorts of things, pleasant things. If you think about it, we haven't sat down and really talked even once.

NURSE: No.

MAN: Come, sit down here. There are all sorts of things I want to talk about. You have a minute, don't you? There really are all sorts of things I've wanted to talk about.

NURSE: Aren't you going to visit your uncle?

MAN: Is there something wrong with my uncle?

NURSE: Not especially.

MAN: Look, I won't talk about the fish . . . or about the sea . . . . I love the sea. It stretches out as far as the eye can see, and the wind blows . . . . How about you? Do you like the sea?

NURSE: I suppose.

MAN: What's wrong? Won't you talk to me about something? There must be all kinds of things you'd like to talk about . . . you'd like to confide.

NURSE: I am going to have a child.

MAN: A child? Why?

NURSE: I want a child.

MAN: Will you get married?

NURSE: Yes.

MAN: To whom? To whom? Tell me, who is it? What sort of man is he? Of course, he's not a survivor, is he?

NURSE: No. He was in the country.

MAN: In the country. Then he must be a farmer!

NURSE: Yes. He's a farmer.

MAN: That's it, he's a farmer. A country bumpkin. He must be round and fat. His arms are heavy and his legs, his legs must be strong as an ox. I'm right, aren't I? And he's always smiling. The tip of his nose is round, and his complexion is good. When he looks into another man's face, he laughs and, bowing his head, says, "Glad to be o' service." How about it, am I right?

NURSE: Yes. He bows his head and says, "Glad to be o' service."

MAN: Have you told him? About your condition, I mean.

NURSE: Yes. He understands.

MAN: He understands. Of course. He understands. You said something like, "I have something to tell you. I am a . . . ." That's what you said, and then the farmer said something like, "What, is that all?" I'm right, aren't I? He said that and beamed generously.

NURSE: Yes, he said that and beamed generously.

MAN: But why?

NURSE: Why what?

MAN: Why do you want to have a child?

NURSE: I want a child.

MAN: When are you leaving?

NURSE: Soon. I'm leaving soon.

MAN: Good-bye.

NURSE: Yes. Good-bye. (*She exits.*)

The sickroom.

INVALID: Hey.

WIFE: What is it?

INVALID: Be careful. I might be murdered.

WIFE: Why is that?

INVALID: I'll be murdered for sure. I can feel it.

WIFE: Everything is all right.

INVALID: Come here.

WIFE: What is it?

INVALID: Won't you tie me up?

WIFE: Tie you up?

INVALID: Yes. It won't take but a minute.

WIFE: What are you going to do?

INVALID: Never mind about that . . . hurry and tie me up, bed and all. There's some rope over there.

WIFE: But . . . .

INVALID: Hurry on with it. Tie me up. I can't stand it any longer. I just can't take it. Come on, I'm asking you, tie me up as tight as you can.

WIFE: With this?

INVALID: That's right. I'll be lying down like this, so bring it over me tight as you can. (*He lies face down on the bed.*) I can't stand it anymore. That's it, tighter.

WIFE: Is this right?

INVALID: Okay, now bring it back over this way. (*Wife binds Invalid.*) Ah, that's it. Ah, that's it. That's it. Listen don't you ever get to feeling lonely?

WIFE: Not especially.

INVALID: You mean you don't ever get to feeling lonely? I wonder why that is. Sometimes I get to feeling so lonely I can't stand it. Ah, it's no good. You'd better untie the rope. I think I'm going to suffocate. I feel as though I'm being choked to death.

WIFE: You mean I should untie it?

INVALID: Yes. I'm sorry, but please untie it. It hurts. I can't breathe.

WIFE: Shall I call the doctor?

INVALID: No, I don't need the doctor. Just untie me and I'll feel better.

WIFE (*untying*): How's that?

INVALID: That's better. That's better. It's nothing at all. (*He gets up and lowers himself to the floor.*)

WIFE: What are you doing?

INVALID: I just thought I'd try walking about a bit. I practice everyday.

WIFE: You know you really shouldn't.

INVALID: Just a bit, you see. Ugh, I've go a bit of a pain in my chest.

WIFE: Now what's wrong?

INVALID: Yeah. (*He touches the floor with his hand.*) It's cool. This is the floor, isn't it?

WIFE: Yes, that's the floor.

INVALID: The floor. It's cool. It feels good. (*He lies down and puts his cheek to the floor.*) It feels so good. It's kind of refreshing.

WIFE: Will you please get up before you catch your death of chill!

INVALID: Listen, what ever happened to that little girl?

WIFE: Little girl?

INVALID: Yes, that little girl. Have you forgotten? You know, there was this little girl who kept asking to touch the keloid on my back.

WIFE: Oh, that little girl?

INVALID: Yes, that little girl.

WIFE: She died.

INVALID: Died?

WIFE: Yes, it happened quite a while ago.

INVALID: Why?

WIFE: That's what they said. They said she died.

INVALID: It's a lie!

WIFE: Everyone said so. They said that little girl died. She just up and died. Why, you said so yourself. The last thing she wanted was a drink of water, that's what you said . . . . You told me so yourself.

INVALID: Lies! Lies! (*He crawls under the bed.*)

WIFE: Where are you?

INVALID: I don't want to hear any more.

WIFE: Now what's the trouble?

Man enters.

WIFE: Oh, it's you.

MAN: What's wrong?

WIFE: He won't come out.

MAN: Why?

WIFE: I don't know. He got all upset and . . . .

INVALID: Get her out of here! Get that fat old woman out!

MAN: What happened?

INVALID: Just get her out of here. Hurry. She killed her. She killed her. Look at her hands. She did it with those hands; she killed her with those hands. Get her out and lock the door after her! (*He crawls out from under the bed.*) It's true. I know it for a fact. You remember that little girl? You know, the cute, fretful little girl who said she wanted to touch my back. She died. She was murdered. And she's the one who did it! It's the truth. She snuck out in the dark of night and did it. I know it for a fact. I'm always talking about that little girl, so she got jealous. It couldn't have been any other way.

WIFE: I haven't killed anybody.

INVALID: You did it! You strangled her with those hands. Now look. I'm telling the honest truth. I'm not lying or anything. It's the truth. I saw her go out to kill her with my own two eyes. That's how I know. That little girl was crying. Painful like. She was crying like she was in pain. And even though she was crying . . . she killed her!

WIFE: I . . . .

INVALID: Ah-ah, get her out of here. Please! That little girl was crying. The tears were pouring down her cheeks. She was looking in my direction and calling out. That's the one she killed!

MAN: Uncle.

INVALID: She killed her!

MAN: Uncle, that little girl is alive.

INVALID: No! She's dead. It happened quite a while ago.

MAN: But she's alive.

INVALID: That little girl?

MAN: Yes, she's all grown up, too.

INVALID: Is that right? Grown up, too?

MAN: Yes.

INVALID: You mean she's alive!

Wife exits.

INVALID: Has she grown into a pretty young lady?

MAN: Yes, she's quite a pretty young lady.

INVALID: Does she remember me?

MAN: Yes, she's been asking how you're doing.

INVALID: You mean she's been asking how I'm doing?

MAN: That's right.

INVALID: She's been alive all along! She'd be happy if I went to see her.

MAN: I'm sure she'd be very happy.

INVALID: Is that right? So she's been alive all this time!

Curtain.

ACT TWO

Carrying a small valise, Wife stands at about center stage with her back to stage right and therefore (obviously) facing stage left.

WIFE: An urgent matter. . . .

Passerby 1 approaches. He is a worn-out schoolteacher type: an older man, wearing a hat and threadbare suit. He passes Wife and walks slowly toward stage right, then turns about and looks back.

PASSERBY 1: Did you say something?

WIFE: What? (*Pause.*) It says, "An urgent matter." (*She extracts a letter from her handbag.*)

PASSERBY 1: Urgent? . . . Perhaps someone's passed away.

WIFE: No, I don't think so.

PASSERBY 1: Oh. Well then, what could it be?

WIFE: I suppose I have to go, though, don't I?

PASSERBY 1: On the other hand, it may not be necessary.

WIFE: I don't want to go.

PASSERBY 1: No, I suppose not.

WIFE: I can't stand it anymore.

PASSERBY 1: No, of course not. I was poor once myself—of course, I still am poor—but, you know, it's not the least bit considerate to look down on people just because they're poor. Don't you agree? There are people with sterling character even among the poor. Actually, the poor may be the only people with sterling character. But tell me, madam, do you think this urgent matter is really urgent?

WIFE: I suppose it must be. I mean, it happens so rarely.

PASSERBY 1: Ah, of course. It must happen very rarely, indeed. That is why it is urgent. That must be it. But how very disturbing for you! Now, I know how this must sound—after all, to you I am nothing more than a passerby—but, if you like, it might do you good to step over here and talk it over with me. That is to say, even though I am poor, I am also old and therefore rich in experience. I may be able to advise you. I ask nothing in return.

WIFE: But, I don't understand very well myself.

PASSERBY 1: What?

WIFE: That's all it says, just "an urgent matter."

PASSERBY 1: Well, then you'll just have to go and see.

WIFE: I suppose so.

PASSERBY 1: Then you'd best be on your way. We can talk any time. I don't have anything better to do. Or, would you like me to go with you?

WIFE: Thank you, but . . . .

PASSERBY 1: Of course not. Perhaps it would be better if I didn't go. After all, you don't know me from Adam. Look, I have an idea! I'll wait for you. I have a bit of an errand to run up ahead here in any case. When I'm finished . . . . It really isn't much of an errand, anyway. If you like, I could even take your address and . . . .

WIFE: My address?

PASSERBY 1: Oh, I am sorry! How forward of me! I really should show more reserve. It's just that I like to lend an ear to people's troubles. When I was younger, I used to advise people all the time. People were always in my debt. It's a sort of habit, I suppose. I'm the type who just can't ignore other people's misery. But, you must be very worried. How about this: you can usually find me sitting on a bench in the park just up ahead here. I spend a lot of time there thinking. If you like, you can drop by and see me at your leisure.

WIFE: You are very kind.

PASSERBY 1: Will you come?

WIFE: All right . . . .

PASSERBY 1: And you'll talk it over with me? Seriously? After all, this is no laughing matter. How about tomorrow? How would that be?

WIFE: All right.

PASSERBY 1: Then it's a promise. Now on your way! Chin up! You know what they say: When the going gets tough, it's time for the tough to get going.

WIFE: All right.

PASSERBY 1: A rather useful maxim. Tomorrow, then, don't forget. I'll be waiting.

Wife exits lifelessly stage left. Passerby 1 walks slowly to stage right and disappears.

The sickroom. Invalid leaves his bed and walks around it. Manually lifting one leg and then the other, he is practicing walking.

INVALID: Left . . . right . . . left . . . right . . . .
Doctor enters.
INVALID: Left . . . right . . . left . . . right . . . .
Nurse enters.
NURSE: Doctor . . . .
DOCTOR: Shhh.
NURSE (*noticing*): What's he doing?
DOCTOR (*to Nurse*): I'll take care of it. (*Nurse exits.*) How's it going?
INVALID: What?
DOCTOR: You're at it again.
INVALID: At what? What are you talking about?
DOCTOR: I see. It was a secret, wasn't it?
INVALID: A secret?
DOCTOR: About your going out to that town.
INVALID: Humph! You'll never understand about that town. (*He crawls back into bed.*) It's the town where I stripped down; I know it like the palm of my hand. Even the shortcut from the station: you turn the corner by the barbecue and take the third alleyway. It's a little narrow, but . . . . That's right, you take that dirty old street, turn left, and go straight by the post office . . . .
DOCTOR: There was a grocery store there, too.
INVALID: You just keep your mouth shut!
DOCTOR: You're awfully touchy tonight. What's wrong? You're tired, aren't you? Everybody gets a little touchy when they're tired.
INVALID: Leave me alone.
DOCTOR: Okay, I'll be going. But don't forget what we said the other night: you're going to shake hands, with everyone. Once you miss your chance, it'll haunt you for the rest of your life.
INVALID: Shake hands? Listen, Doc, what's this about our talking the other night and promises? . . .
DOCTOR: Try to remember. We talked, just the two of us.
INVALID: Just the two of us. Me and you?
DOCTOR: That's right, you remember. We opened our hearts and all but wept together.

INVALID: We did? I'd forgotten.

DOCTOR: But you promised.

INVALID: Promised? What did I promise?

DOCTOR: That if you ever had a problem, you'd talk it over with me.

INVALID: Talk it over? I don't remember that.

DOCTOR: Then you lied.

INVALID: But . . . what should I talk over?

DOCTOR: Anything at all. Just so there are no secrets between us.

INVALID: I don't have any secrets. Really I don't. I'm just figuring to go out to that town, that's all.

DOCTOR: That's fine. Just fine. If you don't have hope, there's nothing left to live for.

INVALID: This is no hope. I'm really going.

DOCTOR: Fine. When the time comes I'll see you off. But just remember that before you go you're to tell me. All right?

INVALID: I'll try.

DOCTOR: No, you must. If you don't you'll be breaking your word. You'll have told a lie.

INVALID: Listen, Doc, could I ask you a favor?

DOCTOR: Me? There's no reason to be so formal. I thought we were friends.

INVALID: Stop looking into my eyes.

DOCTOR: Why?

INVALID: And stop tiptoing around in the corridors. Stop peeping into my room. Listen, why are your hands so warm? And they're always moist. Why is that? Stop touching me with those hands. You understand. Listen to me. I want you to stop it.

DOCTOR: But why? Why is everyone like that to me? Is it because I haven't got a keloid? What do you want me to do? Come on, what do you say we let down our defenses and talk this thing out. Open our hearts, you know. We've known each other for a long time, haven't we? You've been here since way back. Way back. When I was assigned here, you were already curled up there in your bed. Come on, let's talk things over. Come to think of it, you've never shown me that famous keloid on your back. What do you say? How about a good long look? You wouldn't mind, would you? I've heard all about it. They say it's fantastic. I've often thought about asking, but somehow I never had the chance . . . .

INVALID: I don't pose except out in that town.

Invalid stands up in bed and strips to the waist. He raises his hands and poses majestically. Holding the pose, he rotates slowly and bends slightly at the waist. Nurse enters. Doctor raises a finger to his lips, signalling her to keep quiet.

NURSE: His wife is here.

Invalid again stands erect and stretches both his hands straight above his head.

DOCTOR: Bring her here.

NURSE: That's the problem—she says she doesn't want to come under any circumstances.

DOCTOR: Why?

NURSE: I don't know. She just won't come.

Invalid stands with both hands stretched above his head. Doctor exits. Nurse slowly approaches Invalid and sits on the bed at his feet.

NURSE: Your wife is here.

Invalid loftily refuses to move.

NURSE: You sent her a letter, didn't you? That's what she said.

WIFE (*from offstage*): I don't want to! I don't want to!

DOCTOR: Why?

WIFE: I don't want to. I don't want to see him.

DOCTOR: Why? Please tell me the reason.

WIFE: I just don't want to see him, that's all.

DOCTOR: Then why have you come this far?

WIFE: This far?

DOCTOR: As far as the hospital?

WIFE: I got a letter, last night, that's right, I'm sure it was last night. (*She takes the letter from her handbag.*) It's in his handwriting. You see, it says there's an urgent matter and I should come right away. (*She carefully folds the letter and returns it to her bag.*) Please, what's so urgent? The letter said there was an urgent matter. So early this morning I made some rice balls— I don't care for the food in this hospital. I can't eat it. —And then I caught a train . . . and came.

DOCTOR: He's showing his keloid.

WIFE: To whom?

DOCTOR: He showed it to me.

WIFE: It's gotten awfully dirty, hasn't it? Don't you think so? It's gotten awfully dirty.

DOCTOR: He's aged.

WIFE: It's gotten dirty. It didn't used to be that way. It used to have more shine to it. It sort of glistened. It's gone muddy now. Enough to make you weep. It's gone so dirty and all.

Invalid collapses slowly. Nurse rearranges his covers. Doctor takes Wife's hand.

WIFE: Stop it. I beg of you, let me go. Please. I don't want to see him. (*Doctor drags her into the sickroom.*) No! No!

DOCTOR: He's your husband. He's just tired himself out and fallen into bed. He's aged. His keloid has grown dirty with the years. Both the keloid on his back and the one under his arm are stained. You must tell him that. Tell him to forget about going out to that town. Tell him that no one will pay any attention to him. Tell him. If you don't, I can't be responsible. Every day, he gets out of bed to practice walking. Left, right, left, right, he walks around his bed.

Nurse exits.

WIFE: Who was that?

DOCTOR: Do you understand? Tell him that he is to lie quietly in bed. (*Exits.*)

WIFE: Dear . . . .

INVALID (*without raising his head*): Who is it?

WIFE: It's me. I received a letter.

INVALID: Yeah, I wrote it. Received it, did you?

WIFE: It was last night. Last night.

INVALID: Last night, huh?

WIFE: It said there was an urgent matter.

INVALID: Humph.

WIFE: What's wrong?

INVALID: Nothing at all. How about you?

WIFE: Me neither, nothing in particular . . . .

INVALID: Somebody there?

WIFE: What?

INVALID: Is anybody there?

WIFE (*glances around*): No.

INVALID (*getting to his feet*): Smells good.

WIFE: Yes, I'm wearing perfume.

INVALID: It smells good. It's good perfume, isn't it?

WIFE: No, it's cheap.

INVALID: Sure smells good.

WIFE: What is the urgent matter?

INVALID: Oh yes, I figured it was about time I went out to that town. Get my mat ready, will you?

WIFE: You mean your mat?

INVALID: We still have the one from before, don't we?

WIFE: Well, we might at that.

INVALID: And then I'll need some olive oil. To rub on my back. There's a big difference in the shine when you rub oil on your back and when you don't.

WIFE: You mean you're going to rub olive oil on your back?

INVALID: That's right. Everybody used to do that. We all used to rub it on ourselves.

WIFE: And do you want me to borrow a wagon, too?

INVALID: By all means. Borrow a wagon for me, will you? I'm going to do it just like before.

WIFE: Do you think people will really come to see?

INVALID: Of course they'll come. I used to pull the old wagon round the corner and they'd call from this direction and that about how here comes the naked keloid man, and everyone'd come running. Don't you remember? Listen, what if I told them the story about how old Mrs. Yoshida died? I mean, that's a pretty gruesome story, and . . . .

WIFE: Yes, it's a pretty gruesome story.

INVALID: That's it. That's just the story I'll tell. A really horrible story it is, too, that one.

WIFE: It really is a horrible story.

INVALID: They'll all gather round.

WIFE: They'll all gather round.

INVALID: From this direction and that direction, their wooden clogs going clip-clop clip-clop.

As the sickroom fades, Passersby 1 and 2 enter from stage left and right

against a background of light music. Both men are clad in suit, tie, and
white shirt, but they nonetheless appear threadbare and tired. They are
on the brink of old age. Each carries a cane at his side. They approach
each other and face off at center stage.

PASSERBY 1: Good day.

PASSERBY 2: Good day.

PASSERBY 1: Fine weather, isn't it?

PASSERBY 2: Isn't it! Fine weather, indeed.

PASSERBY 1: Blue sky.

PASSERBY 2: Yes, blue sky.

PASSERBY 1: Really fine weather.

PASSERBY 2: Yes, fine. (*Passerby 1 looks at Passerby 2.*) Is there
something I can do for you?

PASSERBY 1: What?

PASSERBY 2: No, it just occurred to me that there might be
something you wanted me to do for you.

PASSERBY 1: Do for me?

PASSERBY 2: You seemed to be staring at me, so . . . . It occurred
to me that you might want me to do something for you.

PASSERBY 1: Of course. It's because I was staring at you.

PASSERBY 2: Yes, but of course there are times when one simply
finds oneself looking at a person, aren't there? Times when
one has no particular business with a person but simply finds
oneself looking. That must have been what happened just
now. No doubt about it. In other words, it was a misunderstanding on my part, to think that you might have some
business with me.

PASSERBY 1: Quite so. It was your misunderstanding. The reason being, you see, that I, in fact, have no business with you.

PASSERBY 2: I see. It was my misunderstanding. The very idea
of your having business with me! Unthinkable!

PASSERBY 1: Quite so.

PASSERBY 2: After all, we're total strangers.

PASSERBY 1: Quite so. One could well say that we are, in fact,
total strangers.

PASSERBY 2: Just as I suspected, then, you were unintentionally
looking in my direction, that's all.

PASSERBY 1: Completely unintentionally.

PASSERBY 2: With no particular business. . . .

PASSERBY 1: No business at all.

PASSERBY 2: Ha-ha-ha, is that so?

Both men are silent. They stand unyieldingly.

PASSERBY 1: What is it?

PASSERBY 2: Nothing, just . . . .

PASSERBY 1: What? If you have no business with me . . . .

PASSERBY 2: No, it's nothing at all really. It's just that, well, I haven't any place in particular to go from here, that's all.

PASSERBY 1: I see.

PASSERBY 2: So you see I am in no particular hurry, and . . . .

Passerby 1 looks at Passerby 2.

PASSERBY 2 (*frightened*): What are you doing!

PASSERBY 1: As you see, I am doing nothing at all. What did you think I was going to do?

PASSERBY 2: Nothing in particular. I just had this feeling and thought that perhaps you were about to do something.

PASSERBY 1: I see, you had a feeling. And that's what you thought.

PASSERBY 2: Yes, that's what I thought.

PASSERBY 1: But, why don't you do something?

PASSERBY 2: Me? Do something?

PASSERBY 1: Yes, or perhaps you think you are doing something?

PASSERBY 2: Not particularly. What do you suggest I do?

PASSERBY 1: How should I know? You are free to do as you please.

PASSERBY 2: But . . . that may well be true, but . . . I'm not entirely sure I understand what you mean.

PASSERBY 1: Understand? What?

PASSERBY 2: What you're saying, I mean.

PASSERBY 1: I'm not saying anything.

PASSERBY 2: Yes, that's true, but I still don't understand.

PASSERBY 1: There is no harm in that, is there? Trying to understand everything! The very idea!

PASSERBY 2: I suppose so.

PASSERBY 1: Shall we, then?

PASSERBY 2: Eh?

PASSERBY 1: Are you ready?

PASSERBY 2: What for?

PASSERBY 1: We're so relaxed, I wondered if we shouldn't.

PASSERBY 2: Relaxed? Me?

PASSERBY 1: Yes. Look at yourself—so calm and self-composed.

PASSERBY 2: Why shouldn't I be?

PASSERBY 1: I didn't say you shouldn't. It's in their nature for human beings to be relaxed. Running away and hiding is the way of the weak.

PASSERBY 2: Running away and hiding?

PASSERBY 1: Yes, there are people who do that.

PASSERBY 2: Why run away? I have no reason.

PASSERBY 1: Quite so. You have no reason.

PASSERBY 2: But why do you say that sort of thing?

PASSERBY 1: What sort of thing?

PASSERBY 2: That I'll call for help or run away?

PASSERBY 1: I just had that feeling, the feeling that maybe you'd call for help, or perhaps were planning to run away.

PASSERBY 2: Listen, please tell me, please explain exactly what you're driving at.

PASSERBY 1: What difference does it make, even if there are a few things you don't understand? Man will never understand everything anyway. Well, shall we begin?

PASSERBY 2: Begin?

PASSERBY 1: Let me see now. (*Indicating Passerby 2's cane.*) Will you make do with that? This one will be fine for me. (*He brandishes his own cane.*)

PASSERBY 2: What is that? In your hand.

PASSERBY 1: It's a cane. It has a lead core. How about yours? Wouldn't you give it a flourish and show me how it handles?

PASSERBY 2: Flourish it? Why?

PASSERBY 1: You don't have to. Flourish it, I mean.

PASSERBY 2: You mean like this? (*He flourishes his cane for Passerby 1.*)

PASSERBY 1: It seems quite light, doesn't it?

PASSERBY 2: Yes, it is light. Canes are best light, I should think.

PASSERBY 1: Indeed, some people do prefer a light cane. Light and strong. For my part, I prefer one on the heavy side. Of course, it has to be strong.

PASSERBY 2: It's strong, all right, this one.

PASSERBY 1: Good. Well then, on with it.

PASSERBY 2: Huh?

PASSERBY 1: Right here. Strike me.

PASSERBY 2: Strike you?

PASSERBY 1: That's right. Here. Actually it makes little difference where you strike me.

PASSERBY 2: Please, just wait a moment. What do you mean to
do exactly?

PASSERBY 1: Fight. I for one do not want to die. So I will fight.

PASSERBY 2: Don't want to die?

PASSERBY 1: Do you want to die?

PASSERBY 2: Of course not.

PASSERBY 1: Then fight.

PASSERBY 2: I don't understand. Why should you fight with
me?

PASSERBY 1: Because I met you.

PASSERBY 2: Because you met me? Just because you met me
doesn't mean . . . . I mean, we hardly dislike each other
enough to . . . .

PASSERBY 1: Of course we don't dislike each other.

PASSERBY 2: Wait. Do you mean to kill me?

PASSERBY 1: It goes without saying. If you don't wish to be
killed, then you must fight, too.

PASSERBY 2: I can't fight.

PASSERBY 1: Of course that is your privilege.

PASSERBY 2: Please wait.

PASSERBY 1: What is it?

PASSERBY 2: Help me.

PASSERBY 1: Why?

PASSERBY 2: I've never done anything bad.

PASSERBY 1: Neither have I.

PASSERBY 2: Oh.

*Passerby 1 slowly brandishes his cane. Passerby 2 falls. Passerby 1
exits.*

WIFE: What's wrong?

INVALID: Nothing's wrong. I was just a little surprised, that's
all.

WIFE: Surprised?

INVALID: Because you're here.

WIFE: I've been here all along.

Carrying a stretcher, Men in White appear along with Doctor. Passerby 2 is on the stretcher.

MAN IN WHITE: Where shall we take him?

DOCTOR: To autopsy.

They exit slowly.

INVALID: Humph.

WIFE: What's the trouble?

INVALID: Dumbest story I ever heard.

WIFE: Is that right?

INVALID: Yes, that's right. (*Invalid dives under the covers.*)

The sickroom. There are two beds side by side. Invalid is lying in one. Man, attended by Doctor, is carried in on a stretcher.

MAN: Wait a moment, please.

DOCTOR: What is it?

MAN: What's happened? Where am I?

DOCTOR: You're in the hospital.

MAN: Hospital . . . I see, the hospital.

DOCTOR: You've been here many times before. And you've always gone home.

MAN: I see, yes, the hospital. But wait a moment, please. I'd just like to rest here for a second.

DOCTOR: But you're in the corridor now. How about getting into your room first? We've already prepared a bed for you in your uncle's room.

MAN: My uncle's room . . . you mean I'm going to my uncle's room?

DOCTOR: There's none other available, so we've taken the liberty.

MAN: Doctor, please give me some other room. I don't care who I'm with. Look, I'm sorry to trouble you, but please do this one thing for me.

DOCTOR: All the other rooms are full.

MAN: Doctor, please. The closet or the hallway, put me anywhere, but not here.

DOCTOR: We can't always have things exactly as we please. It's the same with everybody. The room you're to occupy has been decided in advance.

MAN: Anybody's room would do. I don't care who I'm with!

Man is carried into the sickroom and laid in bed.

DOCTOR: Now, isn't that better?

MAN: My uncle, how about my uncle?

DOCTOR: He's asleep.

MAN: Please don't wake him.

DOCTOR: Why not?

MAN: Shhh. It's all right. I'm fine just as I am. Only let me rest in peace. Did my uncle know?

DOCTOR: What?

MAN: That I'd be coming here?

DOCTOR: We haven't told him. There was no need.

MAN: Of course, there was no need, but . . . . Then, I suppose he'll laugh.

DOCTOR: Laugh? Why should he?

MAN: He'll laugh, all right. That's the way he is. Now won't you go about your business? I know what's expected of me.

DOCTOR: Then I'll be on my way. You know you can't overdo it with this disease, don't you?

MAN: Of course I know. Now please leave me.

DOCTOR: Then I'll be on my way. Good-bye. (*He exits.*)

INVALID: Has he left? (*He rises slowly and looks at Man.*)

Man remains silent.

INVALID: Why are you looking at me like that?

A moment passes.

MAN: I vomited blood.

INVALID: Why didn't you run away?

MAN: Run away?

INVALID: If I were you, I'd have run away before they had a chance to bring me here. I'd go to some town I'd never known before. I'd go by train. I'd have found myself an attractive, cozy little town and hidden out. I might even have made a success of myself there, for all I know. At something else of course. There'd be plenty of ways to get a huge round of applause—I wouldn't have to show off my keloid. That's what I'd have done. I'd have made a success of myself, even if I died doing it.

MAN: Is that right?

INVALID: Of course that's right. I wouldn't have been as stupid as you, getting carted in here on a stretcher. You can bet on that!

MAN: Of course.

INVALID: Didn't you feel like going any place?

MAN: Yes, I mean, I thought I'd like to go to the sea once before I came here.

INVALID: To the sea? A sailor, is that it?

MAN: No, just to look.

INVALID: Hm . . . and did you go?

MAN: No, I didn't. I was walking around town and, I remember, I got on a train.

INVALID: You got on?

MAN: Yes, it was dark. The train was small and dirty. The passengers were looking at my face, all of them.

INVALID: Your face?

MAN: Yes.

INVALID: Why did they do that?

MAN: I don't know. So I got off the train.

INVALID: You did? You shouldn't have done that. You really shouldn't have done that. If I were you, I'd have been a little more perseverant and ridden on. What difference does it make if they look at your face? What difference? Why couldn't you ask them if there was soot on your face or something? And if I got on a train, the first thing I'd do is I'd say, "I'm a survivor!" Right to their faces. Then, see, they'd get up and offer me their seats, make sympathetic conversation, offer me fruit and candy. When was it, now, somebody said how I must suffer and wrapped up some money in a bit of paper? Kind of a high-class lady. I got her address and sent her a picture afterwards, one of me standing with my arms spread apart like this, taken from just about this angle. She said it was a good picture. Sent a thank-you note later.

MAN: Uncle.

INVALID: Hm?

MAN: Would you be quiet for a minute?

INVALID: What's wrong?

MAN: I'd rather you didn't talk to me.

INVALID: Why not?

MAN: Please. Let's just rest here in peace and quiet. We ought to hold our breath and lie here without moving a muscle.

INVALID: But why? Why?

MAN: We're tired. Dog tired.

INVALID: What's that? Tired? Dog tired? Is that what you said? Exactly what is it you think you've done? What are you trying to tell me you've done? Huh? You work? You strip down? Did you study? Did you read books? Did you make any use of them? What do you think you've done? What? You haven't done a goddam thing. You've just walked around in a daze, and in a daze you got yourself dragged in here, flat on your back. And then what? Let's just rest here in peace and quiet, is it? Is that what you're trying to say?

MAN: Yes, that's what I'd like.

INVALID: That's not what it's all about. That's just not what life's all about. A man's got to see a thing through. Look here, even me, even an old man like me gets up every day and practices walking. That's right, every single day. I walk around this room. Then, when I get a little meat on these legs, I'm going out to that town once more. That's what I'm figuring. The wife's preparing my mat and wagon. I'm not kidding. She's getting my stuff together, just like it used to be. Do you understand? I'm going to ride into that town, pulling my wagon, dressed just like before. I'll turn the corner and call. "I'm the naked keloid man!" I'm going to call out, you see, "I'm the naked keloid man!" I'll say. The place'll be in an uproar. They won't take it serious at first. Because, see, it'll be like they can't believe it. They'll ask each other, "I wonder if it's true?" Then they'll come running. From this direction and that. A great wall of faces will form. I'll shake hands with them, one by one. And then . . . and then, I'll start weeping. Then all of them, everyone of them, they'll rejoice and wrap their arms around my back.

Nurse enters, dragging a large bag. She walks across the stage. Startled, Man jumps to his feet.

MAN: What happened?

NURSE: It died.

MAN: Died?

NURSE: It just died, that's all.

MAN: I'm sorry.

NURSE: As soon as it was born. We did what we could, but it was no use.

MAN: What are you going to do now?

NURSE: Throw it away. In the river.

MAN: You mean you're going to wash it down the river?

NURSE: Yes.

MAN: What about your husband?

NURSE: He wept.

MAN: Wept?

NURSE: Yes.

MAN: Good-bye.

NURSE: Good-bye. I'll have another child. I'm sure I'll have another child.

Nurse exits. Man returns silently to bed.

MAN: Uncle. When was it now? I told you that little girl who wanted to touch your back was alive?

INVALID: Yeah, she's still alive, all right.

MAN: I lied.

INVALID: What?

MAN: It was a lie.

INVALID: What are you trying to do? Who do you think you are?

MAN: What?

INVALID: What are you getting at?

MAN: I told a lie.

Wife enters dejectedly, her eyes downcast. Invalid addresses her, almost pleading.

INVALID: I'm going. Things have finally worked out, and I'm going. Look, you only have to help me a little, that's all. Then I can do for myself. If you'd just lend me a hand when I go down those stairs—that's all I'm asking. Will you do that much for me?

WIFE: I'm going back to my parents' place in the country.

INVALID: Your parents' place? You're going to your parents' place? Why?

WIFE: I'm bored. There's nothing left for me to do anymore.

INVALID: How about books? You could read books, couldn't you? There are all kinds of interesting books. And then, there's something to be gained from books, too.

WIFE: I've read books.

INVALID: How about movies? You could go to the movies. They say there are lots of interesting movies.

WIFE: They're all filled with nonsense.

INVALID: Is that right? Okay. Hurry back, then. It's good to go home sometimes, see old friends and all. It's been a long time, anyway. Everyone will be glad to see you. They might even hug you and weep on your shoulder. "Sure is good to have you home again," they'll say. Go ahead and hurry back. I'll be all right on my own. Just when I go down those stairs, that's the only part that'll give me trouble. What am I talking about! If I put my mind to it, there's nothing impossible! I was just thinking, a minute ago, how it might present a bit of a problem, that's all. Once I get down to it, it'll probably be a lot easier than I think. If you'll just get the matting and wagon ready, that'll be fine. Okay? Just do that much for me. It won't be too much trouble. Just the wagon and the mat.

WIFE: I want to leave today, straight from the hospital.

INVALID: Listen, what about the wagon? Huh? How about the wagon and the mat? Is that too much to ask?

WIFE: I can't do any more.

INVALID: What? Not even the wagon? All you have to do is borrow it for me. Just borrow it, that's all. We still have the mat from before, don't we? Just the wagon, that's all. That's all I ask.

WIFE: I just can't help you anymore.

INVALID: Not even with the wagon? You couldn't just borrow it for me?

WIFE: I can't.

INVALID: I see. Well, in that case, hurry back. Give everyone my regards. Tell them that I'll be going, too, after I get myself together. Tell them that for me, will you?

WIFE: All right.

INVALID: You're leaving straight from here?

WIFE: Yes, straight from . . . . Good-bye.

MAN: Aunty.

WIFE: Oh, you're here, too.

MAN: You going?

WIFE: Yes.

MAN: If anybody asks about me, tell them you don't know. I don't want anybody talking about me.

WIFE: All right. If anybody asks about you, I'll say I don't know.

MAN: Thanks. And when you think of me, please rest assured that I'm still in the same dim hospital room, my eyes half open, staring at the ceiling.

WIFE: I will. That'd be best for everyone.

MAN: Good-bye, Aunty.

WIFE: Good-bye. (*She leaves.*)

Invalid uncovers his legs and examines them. Then he chuckles under his breath.

INVALID: These are my legs. They've got a little more meat on them now. That's what you call the fruit of practice.

MAN: Aunty's gone.

INVALID: It's because I practiced. Because I worked at it every day.

MAN: Uncle.

INVALID: Listen, you wouldn't know somebody in this neighborhood who'd lend me a wagon and some matting, would you? Just a simple, little one would do. Wouldn't have to be much bigger than about this much of my bed.

MAN: No.

INVALID: Just a little one like this. Yes, one about this size would be plenty.

MAN: Uncle, the keloid on your back is covered with spots. It's stained and covered with spots.

INVALID: There used to be a bicycle store up the way. Remember, just up the way? Out of the hospital and toward the street—wasn't the store on the corner there a bicycle shop? It was, I'm sure of it. It was a bicycle shop. I'll borrow my wagon from there. Wagons go with bicycles, so they're

bound to have one. Then the matting. Matting comes from
the flooring shop. They use it to cover floors. I'll have to
search for a flooring shop. That's it, I'll have to ask somebody. And that'll be my wagon and mat.

MAN: Uncle.

INVALID: Olive oil, got to have olive oil. Rub it on my back. To
bring out the shine. On my back. When I rub it on my back, I
may have to ask you for a little help. My arms won't reach,
you see.

Man remains silent. Invalid hugs his knees and sits on his bed, lost in
thought. Then he lowers himself to the floor and stands.

INVALID: Good. No problem with these sturdy legs. Didn't
used to be like this. Used to be that if I wasn't holding on to
something I'd lose my balance. (*He lifts his legs and tries to*
walk. He stops and returns to his bed.) Feel heavy. I must be
tired. I'm a little tired today. That's all it is. That's all there is
to it. This sort of thing happens sometimes. I'm tired. (*He*
climbs back into bed.) Okay, here and now let's decide. If it
doesn't rain, I'll leave in the evening, day after tomorrow. In
the evening, day after tomorrow. If it doesn't rain. If it rains
I'd need some rain gear, see. I'd need some rain gear, and the
onlookers aren't likely to be out either. If it doesn't rain. If it
doesn't rain, I'll go out in the evening, day after tomorrow.
You know, I might be murdered out in that town.

MAN: What?

INVALID: I might be murdered. Out in that town.

MAN: Murdered?

INVALID: Somebody's out to get me.

MAN: Who?

INVALID: Somebody, a bad guy, that's who.

MAN: Why?

INVALID: He's been wanting to murder me.

MAN: But why should he?

INVALID: I'll die for him anytime. I've got the word out. Just
come and get me, I say!

MAN: You mean you're going to be murdered?

INVALID: That's right. What? You think I'm gonna start shaking
in my boots? Hell, there's nothing to be afraid of. I'll be

standing there with my feet planted on the ground, my hands on my hips, scowling at the sky. Then, out of nowhere this bad guy's gonna come carrying a knife, and he's gonna run right into me and drive that knife through my belly. Blood'll come gushing out. I'll fall over. Everyone will gather around and they'll carry me in their arms, but by that time I'll already be dead. They'll get incensed. And they'll trample on the guy that stabbed me; they'll turn into a mob and torture him within an inch of his life. They'll beat him and kick him and spit on him and pull out his hair and throw him around. My wife, even my wife'll be sorry when I'm gone. She'll regret ever having gone home to the country. She'll be sorry all right. But it'll be over and done with. Everyone'll blame her. Because it's not such a good thing to leave a sick man and go back to the country. That's right, isn't it? It'd be natural for them to blame her, wouldn't it?

MAN: Supposing nobody came to murder you?

INVALID: What's that?

MAN: What if nobody came to murder you?

INVALID: Nobody? Not a single solitary person?

MAN: Not a single solitary person.

INVALID: If not a single person came? If nobody came, then I'd go out looking. I'd do out looking and let them know where I was, that's what I'd do.

MAN: What if nobody listened?

INVALID: If nobody listened? Then I'd yell out in a loud voice. "Here I am, you bastards, come and get me!" I'd say. I'd say it in a real loud voice.

MAN: In a real loud voice?

INVALID: That's right. And everybody'll sit up and listen, too. And they'll all gather round me. He'll change colors and jump out of the crowd. And then he'll take this long, silvery knife and gash me in the belly. I'll bet I die laughing! Laughing, you see. After I'm gone they'll realize for the first time. The fact that I'd suffered, I mean. They'll catch on then for the first time that every day I'd been throwing myself into my work body and soul for them. That's why they might lynch the guy that murdered me. But I'll forgive him. I'll forgive him, all

right. He didn't know anything. He's to be pitied. See what I
mean? I'll forgive him. But, they might blame my wife. No
matter how you look at it, she did go off and leave a sick man
behind. Don't you think so? Don't you think they'll blame
her? But I'll forgive her, too. She wanted to be with me. It's
only a matter of . . . she just went back to the country to kill
time. She even went to borrow the wagon for me, but the guy
didn't respond well, that's all. He must have said something
to make her feel ashamed, like how he wouldn't want to be
responsible if somebody catches keloids from me. So she
went back to the country. Poor thing. Huh? You see what I
mean? This time, when I go out to that town, I'm going to
tell them that right to their faces. I've got to make her situation clear to them, see?

MAN: Uncle.

INVALID: What?

MAN: Let's stop fighting windmills.

INVALID: What's that?

MAN: I've thought about things like you do, but there's no one
out there to murder us anymore. It's the truth. Is there anybody left who'd say that it wouldn't do to have our keloids
spread? Nobody says that anymore. It's not like that. Listen,
here's a true story. There's a girl out there who says she won't
marry anyone but a man with A-bomb disease. A pretty,
ordinary sort of girl she is, too. And they say there are men
who won't marry anyone but a woman with a keloid scar. As
a matter of fact, the nurse who was working here until recently married a man like that. See, it's as if we were in love
with each other. It's forbidden to murder us or say vile things
about us. It's a regular conspiracy. That's why everybody's
smiling. It's as if they were in love with us.

INVALID: That's right, there are even people out there who'll
love us.

MAN: That's not what I mean!

INVALID: You're right, you're absolutely right. We're in love
with each other. You've made a fine point. There are lots of
bad guys in the world, but there are lots of good guys, too.
And there's a spot of good in even the worst of them. I mean,

that's what everybody says, isn't it—that no matter how bad a guy might be, he'd throw a rope to a drowning child without a second thought. See, that's the point. That's what I'd forgotten.

Giving up, Man falls back into bed.

INVALID: Ah, you know it feels good to get this off my chest. Yes, no matter what happens I'm going out to that town. I'll go out and shake hands with everyone. That's all I'll have to do. To tell the truth, I was beginning to think about forgetting the whole thing. But that won't do. That won't do at all. Come what may, I'm going. It'll make everybody so happy!

MAN: Uncle.

INVALID: Yes?

MAN: Come on, as a favor to me, stop it now.

INVALID: What?

MAN: Everything, just stop everything. Don't yell out in a loud voice and don't run around calling attention to yourself. Don't get excited, don't weep, don't laugh! Stop, once and for all! Just be quiet! And then rest here peacefully. That's all there is. That's all there is, don't you see?

INVALID: You don't understand. There are lots of things that you don't understand. You're frustrated, aren't you? That's not good. Look at me. I'm relaxed. You see, I've got a plan. Heh-heh, a plan, you see. I just was thinking about it a bit, and, you know, it's a great plan. Listen. I arrive in that town and strip. I strike a pose. There's terrific applause. Okay? Up to there nothing's changed. But then I take out this razor. You see what I mean, a straight-edge razor. I'll have gotten this razor ready in advance, that's it. I'll pull it out, see, and then ZIP, right across my arm, about here. See what I mean? I start bleeding. Fantastic. Everybody's watching with their eyeballs popping out. I rub the blood all over my body. I'm dripping with blood. Then I strike another pose. Absolutely fantastic. The crowd roars. They'll roar for sure. That's when I'll tell them. I'll say, "Ladies and gentlemen, I've lived my life with all I've got. I've borne the pain of the last ten years and fought with all my might. Ladies and gentlemen, I've lived my life with all I've got. I've fought my way to this day with death on my doorstep. I've tried. Look at this blood-drenched body of mine. Look at this body of mine, covered with blood. I have done it!"

MAN: Uncle.

INVALID: Wait a minute . . . wait just a minute. "Ladies and gentlemen. I've come all this way. I've come fighting. I've worked. I've worked with my body and my soul. Look. Look at this bloody flesh, this blood-soaked body. Ladies and gentlemen. Ladies and gentlemen. I have suffered. My wife, my wife returned to the country. Forgive my wife. Look at me. I'm covered with blood."

MAN: Uncle!

INVALID: Just wait a minute. It'll only take a minute. Wait. "Ladies and gentlemen. Tears flow from my eyes. Ladies and gentlemen. On my back I've carried . . . ." Who is it? Who's there?

Doctor enters.

DOCTOR: What's going on?

INVALID: Just a minute. I'll be finished in no time. Right away. Won't take but a minute. "Ladies and gentlemen, all of you who have gathered around me, look at me. Look at me well." (*To Doctor*): Don't touch me. Please don't touch my back. "Ladies and gentlemen. Ladies and gentlemen. At this very moment, I am about to be murdered. I will be killed. I've tried. I've tried with all my might."

MAN: Stop it!

INVALID: "Ladies and gentlemen, I have tried. Nevertheless, nevertheless, at this very moment someone is preparing to murder me. Ladies and gentlemen, do you understand? I've come all this way covered with blood. Ladies and gentlemen, ladies and gentlemen, please applaud. Please applaud! Please! Give me a round of applause. I've come, pulling my wagon behind me. Applaud. Please applaud me. Applause, an impassioned round of applause! Please, applaud me!

He falls back into bed and continues, babbling to himself.
Curtain.

ACT THREE

Invalid's bed is empty. Man is alone, sitting on his bed, his legs folded under him in a formal posture. Doctor enters.

DOCTOR: He's not here, is he?

MAN (*vacantly*): Not here?

DOCTOR: No.

MAN: But it's raining. It's raining, isn't it?

DOCTOR: Yes, it's raining. Raining cats and . . . . What exactly happened anyway?

MAN: How should I know. When I opened my eyes, I heard the sound of rain falling. And when I looked around, he wasn't here.

DOCTOR: You say when you opened your eyes he was already gone? But listen, didn't he say he'd forget the whole thing if it rained?

MAN: That's what he said.

DOCTOR: That's right, that's what he said. He said if it rained, the onlookers wouldn't be out. That's the way it used to be, I suppose.

MAN: It really is coming down, too, isn't it?

DOCTOR: It's a regular flood.

MAN: Are you searching for him?

DOCTOR: The whole staff's out looking.

MAN: What if you stopped looking?

DOCTOR: We couldn't do that. He might already be dead. He might be lying in the mud someplace, face down, pelted by the rain. At first glance, nobody'd realize he was a human being. He'd only look like a little pile of something. Like a gutter rat, drenched to the skin. Of course, there's no point talking to you about it. It's not your fault. There's no reason for you to feel responsible or get excited. You only shared his room, that's all. What about you?

MAN: Me?

DOCTOR: Aren't you going to leave?

MAN: I'm not going anyplace. I'm lying right here.

DOCTOR: Why?

MAN (*thinking about something else for a moment*): Listen, Doctor

. . . you remember the nurse who was working here, the one who got married?

DOCTOR: A nurse who worked here?

MAN: That's right . . . the one who said she wanted to have a baby.

DOCTOR: Oh, that one. She never got married or anything of the sort.

MAN: What?

DOCTOR: Of course not. She's still here.

MAN: Here?

DOCTOR: In the hospital.

MAN: Why?

DOCTOR: Her body gave out on her. She's resting in the sickroom a couple doors ahead.

MAN: I see.

DOCTOR: Did she say she was getting married?

MAN: That's not the way it was at all, was it?

DOCTOR: She probably just wanted to see what it would feel like to say so. You can hardly blame her.

MAN: No . . . you can hardly blame her . . . .

Passerby 1 enters.

PASSERBY 1: Good day.

DOCTOR: Yes?

PASSERBY 1: I've come to pick him up.

DOCTOR: Pick him up?

PASSERBY 1: Isn't this the right place?

DOCTOR: For what?

PASSERBY 1: I was requested, by a certain lady, to transport one of the patients here out to the town by wagon. The wagon should be here any minute.

MAN: Aunty asked you?

PASSERBY 1: Quite so.

DOCTOR: I'm afraid he's already left. Walked out under his own steam.

PASSERBY 1: Walked? Is that so? I was afraid something like this might happen. That's just the way life is. I had a funny feeling.

DOCTOR: A funny feeling? About what?

PASSERBY 1: Both that lady and this place . . . . Well, the wagon

may very well arrive later. I cannot be responsible. The lady
requested it separately. (*Exits.*)

DOCTOR: What are you looking at me like that for?

MAN: Everybody knew. About today. You knew, too, didn't
you? What's really happened? Has my uncle died?

DOCTOR: I don't know. I have no idea. Really.

MAN: Then why should a man like that show up here?

DOCTOR: Your aunt must have asked him to come before she
left for the country.

MAN: But why today?

DOCTOR: I don't know.

MAN: Doctor, how is that nurse doing?

DOCTOR: Mm.

MAN: Is she really here?

DOCTOR: Yes, she's here. Why?

MAN: Where?

DOCTOR: In the sickroom a couple doors ahead here. Do you
want to see her?

MAN: Everybody's listening. Tell me, Doctor, where is the
intercom?

DOCTOR: Intercom?

MAN: Yes.

DOCTOR: There's no intercom here.

MAN: No?

DOCTOR: Look for yourself.

MAN: Do you think my uncle really made it out of the hospital?
Is he really gone?

DOCTOR: It certainly looks that way. If we haven't found him
by this time . . . .

MAN: Shhh!

DOCTOR: Mm?

Pause.

MAN: Doctor, you mustn't say anything. Don't say anything.
Then please leave the room.

*Invalid returns, crawling along the floor. He approaches the bed and
crawls up into it. Doctor watches the whole process, then leaves in
silence. Invalid gives a low, groaning laugh. And he continues to
laugh.*

MAN (*in a low voice*): Where were you?
Invalid raises one hand up high. He is gripping something shiny—a razor.
MAN (*in a low voice*): What happened?
Invalid points off stage right. His choked laughter continues.
MAN: Everybody's been looking for you.
Invalid sits up in bed. He is not laughing anymore. He holds the blade of the razor up to the light.
INVALID: It's shiny.
MAN: Tell me what happened.
INVALID: Mm.
Invalid hones the razor on his cuff and holds it up to the light again. Then he hones it again, repeating the process.
MAN: Even though it's raining today, I thought you'd gone for sure.
INVALID: What's so special about today?
MAN: What?
INVALID: That's right! It's today!
MAN: Are you going?
INVALID: Today! Of course! I knew I had a funny feeling, but
. . . .
MAN: But it's raining!
INVALID: But today's the day.
MAN: Why today? It's raining, you know. It's a regular flood. I thought you said that if it rained you'd forget the whole thing. There won't be a spectator out there.
INVALID: Humph. But listen, it's been ten years.
MAN: You'll get wet, you'll get drenched to the skin.
Invalid takes a package wrapped in a kerchief from under his blankets and arranges its contents.
MAN: Uncle, will you listen to me? Let's just suppose you were able to go out to that town.
INVALID: Ah . . . .
MAN: If you were able to go—all right?—it'd still be raining cats and dogs. The roads are bad over there, so you'd be in mud up to your knees, and the rest of you'd get soaked right down to your underwear. It would cling to your skin, and it's cold, so your knees'd begin to shake together. You know it's the truth!

And what's more, there won't be anybody out there! And on that road, even if you called out, nobody'd hear you. Because it's raining, see. You'll be standing out there beaten by the rain. For nothing! It's the truth. And even if someone did happen to pass by, you think they'd notice anything? They'd be carrying umbrellas. And even if, chance in a million, they did notice you, they wouldn't know you from Adam.

INVALID: Don't worry. I've got the answer.

MAN: To what?

INVALID: You know, how to go about it. I saw my chance, so I took it. Now all I have to do is shake hands.

MAN: With whom?

INVALID: This morning, I opened my eyes. Then I thought, it's today! I wonder why? That's why I wanted this razor. So I went down the stairs to the bathroom. I figured that they'd have a razor there. I couldn't reach the shelf. Finally, I got it. And then I put the razor in my pocket. I was completely beat, so I just sat there in the shadows behind the lockers for a while.

MAN (*after a moment*): A strange man came by a while ago. He said he'd come to pick you up. The wagon's ready, too.

INVALID: He's an imposter.

MAN: An imposter?

INVALID: Now let's see, is this all I'll need? All that's left is the wagon and the mat.

MAN: Uncle.

INVALID: Yes?

MAN: I really want you to stop it now. Please. Listen, there's no reason in the world why you have to go and get soaked into the bargain, is there? I can't stand it. The very idea upsets me. Now come on, let's forget the whole thing. Everything would be all right, don't you see, if we just rest here. You just don't understand anything!

INVALID: I don't understand?

MAN: You don't understand anything at all. But, never mind, just never mind about that. The only thing is that I don't want you to go. Everybody feels the same way. They rest easy because they know that you're lying here.

INVALID: You're absolutely right, but, you know, they still want to see me. They want to meet me and see how I've been. (*He places his bundle over his shoulder.*)

MAN: Uncle, please stop. If you don't I'll call the doctor. I'll yell out in a loud voice and call the doctor. Do you understand?

INVALID: Hey, what's come over you? What are you saying? I've been planning this for ten years. And now you're trying to tell me to forget the whole thing?

MAN: That's right. I want you to forget the whole thing.

INVALID: You . . . .

MAN: I'll call the doctor!

INVALID: Don't you see? You can't do that to me. Look, I know. I've come to understand. If I don't go today, I'll never go. You know it's true. I've got to go today even if I have to crawl. Please, I'm asking you, let me go. Look, I've made up my mind, I'm going. Can you understand that? (*He descends from his bed.*)

MAN (*also leaving his bed*): Uncle, get this through your head. Listen. We mustn't do anything anymore. Not anything. To do something is the worst thing of all. No matter how hard it is, we've got to lie here patiently and keep our mouth shut. It's not because we're sick. That's not it. I don't say that. I'm no doctor. It's just that we mustn't try to do things, that's all. We are incapable of doing anything except being persecuted, hated, and destroyed. We cannot even think about being loved. When we're not being murdered, hated, or tormented, we wait. There's nothing left for us but to wait. We rest quietly.

Invalid gets down on all fours and begins to leave. Man approaches, ready to stop him.

MAN: Stop!

INVALID: Don't come any closer. I'm warning you. (*He holds the razor in his hand.*)

MAN: What exactly do you expect to accomplish?

INVALID: I'm going, no matter what.

MAN: Listen to reason! Everybody's the same. They're all acting as I say. You remember the nurse who used to work here? She never got married. She's here. In the sickroom a couple doors up the hall. She rests quietly. She doesn't move a muscle.

INVALID: They brought her back.

MAN: What?

INVALID: She left. And then she came back. Together with the doctor. It was night. They say she ran away. They say she almost flew.

MAN: Ran . . . .

INVALID: With all her might, barefoot . . . barefoot.

Invalid undoes the bundle strapped to his back, throwing it and the umbrella aside.

INVALID: This junk! I'm going. (*He crawls, slowly.*)

MAN: Uncle!

INVALID (*without turning around*): What is it?

Screaming "Stop it! Stop it! Stop it!" Man flings himself upon Invalid. Invalid crumbles. For a moment both men are motionless. Then, Man picks up the umbrella and gets dazedly to his feet. He opens the umbrella.

Doctor enters, goes to Invalid, and examines him. Then he gets to his feet. Man, concealing his face under the umbrella, speaks.

MAN: Why don't you applaud? He thought you would. He said you'd applaud. I wonder why? Perhaps it all happened too quickly. It must have come as a complete surprise—for him, too.

Wife, Nurse, Passersby 1 and 2, and the other characters emerge vaguely upstage. Downstage, a man appears, pulling a wagon behind him. He halts stage center.

WAGON MAN: I've brought the wagon.

DOCTOR: Thank you. You're just in time. Here's your passenger.

Wagon Man, Doctor and Passerby 1 and 2 lay Invalid's corpse in the wagon.

DOCTOR: You know where to take him.

WAGON MAN: To that town.

DOCTOR: Yes, with joy.

The wagon slowly begins to move. Doctor, Wife, Nurse and Passersby 1 and 2 follow it.

MAN (*shouting after them*): Take the shortcut. Don't forget. Turn the corner by the barbecue in front of the station and take the third alleyway. It's a little narrow, but . . . . You take that dirty old street, turn left, and go straight by the post office

. . . . The moon. A sad fish. I grow lighter and lighter. I wonder why? . . . Just now . . . I'm somehow feeling heavier. How can I stop becoming lighter? What might be the way? Sometimes, I try lifting one leg. Like this. This is quite a risky venture. It's quite possible that, sometime, I might lift both legs off the ground . . . . If I do like this, for this leg at least, I'm heavier. For a moment, I feel secure. Moon, you are too bright! It might as well be broad daylight!

Still carrying the umbrella, he spreads his arms upward and out. Curtain.

NEZUMI KOZŌ: THE RAT

Nezumi Kozō: The Rat: Holocaust as Metahistory

By formulating the unique situation of atomic bomb survivors
as a crystallization of the universal dilemma of survival in the
nuclear age, Betsuyaku Minoru had in *The Elephant* taken the
first steps toward a radical transformation of the atomic bomb
experience. Satoh Makoto goes even further in *Nezumi Kozō:
The Rat.* He rejects the need felt by previous writers to remain
bound by historical events as such and instead integrates Hiroshima and Nagasaki into the great pattern of human metahistory. Satoh's play is the most radical Japanese dramatic work on
the atomic bomb experience to date. It utterly rejects shingeki
orthodoxy and passivity and offers in its place a dramaturgy of
mystical activism akin to the revolutionary messianism of Walter
Benjamin.

A LIFE UNDER THE NUCLEAR UMBRELLA

Born in 1943, Satoh (who prefers to spell his name with an *h*
rather than the more usual macron) never knew a world free
from nuclear weapons. Growing up under the U.S. nuclear umbrella, Hiroshima and Nagasaki were to him not events but
conditions. He grew up with a terror of the bomb and became
involved in the demonstrations of 1960 while still in high school.

Satoh's concern with Hiroshima and Nagasaki was reinforced
during his theater training. At the Actors' Theater Training
Academy (*Haiyūza yōseijō*) he studied with Tanaka Chikao,
serving as stage manager on his class's graduation production of
The Head of Mary; and in July 1965, immediately after graduat-
ing, he was assistant director on the Youth Art Theater (*Seinen
geijutsu gekijō*) production of *The Elephant.*

Already in his earliest plays, Satoh displayed a profound pre-
occupation with the threat of nuclear holocaust. He presented

the specter of atomic destruction explicitly in his first produced work, *The Subway* (*Chikatetsu,* 1966), and it has remained an implicit theme in all his subsequent plays.

The turning point in Satoh's thinking about nuclear issues came during the summer of 1966, when he was involved in the demonstrations against the entry into Japanese waters of the nuclear-powered Polaris submarine that docked at Yokosuka on May 30. During the demonstrations Satoh began to feel that demonstrations against inanimate objects like bombs and submarines were fundamentally absurd; and he concluded that the atomic bomb exists, not because of an inherent life force, but because people allow it to exist. It followed that the most effective means of eliminating nuclear weapons would be to alter the structure of the human imagination that permits them. Satoh's theater is therefore an attempt at symbolic action intended to alter the structure of the human imagination in politically meaningful ways, in particular, to eliminate the threat of atomic destruction.

TWO SETTINGS

Spectators who attended the first production of *Nezumi Kozō: The Rat* in 1969 descended the steps into the Freedom Theater, located in the basement of a plate glass store in central Tokyo, to find themselves in a room painted entirely black. Seating was arranged on three sides of the room on tatami mats. On the fourth wall were Chinese characters reading "mixed bathing" (*danjo konyoku*) written in the *kantei* style of calligraphy associated with kabuki and the Edo period. The room was dimly lit to suggest candlelight, and over the door hung a *shitodachi,* the twisted rope decorated with folded paper hangings that is found at the entrance to Shinto shrines.

The inscription "mixed bathing" and the *shitodachi* correspond respectively to the bath and the *temenos,* the two overlapping spaces in which the action of the play takes place.

The inscription "mixed bathing" in a style of calligraphy straight out of the Edo period evokes the image of the public bath and the traditional Japanese community. For the Japanese, the public bath is a powerful symbol of the Japanese community and its mentality.

The chase that constitutes the basic story of *Nezumi Kozō* takes place within this watery world. Five characters (Nezumis 1–5) pursue the Guardian through subterranean passages, the sewers of Japanese history. These five dispirited figures are "sewer rats" (*dobu nezumi*), and these sewers, the lower depths of Japanese society, are their lair. The Guardian flees, searching for a new public bath and the safety of the traditional community, where his charge, the Lord of the Dawn, will be safe.

The five characters represent the Japanese masses; the Guardian and the Lord of the Dawn represent the Japanese emperor system. The Lord of the Dawn is the transhistorical, legitimizing spirit of the emperor system; the Guardian is the present human investee of that spirit, in other words, the current emperor. The chase through the sewers of Japanese history should therefore be understood as an abortive attempt by the Japanese masses to seize and destroy the emperor system that oppresses them.

The chase begins at the end of World War II, "when the bottom fell out of traditional Japanese society," and the emperor system is washed into the sewers and is in temporary limbo. Eventually, the Guardian succeeds in eluding his pursuers and proceeds toward the hot springs resort of Atami. The transition from the public bath, through the sewers, to the Roman baths of Atami represents the history of Japan from the loss of the war, through the chaos of the immediate postwar period, to the reestablishment of the traditional imperial order on a new, prosperous, streamlined basis.

Superimposed on this first setting is another, signified by the ritual rope hanging over the door. The *shitodachi* is a ritual article of the Shinto religion having its origins in the earliest days of Japanese civilization. Its purpose is to delineate a *temenos,* a sanctified space where gods may appear. *Shitodachi* hang over the entrance to Shinto shrines, demarcate the ritually purified site of new construction, and adorn rocks, trees, and other natural objects believed to harbor exemplary power. Anyone who entered the Freedom Theater and noticed the *shitodachi* hanging over the threshold was immediately aware that he had entered a ritually purified space where divinities were to be welcomed.

TWO MODES OF TIME

Within these two overlapping spaces, Satoh describes two competing temporal modalities that he believes coexist within the Japanese imagination. These are historical, goal-oriented time represented by the five Nezumi characters; and ahistorical, cyclical time represented by Heh-heh, So-so, and Bo-bo.

The five sewer rats are poor and oppressed and dream of release from their condition. They envision a moment, "The Hour of the Rat," when a savior (Nezumi Kozō) will appear to redeem them. The Hour of the Rat is in their minds the moment of eschatological redemption, a fiery Apocalypse, the Advent of the Messiah, the culmination of history when final justice will be done and all wrongs set aright.

When they sight "a falling star in the southern sky," each of the five makes a wish upon it, and this binds them together in a brotherhood of faith. Ironically, "the falling star" in which they have invested their hopes and dreams is in fact "the silver pod" of the atomic bomb. They have wished upon the mechanism of their own destruction, and at the end of the play, they remove their robber's masks to reveal profiles deformed by the keloid scars that have been emblematic of A-bomb survivors. In effect, they have wished atomic destruction upon themselves. It is the dynamics of this self-delusion, this self-betrayal that Satoh wishes to explore in this play.

The five characters exist in a historical universe. They imagine themselves to be in a world where action has historical consequences, and they seek to act to achieve a historical goal: a revolution that will result in their redemption. Their pursuit of the Lord of the Dawn, their belief in the imminent appearance of a savior at an appointed time, and the coincidence of that time with a fiery Apocalypse that will save them and validate their suffering makes them quintessentially historical beings and places them in a well-established messianic tradition that stretches from ancient Iran, through Judaism and Christianity, to Marxism and contemporary revolutionary theory.[1]

Opposing the five characters and representing the ahistorical, cyclical perception of time are Heh-heh, So-so, and Bo-bo. There are basically four aspects to the highly complex identity of these characters. They are Shinto mediums (*miko*), incarnations of the female genitalia, guides to hell, and cats. These apparently unconnected aspects of their identity are bound together by the associational logic characteristic of Japanese religion which is given free rein in the sanctified space of Satoh's theater.[2]

There is a sex-specific division of labor in Japanese shamanism. Male shamans are active, traveling to the Other World to commune with the gods. Female shamans are passive mediums through whom the gods speak. When Heh-heh, So-so, and Bo-bo first appear, they are dressed as *miko,* and are performing a ritual invocation of the Japanese gods.

The relationship between the female shaman and her tutelary deity is implicitly sexual. The deity (male) possesses the shaman (female) in a sexual fashion. The deity is frequently represented in Japanese mythology as a supernatural snake that penetrates and impregnates the female medium.[3] In their most basic form, therefore, Japanese female shamans are incarnations of female sexuality: they are receptacles for the divine oracles of masculine divinities. The names Heh-heh, So-so, and Bo-bo underscore this fact: all three names are euphemisms for the female genitalia.

If the *miko* is the sacred manifestation of female sexuality, prostitutes are its profane manifestation. Heh-heh, So-so, and Bo-bo thus also appear as procuresses, the babies of Jenny the prostitute on their back, using their wiles to lure customers into a dead-end street of bordellos (*nukeraremasu*).[4] Tsuno Kaitarō has pointed out that "the Japanese word for hell, *jigoku,* is also argot for both prostitutes and their brothels."[5] Thus, in their guise as procuresses, Heh-heh, So-so, and Bo-bo are also guides to hell. This hell is not merely personal. It is the real historical inferno into which the Japanese as a people were led in World War Two.

Heh-heh, So-so, and Bo-bo's identity as cats explains their maliciousness and their ability to metamorphose into whatever form best serves their mischievous purposes. The ornithological symbolism characteristic of Japanese male shamans is conspicuously absent in their female counterparts. Instead, female shamans are frequently identified with cats. In Japanese legend, the benign passivity of the domestic cat is thought to conceal an active, malignant side. Cats are reputed to eat small children, and they have the ability to assume the identity and form of the human beings they devour. These metamorphosing felines are known generically as *bake-neko* and are the perennial subject of Japanese horror films. Heh-heh, So-so, and Bo-bo reveal at the end of the play that they are *bake-neko*. They wear blond wigs, chew gum, and claim to be Santa Claus because they are the most recent, American-style manifestations of these hoary Japanese archetypes.

These four interrelated aspects of the identity of Heh-heh, So-so, and Bo-bo correspond to the other characters in the play. As *miko,* they correspond to the Guardian, priestly protector of the Lord of the Dawn. As incarnations of the female genitalia, they corresponds to the phallic identity of the Lord of the Dawn. As procuresses, they lure the five characters into "hell"; and as cats they systematically oppose the aims of the rats, the five Nezumi Kozōs.

Miko_____Guardian

Female Genitalia_____Lord of the Dawn

Guides to Hell_____Five Characters

Cats_____Rats (Nezumi Kozō)

NEZUMI KOZŌ JIROKICHI

The five characters' confusion of the atomic bomb for a wish-fulfilling falling star is reflected in their confusion of Nezumi Kozō for a messianic redeemer.

Nezumi Kozō Jirokichi (real name: Nakamura Jirokichi) was a nineteenth-century burglar who, like Robin Hood, stole from the rich and gave to the poor. He was known as "The Rat" (Nezumi Kozō) because it was thought that the wealthy were as powerless to prevent his entry as they were to prevent the incursion of mice.

Nezumi Kozō was beheaded on August 18, 1831, but death only led to his apotheosis. To this day, he continues to be worshipped as a god who will aid those who appeal to him. In fact, so many pilgrims to his grave at the Ekōin Temple in the Ryōgoku section of Tokyo chip away pieces of his tombstone for charms that substitute stones (*omaedachi*) have had to be constructed since shortly after his death. The *Asahi* newspaper of January 9, 1981, reported that the most recently constructed substitute stone, set up on December 25, 1980, was not expected to last beyond March.

Nezumi Kozō is thus not only a legendary Japanese hero but also a nineteenth-century manifestation of the archetypal redeemer in Japanese tradition, a plebian counterpart to aristocratic divinities like Kitano Tenjin, the apotheosis of Sugawara no Michizane, a martyred nobleman of a thousand years earlier. In short, Nezumi Kozō's apotheosis into a saving divinity capable of interceding in human affairs links him directly into the mainstream of Japanese religious experience.

If the five characters' confusion of the atomic bomb with a falling star is a disastrous misunderstanding, so is their confusion of Nezumi Kozō with the redeemer, however. The legend of *Balls-of-Fire Georgie: Knight of Liberty* underscores this point. Just as the three blond, gum-chewing, feline Santa Clauses are the postwar manifestation of the *miko* archetype, so Balls-of-Fire Georgie is the appropriately Americanized postwar version of the archetypal Japanese redeemer, whom Nezumi Kozō also represents. What is revealed in Balls-of-Fire Georgie is that the archetypal redeemer "is on the wolves' side," that his aim is not the salvation but the eternal damnation of the lambs who worship him.

It is not at all surprising, therefore, that Nezumi 1 (The Novelist) identifies the falling star with Nezumi Kozō. Both are thought to be redeemers who will fulfill the masses' fervent prayers for salvation; and both turn out to be monsters intent on their destruction.

What Satoh is saying, in effect, is that the Japanese have a catastrophic proclivity for confusing oppressors with liberators, demons for gods, atomic holocaust for fiery apocalypse. Moreover, in Satoh's view, this proclivity is rooted deeply in Japanese religious tradition, the very essence of what it means to be Japanese.

SELF-BETRAYAL

The problem according to Satoh is that the Japanese betray themselves; that so long as they remain Japanese they will continue to do so; and that the only way out of their predicament, the only way to prevent recurrent holocausts like the one that enveloped Hiroshima is to cease being Japanese, to die as Japanese, to commit symbolic suicide so that they can extirpate the fatal core of their collective personality. Satoh is of course aware of the irony in this prescription of suicide for the Japanese, always so prepared for self-immolation, and this accounts for the humor in these scenes.

Nezumi 5 embodies the self-betraying aspect of the Japanese personality and the will to expunge it. Her lament that she cannot die, her abortive lovers' suicide with Nezumi 4, her wish for a male child to end her life, and her final attack on the Guardian are all aspects of this important motif.

Nezumi 5 (The Prostitute) calls herself Jenny. She is named for "Pirate Jenny" in Brecht's *Threepenny Opera,* who also waited for pirates to save her from her unhappy life. As a woman, she represents the ineluctable reproductive capacity of Japanese culture that dooms it to reproduce itself generation after generation without change. She embodies the imagination that awaits the outlaw Balls-of-Fire Georgie even as it recognizes his true character, the imagination that cannot conceive of true liberation but only alternative forms of subjugation.

Jenny is aware that she "betrays herself" and that this is why she cannot die. As the personification of the self-betraying characteristic of the Japanese personality, she is aware that she is responsible for reproducing and, by bearing only female children, ensuring the continual reproduction of a culture that deludes itself into mistaking gunslingers for messiahs, an atomic holocaust for redeeming apocalypse. She wishes to bear a son who will end her life, who will, to borrow Walter Benjamin's phrase, remain "in control of his powers, man enough to blast open the continuum of history."⁶

At the end of the play, a dramatic revelation is made: The Guardian is none other than Jenny's son. Far from "blasting open the continuum of history," her male offspring is the staunch defender of the avatar of that continuum. This fact, while startling, is the logical extension of Jenny's limitless capacity, the Japanese people's limitless capacity, for self-betrayal. Not only does Jenny betray herself and guarantee the undying continuity of Japanese culture through her female offspring; she also betrays herself through her male offspring, who, rather than make a concerted effort to end the continuum of Japanese history and culture, actually defend it.

Faced with this realization, Jenny hesitates—then stabs the Guardian decisively. Jenny acts. She makes the only protest she can against the redundancy that Satoh believes characterizes Japanese history.

UR-HOLOCAUST AND HIROSHIMA

One of the unique things about Satoh's play is that it does not treat the bombings of Hiroshima and Nagasaki as a unique occurence. Rather, it conceives of the bombings as the recurrence of an archetypal event. Like the gum-chewing feline trio and Balls-of-Fire Georgie, the atomic bombing of Hiroshima and Nagasaki was simply the most recent manifestation of an ur-holocaust anticipated—and indeed longed for—in the most profound recesses of the Japanese imagination.

At the outset of the play, Heh-heh, So-so, and Bo-bo describe an immense conflagration. It immediately brings to mind Hiroshima and Nagasaki. But upon examination we realize that this is a more generic depiction of hell, akin to the images found in the late twelfth-century Japanese "hell scrolls" (*Jigoku zōshi*).

BO-BO: They're screaming amidst it all: Aaaa!! It's as if the earth itself were trembling, as if the earth itself were wailing! I can hear something crackling. Could it be the sound of human flesh burning?

SO-SO: Dance around amidst the flames. Little blue flames. Tens upon tens of thousands. That's right, those are human beings, human beings going up in flames!

Hiroshima, the contemporary manifestation of this hell-on-earth, is depicted in the scene ironically titled "Dream." The scene is so called because in Satoh's mind the bombing of Hiroshima and Nagasaki had so little effect on the course of Japanese history or the structure of the Japanese imagination that it seems almost as if the events never happened, like a dream. And of course contrary to the expectations of the five rodent revolutionaries, it is not the oppressive emperor system that suffered the effects of the atomic blast but themselves.

THE LORD OF THE DAWN WAS NOT THERE WHEN IT HAPPENED. BENEATH THAT SLOWLY FALLING STAR, BENEATH THAT BRILLIANT FLASH OF ENERGY, THE LORD OF THE DAWN WAS NOWHERE TO BE FOUND.

Finally, the holocaust is described a third time, as the adumbration of a future cataclysm.

In swamps and quicksand marshes
Man's slipshod cityplanning
Explodes:

Glass shatters,
Asphalt ruptures,
Concrete crumbles.

White shadow ghosts
Saturate stones,
A blood brotherhood
Till the end of time.

This could be mistaken for a description of the destruction of Hiroshima or Nagasaki, but from the imagery and the position of the poem toward the end of the play, it is clear that the cities being destroyed are not Hiroshima and Nagasaki but the metropolises of contemporary Japan. "Slipshod cityplanning" (*nurari to/ toshikeikaku*) is a reference to the postwar reconstruction Satoh describes in other plays, which conceals beneath its prosperous facade a rotten and festering substance.[7] Nevertheless, the passage clearly describes an atomic holocaust, and the reference to "white shadow ghosts" that "saturate stones" is a gruesome reminder of the ghostly silhouettes left by the bomb in Hiroshima.

In short, three distinct holocausts are described in the play: one past, one present, and one future. What is being described, in fact, is the ubiquitous vision of imminent, existential peril that has simultaneously terrorized and fascinated mankind since time immemorial. It is the cataclysmic event incessantly repeated in myth and imagination that the ahistorical, cyclical, "lunar" mentality rationalizes as the necessary beginning of a new cycle of time. As Mircea Eliade explains,

In the "lunar perspective," the death of the individual and the *periodic* death of humanity are necessary, even as the three days of darkness preceding the "rebirth" of the moon are necessary. The death of the individual and the death of humanity are alike necessary for their regeneration.[8]

Heh-heh, So-so, and Bo-bo's vision of an all-consuming and constantly repeated holocaust is as appropriate to their cyclical

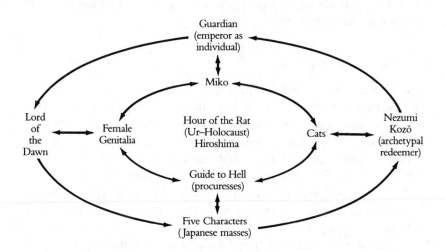

The model of Japanese history Satoh presents in
Nezumi Kozō: The Rat.

mode of being-in-time as the five characters' vision of the holocaust as a one-time, final event is to their historical mode. The interaction between the five Nezumis and Heh-heh, So-so, and Bo-bo is in fact a cosmic struggle between rodent proletarians battling for messianic redemption and the feline defenders of the myth of the eternal return.

Satoh's initial answer to the question why the atomic bomb was dropped was that the Japanese wished it upon themselves. In earlier plays, Satoh tried to account for this betrayal through the activity of omnipresent but unacknowledged forces that inhabit the Japanese imagination and neutralize its historical, redemptive impulses.[9] In contrast to these earlier plays, where the relationship between these forces and the Japanese religious tradition had been tenuous and conjectural, in *Nezumi Kozō* this relationship is fully stated and acknowledged. According to the formulation in *Nezumi Kozō,* the reason the five characters fail to capture the Lord of the Dawn, the reason the Japanese fail to effect a revolution and throw off the yoke of the emperor system is that they betray themselves, yes, but the specific nature of that betrayal is the powerful centripetal influence of the indigenous Japanese religious system, which pulls the messianic élan out of its straight trajectory toward the end of history into its own repetitive orbit.

THE HOUR OF THE RAT

The climax of *Nezumi Kozō: The Rat* comes at the point where the Nezumis' messianic élan is pulled out of its trajectory into the redundant orbit of Heh-heh, So-so, and Bo-bo. This happens during a banquet sponsored by the three women in the "hell" to which they have lured the Nezumis. We know from the broadcast of the Emperor's surrender speech that the war has ended. A popular song informs us that the time is the present. The Nezumis have full stomachs and are reciting prayers. They believe that they are close to their goal of salvation. However, they are blindfolded and thus blind to the truth: they have just consumed Jenny's baby girls.

When the truth is revealed, the five characters rise, remove their blindfolds, and wrap them around their heads. The headbands are white and emblazoned with a crimson "Rising Sun." The rodent revolutionaries have become kamikaze pilots.

Now they set off for "that object in the sky beyond," their ideal, but they do so as servants, not opponents, of the Emperor. The Hour of the Rat has arrived *and passed*. Instead of being a one-time, final event, it is the beginning of a new cycle. The long-awaited moment of redemption is revealed to be the point at which the messianic élan of the Nezumis reenters the eternally repeating orbit of Heh-heh, So-so, and Bo-bo.

The five characters have eaten Jenny's children, consuming the next generation, and the souls of the dead stream back, possessing them, transforming them into *ashura,* warrior spirits in Buddhist hell condemned to war for all eternity. Duration is annulled. Past and present coexist. History has been abolished.

It is significant that all this happens during an orgiastic banquet. The setting is appropriate to the Nezumis' reentry into the cyclical regimen of Heh-heh, So-so, and Bo-bo, which functions on the following assumption:

Any form whatever, by the mere fact that it exists as such and endures, necessarily loses vigor and becomes worn; to recover vigor, it must be reabsorbed into the formless if only for an instant; it must be reabsorbed to the primordial unity from which it issued; *in other words, it must return to "chaos" (on the cosmic plane), to "orgy" (on the social plane), to "darkness" (for seed), to "water" (baptism on the human plane, Atlantis on the plane of history, and so on).*[10]

The Hour of the Rat is that instant when "revolution" conceived as the culmination of history and "revolution" conceived as the initiation of a new cycle of time intersect, when those who aspire to an end to history are "reabsorbed into the primordial unity from which they issued." Thus, when we hear "The Jirokichi Theme" repeated at the end of the play, it has lost the tone of the revolutionary anthem it had at the outset and resounds as an ironical dirge.

A dim and steamy bath to wash away the past
Like slipping from the womb, naked slipping in
Only this time the markings of a man
Beneath the hot water, the silver blade of revenge!

Ah, just to strike once, to strike back just once!
To take the place of God
And strike back at all injustice!

A struggle to the death, how happy I would be!
To wallow in the gore, it would be true bliss!
And then to cleanse myself all over again
In frothy sewers deep and dark and dank.

Ah, just to strike once, to strike back just once!
To take the place of God
And strike back at all injustice!

On the tip of my tongue a twattled jelly-bean,
Can't get no satisfaction, sweet though it be.
Out of drive and duty I crawl from hole to hole—
I can still remember the taste of my first true love!

Ah, just to strike once, to strike back just once!
To take the place of God
And strike back at all injustice!

It sparkles a steely blue, oh yeah.
It sparkles a steely blue, oh yeah.

As we listen to this song repeated, we realize that from the outset the five characters' revolutionary cabal had been conceived, not in true messianic terms, which would have envisioned an absolute end to history, but in the terms of cyclical renewal. "A dim and steamy bath to wash away the past" (water), "a struggle to the death" (chaos), a "crawl from hole to hole" (orgy) are all images of "the primordial unity" into which the five characters, representatives of the Japanese masses, long to be reabsorbed. Their dream of a revolution was from the outset cast in terms of the myth of eternal return.

As the Nezumis are reabsorbed into primordial chaos, they spew forth lines that describe the madness that envelops them. Two of their speeches are of particular interest.

NEZUMI 4: Sta-sta-sta-sta-sta-sta-sta. When the sta-sta priest comes around, hang five and seven talismans from your belt, wrap your head tightly round; give up on life, give up on death. The Buddha is in life and death. Where there is the Buddha, there is neither life nor death. The cycle of life and death is nirvana. One should not eschew this cycle, but embrace it! Then the distance between life and death is the sole great Karma of all things. Ah, well, well . . . .

NEZUMI 2: Contradictions are universal and absolute, but the way in which contradictions are reconciled, that is, the form of struggle, differs in accordance with the quality of the contradictions themselves. There are contradictions which are characterized by outright antagonism, and there are others which are not. Based on our concrete discoveries concerning the nature of the world, we know that there are cases where originally non-antagonistic contradictions develop into antagonistic contradictions, and, furthermore, where originally antagonistic contradictions have developed into non-antagonistic . . . . (*He stops in midsentence, looks up at the sky and grins.*) I'm strong, I'm really strong. Balls-of-Fire Georgie! One-hundred million Balls-of-Fire Georgies! One-hundred million Balls-of-Fire, attack!!!! Yaaaaa!!!!

Both of these diatribes sound crazy, but there is method to their madness. Both describe major world movements active in Japan that succumbed to Heh-heh, So-so, and Bo-bo's sirens' call: "Revolving you come to relative truth:/ Clean is dirty, dirty is clean/ And all is a limitless grey." The first refers to late Mahayana Buddhism's doctrine of *bonnō soku bodai* (passion equals Buddhahood), which was the diametric opposite of the Buddha's original teaching; and the second is a typically prolix Maoist pronouncement that indicates the degeneration of Communism into a relativist, historicist doctrine.

In other words, in Satoh's view, even the most powerful soteriological movements like Communism and Buddhism inevitably degenerate into their opposites and compromise with the cycle of time they originally sought to escape. Satoh is saying that we are all doomed to repeat forever the cycle of incessant death and destruction until, inevitably, atomic cataclysm ends human life on earth permanently.

Does Satoh hold out no hope at all, then? In the last moments of the play, Jenny confronts the Guardian, who is wearing a clock whose hands are permanently fixed at twelve o'clock, the Hour of the Rat. He begs Jenny, his mother, to remove the clock. Otherwise, he wails, "it will be the Hour of the Rat forever!"

Jenny's answer is to attack the Guardian. This is not *dues ex machina* but an authentic contemporary, secular messianism. Satoh has just demonstrated that all movements no matter how formidable are necessarily foredoomed to compromise before achieving their goal. Nevertheless, he insists upon the legitimacy of the messianic promise and the possibility of true revolution. Tsuno accurately interprets this ending.

What sort of history is it the rhythms of which neither revolution nor nuclear war can affect? Amidst the dull continuity that paces these rhythms, what sort of action is available to us? Jenny stabs the Guardian to death. But . . . I cannot help thinking of her violent act—less, I admit, because of its meaning than because of its tone of desperation—as something very close to political agitation calling for the immediate rupture of that continuity that damns us. In analyzing Marx's language, Maurice Blanchot discovered in it a tendency to discuss the revolution not as a necessity to be achieved within time limits but as an "immanence." And he goes on to comment to the effect that "if revolution is to carve time, cross-section it, and persist as a requirement of life, then the refusal of respite itself must be the signal characteristic of the revolution." It almost seems that by placing this pathetic, violent scene at the end of his play, Satoh has tried to once again call back the revolution which should always remain alive, promised neither by calendars nor stars, into our precarious lives.[11]

Satoh, while rejecting the Hour of the Rat and false messiahs like Nezumi Kozō, nevertheless insists on the possibility of revolution "as immanence" and on the legitimacy of the messianic promise. He shares the mysticism of Walter Benjamin, whom he quotes frequently in the epigraphs to his plays. Benjamin argued that in order for the "puppet called 'historical materialism' . . . to win all the time . . . [it would have to enlist] the services of theology." Satoh also wishes to view "every second of time [as] the strait gate through which the Messiah might enter." And like Benjamin's ideal historical materialist, he seeks in *Nezumi Kozō: The Rat* to remain "in control of his powers, man enough to blast open the continuum of history" and establish "a conception of the present as the 'time of the now' which is shot through with chips of Messianic time."[13]

NEZUMI KOZŌ: THE RAT

by Satoh Makoto

Jiyū gekijō (The Freedom Theatre) first performed *Nezumi Kozō: The Rat (Nezumi Kozō Jirokichi)* in October 1969 in a production directed by the playwright. This translation is from the text included in Satoh Makoto, *Atashi no biitoruzu* (Tokyo: Shōbunsha, 1970).

CAST OF CHARACTERS

Heh-heh
So-so
Bo-bo
Nezumi 1
Nezumi 2
Nezumi 3
Nezumi 4
Nezumi 5
Guardian
An Object Worshiped as "The Lord of the Dawn"

There is absolutely no need for the place to resemble a theater. Any relatively large room will suffice. Aside from a talismanic Shinto rope (shitodachi) hung over the entrance, the room is left untouched. Thus, the performance area will be perhaps 18 feet across and empty. It would be best if lighting were done as much as possible with candles.

OVERTURE

CHORUS:*
Across the complacent face of peace
Let us white blood spatter:
As Great Japan wanders from gloom
To yet another gloom,
Suddenly,
Neither close to home nor far away,
The rising sun on aged pines and young bamboo
Turns to midnight black!

This is a realm where
Heaven revolves about the earth
And souls transmigrate:
One on top and six a-bottom,
The dice roll of
A hundred black mouse-heads,
The heads of actor-beggars.

Between the world of men and of heaven,
A thirteenth floor.
We are the fantasy mingling of reverie and truth
Who perform here the limits of distraction.

Treading the ever-changing dark,
The wind about us swirls,
And as lost to ourselves as to the world,
Into frenzy dance we.

*In the original production, the lines of the chorus were performed in the classical *nagauta* style of Kabuki chanting by professional musicians taped beforehand. The music was composed by Miyama Masaya, a member of the Kineya family of *shamisen* virtuosos.

ONE

Heh-heh, So-so, and Bo-bo enter casting salt before them in a ritual of purification. They are dressed to give the impression they are Shinto priestesses.

HEH-HEH, SO-SO, AND BO-BO:
Purify heaven. Cleanse the earth.*
May the within and the without be purged of all
    contamination,
And may the six senses be free of distortion.
Gods! Hear thy names called!
From the four emperors of heaven above
To Enma, Dark Consul of the Five Roads, King of the Law,
    below.
The gods of heaven, the gods of earth;
In the home, the gods of the well and deities of the hearth;
In Ise, the Goddess of the Sun, Amaterasu;
In the land of Sanuki, Kompira, bodhisattva, savior, Lord
    of the Sea;
In Settsu, the great light Sumiyoshi,
And Kasuga in Yamato;
In Yamashiro, Giongozutennō
And Kashima Katori in Shimo-Osa.

But beside all these, the gods of our land:
Ichinomiya's Hikawa, light of the world;
Hiesannō, his divine highness;
Kanda Daimyōjin;
The god of Tsumakoi Inari and of Inari in Ōji.
The panetheon of all the gods in the more than sixty
    provinces of Japan: The Great Shrine of Izumo.

We tremble before the numberless Buddhas,
The myriad gods,
And the infinite road of darkness.
But we call upon the gods to come before us here and now
And tell us all there be in the world!

---

*This is an adaptation from the Shinto liturgy of an actual *kami-oroshi* ritual for "bringing down the gods."

The spirits of the six relations:
Father, children;
Elder brothers, younger brothers;
Husbands and wives—
Both our own and those of others.
The spirits of all the forebears of every generation.
Parents paired like arrow and bow.
Brothers first to last.
All men will part some day as will the waters of the world.

Only power remains unchanged,
The altar of every temple resounding in sympathy with its
 tone.

Ululating, they prostrate themselves. Cicadas begin to sing raucously.
The Guardian enters with an austere gait. He is dressed in a richly
brocaded divided skirt (hakama) *over a formal kimono; and he sol-*
emnly bears the Lord of the Dawn. He halts at an appropriate place.*

GUARDIAN: It was a fine way to meet the day! And a perfectly
 lovely morning as always. Plenty of sleep and just enough
 appetite. I'm the peaceful Guardian. A blessed, joyous calling. We proceeded to the toilet, performed the lavabo, exer-
 cised to *Everyone's Physical Fitness* on the radio, and recited
 the rosary a hundred times, no less. Truly refreshing for body
 and soul! Casting our gaze abroad from our vantage point
 atop this hill, we can see the smoke of humble morning
 chores climbing skyward from houses in the village.† How

---

*In the original production, the Lord of the Dawn was a five-foot tall phallus
constructed of foam rubber and decorated with Shinto regalia.

†This line, *"Kono oka no ue kara miwataseba, machi no ie-ie kara wa tsutsumashii
asa no shitaku no kemuri ga tachinobori , . . ."* echoes a universally recognized
"land-praising song" found in the *Shinkokinshū,* an anthology of Japanese poetry completed in 1201: *"Takaki ya ni noborite mireba/ Kemuri tatsu tami no
kamado wa nigiwainikeri."* The poem is attributed to Emperor Nintoku (r.
885–889), and we are meant to understand from this paraphrasing that the
Guardian represents the Japanese emperor and the Lord of the Dawn, whose
name clearly indicates "the spirit of the rising sun," is the transhistorical Imperial Spirit that legitimates each succeeding emperor and imbues him with
sacerdotal authority.

green the rice paddies! How sparkling the rivulets! Not a
thing missing. Isn't it just the picture of perfection? To all a
good morning! A fine day today! A fine day today! (*He takes a
deep breath and then intones*): Make way for the Lord of the
Dawn!

*Instantly the cicadas stop singing. Guardian sets Lord of the Dawn
down and majestically stands beside it.*

HEH-HEH: In the sky, sparkling brilliant. Did you see it? Yai!

SO-SO: Indeed I did! Red-red-red!

HEH-HEH: Did you hear it? Yai!

BO-BO: Indeed I did! Boom-boom-boom!

HEH-HEH: Oh! In the name of heaven!

SO-SO AND BO-BO: Red-red-red and boom-boom-boom!

GUARDIAN (*repeating*): Make way for the Lord of the Dawn!

SO-SO: Beyond all imagination! Dazzling! Blinding!

BO-BO: Like an enormous fire!

GUARDIAN: I say, fire? (*He looks around.*)

BO-BO: Everything's on fire! Hither and yon: boom-boom-
boom the forests roar!

SO-SO: A deep red flood of floods!

BO-BO: They're screaming amidst it all: Aaaaa!! It's as if the
earth itself were trembling, as if the earth itself were wailing! I
can hear something crackling. Could it be the sound of human flesh burning?

SO-SO: Dance around amidst the flames. Little blue flames.
Tens upon tens of thousands. That's right, those are human
beings, human beings going up in flames!

GUARDIAN: May I remind you that you are in THE PRESENCE!!!

HEH-HEH: With fear and trepidation, may we ask? . . .

GUARDIAN: What is it?

HEH-HEH: With fear and trepidation, was the Lord of the
Dawn's awakening this morning as incomparable as always?

GUARDIAN: Get to the point. (*There is annoyance in his voice.*)

HEH-HEH: With fear and trepidation, there seems to be something different about the Lord of the Dawn this morning.

SO-SO: Red-red-red!

BO-BO: Boom-boom-boom!

GUARDIAN: As you well know, I'm the Guardian, the one and

only Guardian. You trying to make a fool out of me or something?

HEH-HEH: From the edges of the sky, a silver pod . . . like the
wind . . . .

GUARDIAN: Look, if, chance in a million, there were something
wrong with the Lord of the Dawn, it would be your humble
servant's fault, see. I'm always close by guarding Him, so
there's not likely to be anything amiss. (*Firmly*): The Lord of
the Dawn's awakening this morning was, as always, a truly
enriching experience!

BO-BO: Boy what a bureaucrat!

SO-SO: The only one who had a pleasant "good morning"
around here is you. You've got a lot of nerve bringing the
Lord of the Dawn in on the deal.

GUARDIAN: Shut up, goddamit! You sure you people are all
right this morning?

SO-SO AND BO-BO: Yes, we're fine, just fine. (*Looking at each
other*): Aren't we?

SO-SO: Red-red-red!

BO-BO: Boom-boom-boom!

SO-SO AND BO-BO: Red-red-red and boom-boom-boom! Fire!
Fire! An enormous conflagration!

GUARDIAN: Not again!

HEH-HEH: With fear and trepidation . . . .

GUARDIAN (*irritated*): You don't have to fear and trepidate all
that much!

HEH-HEH: Indeed, we are most abysmally sorry. But with fear
and trepidation, it is a matter of the most ominous oracle.
Scarlet flames enveloping this reign of peace. Red-red-red and
boom-boom-boom!

BO-BO: With these very eyes!

SO-SO: With these very ears!

GUARDIAN: Don't be silly.

HEH-HEH: That is the omen. Believe it or not as you wish, but
beware of negligence, Mr. Guardian.

GUARDIAN: Are you threatening me?

SO-SO: Heavens no! It is the oracle of the numberless Buddhas
and the myriad deities. We heard it, all of us.

BO-BO: It gave us the creeps all over. We got exhausted.

GUARDIAN: Miss Heh-heh?

HEH-HEH: Yes.

GUARDIAN: Miss So-so and Miss Bo-bo?

SO-SO AND BO-BO: Yes.

GUARDIAN: This is a matter of some importance. A matter of grave importance. However humbly, we are speaking of the exalted manifestation of the Lord of the Dawn.

HEH-HEH: A point well taken. All the more do we humbly recommend to you, Mr. Guardian, the one and only legitimate Mr. Guardian, the reaffirmation of the Lord of the Dawn's exalted manifestation. Come, come! Goodness is best served quickly.

GUARDIAN: Well, if you put it that way. (*He approaches the Lord of the Dawn but stops.*) But, . . .

HEH-HEH: Is something wrong?

GUARDIAN: I'm scared! If something's really happened, what am I going to do? I'll be in some fix!

BO-BO: Oh my, where's your gumption?

SO-SO: I'll say!

GUARDIAN: Listen, I'm different from you. I've got responsibility, see, responsibility. I'm the Guardian!

HEH-HEH: So please fulfill that responsibility, Mr. Guardian!

GUARDIAN: I got the message already. My dreams weren't bad, but this has turned out to be one hell of a morning. I have an awful feeling about this.

So saying, he resigns himself and begins to examine the Lord of the Dawn. At first he is frightened, but slowly regains his confidence.

GUARDIAN: There doesn't seem . . . to be . . . anything wrong. As I suspected, this is some sort of mistake, isn't it?

HEH-HEH: Please look more carefully. Fearsome secrets sometimes lurk in unexpected places.

GUARDIAN: That's true, but . . . there's nothing missing . . . Aaaaaaa!!! (*He flees from the Lord of the Dawn and begins to shake violently.*)

HEH-HEH: Mr. Guardian, is something wrong?

GUARDIAN: It's . . . it's . . . .

The Lord of the Dawn has fallen over, and on the bottom is pasted a single sheet of paper. Heh-heh removes the paper and reads the message. She is eerily calm.

HEH-HEH: "By the Hour of the Rat!"*

GUARDIAN: The Hour of the Rat!!!

BO-BO: That's him all right, The Rat!

HEH-HEH: The Rat?

SO-SO AND BO-BO: Nezumi Kozō, The Rat!

Blackout. And then loud, mocking laughter. Nezumi Kozō (Nezumi 5) appears out of the darkness dressed in robber fashion.

NEZUMI 5: Give me room! Give me room! (*She scans the audience with a chilling glance.*) Thank you for your quick consideration. I am dressed inappropriately to greet you, but I beg your indulgence. May there be no ill will between us. My home is in Edo, my lowly robber's trade in the underworld. Lowly though it be, my technique requires no little prowess, for I always leave a notice of what I intend to steal and the time by which I will perform this self-appointed task. My victims seldom elude me, try though they might. My booty goes to those whose dreams may, by no other means, be fulfilled. My name? Nezumi Kozō Jirokichi, The Rat!

Music: The Jirokichi Theme. Dressed in identical robber's costumes. Nezumis 1–4 join Nezumi 5.

A dim and steamy bath to wash away the past
Like slipping from the womb, naked slipping in
Only this time the markings of a man
Beneath the hot water, the silver blade of revenge!

Ah, just to strike once, to strike back just once!
To take the place of God
And strike back at all injustice!

A struggle to the death, how happy I would be!
To wallow in the gore, it would be pure bliss!
And then to cleanse myself all over again
In frothy sewers deep and dark and dank.

---

*"The Hour of the Rat" is midnight according to the traditional Japanese system of telling time. Since *nezumi* means "rat," here the term also refers to the promised hour when Nezumi Kozō will arrive to steal the Lord of the Dawn.

Ah, just to strike once, to strike back just once!
To take the place of God
And strike back at all injustice!

On the tip of my tongue a twattled jelly-bean,
Can't get no satisfaction, sweet though it be.
Out of drive and duty I crawl from hole to hole—
I can still remember the taste of my first true love!

Ah, just to strike once, to strike back just once!
To take the place of God
And strike back at all injustice!

It sparkles a steely blue, oh yeah.
It sparkles a steely blue, oh yeah.
Blackout.

TWO

A burst of shamisen music like a drum roll. Then Heh-heh, So-so, and Bo-bo appear. As if they were pompoms, they wave the staves decorated with strips of folded paper (gohei) used in Shinto rituals and intone:*

HEH-HEH, SO-SO, AND BO-BO (*as if cheering at a football game*):
Come on, you can do it! Push harder! That's it, just a little more! Bear it! Bear it! Siss-boom-bah!

A gust of wind. Another burst of shamisen music which abruptly ceases as if drowned out by the wind. The three women stop what they're doing and listen. Silence. Then, the choked cries of newborn infants.

SO-SO: She did it!

HEH-HEH: Look more like greasy slices of bacon than human beings. Girls, all three of them.

BO-BO: The riverbed† hooker Jenny becomes a mother!

SO-SO: Did you know that at dawn she secretly made a wish on a falling star that pulled its silvery tail across the southern sky?

HEH-HEH: Big deal.

BO-BO: She mistook that star that got sucked up in the crud of the southern sky for a rain drop. She stuck her hand through the bars on the closet window and grasped at it.

SO-SO: Baloney. I heard her.

BO-BO: Her delirious rantings?

SO-SO (*mimicking*): "Dear falling star! I will become a strong woman. I promise to marry Georgie and protect the child, so . . . ."

BO-BO: If that's not delirious ranting, I'd like to know what is.

---

*Here and elsewhere, when I have felt it would enhance understanding, I have taken the liberty of supplementing the published text of the play to indicate how Satoh construed his own words when he directed the original production.

†In premodern times, dry riverbeds were one of the places where prostitutes of the lowest class, traveling theater troupes, and other pariahs could ply their trade. Jenny's nickname indicates that she and the others who identify with Nezumi Kozō belong to the lowest strata of Japanese society and represent the Japanese masses.

That Georgie isn't about to settle down with no bitch and babes. In the first place, where's he going to get the money to buy her contract with the brothel?

SO-SO (*paying no attention*): ". . . So, dear star, I implore you! Make my baby a boy. Not a girl, a boy! A round, fat boy with a fine little wee-wee all attached. I beg of you!"

BO-BO: See! Just like I said—three kids and not a single wee-wee among them.

HEH-HEH: Everything in this world is retribution for past deeds. All was determined during her previous life, no doubt about it. There's no point in wishing on stars. The fact that she doesn't know better is just her woman's foolishness.

BO-BO: Oui, oui.

SO-SO (*still paying no attention*): ". . . A boy! Absolutely and positively a boy! You see . . . I want him to avenge me!"

Nezumi 5, "The Hooker," enters haltingly. She looks haggard. Her clothing thrown about her in disarray, she is fearsome to behold.

HEH-HEH: Jenny! You wouldn't be sneaking out to register the births now, would you?

Nezumi 5 laughs forlornly and shakes her head.

HEH-HEH: Good, good. Of course you're not. But I'm glad to hear it. Premature, illegitimate, and female. You've about reached the end of your tether. The hooker falls in love with a customer and gets pregnant into the bargain. You can't stray much farther from the primrose path. Fate sees through everything. It was in the cards that you'd end up like this.

NEZUMI 5 (*vaguely*): I'm . . . I'm a very unhappy woman, aren't I?

HEH-HEH: That's the spirit! That's the spirit! Can't complain about that attitude. By the way, the kids are in the closet, right?

Nezumi 5 doesn't answer but nods.

HEH-HEH (*to So-so and Bo-bo*): Shall we?

The performance area darkens with light falling only on Nezumi 5.

CHROUS:

Only spring flowers protest her passage
Along Famine Road
To beg, to bless, to mourn.

Blizzard blossoms for winter snow mistaken
Not mad but halting helpless
Pressed on by the wind
She wends her dizzy, fated way.*

Nezumi 4, "The Actor," is squatting facing backwards.

NEZUMI 4: The wish to die is written all over your face. Nevertheless, you cannot die. Why? (*Nezumi 5 notices him.*) Because while you are eating your body, without knowing it, you are prolonging your life. It's as simple as that. It's because you're a female, see. This sort of talk's impossible for men. A man can't eat his body. What a man eats is soul. No vitamins in soul. And baby, once you've consumed it, that's the end. It just ain't gonna grow back.

NEZUMI 5: Who're you?

NEZUMI 4: Student of "Agrodramatics," actoragronomist . . . (*Turning around*): Ah!

NEZUMI 5: What's wrong?

NEZUMI 4: There . . . there's a star in your eye!

NEZUMI 5: A star?

NEZUMI 4: Look! In your left eye, see? A little black spot.

NEZUMI 5: Really? (*She takes out a compact and looks at herself in the mirror.*) How disgusting! I wonder what happened. I never noticed it before.

NEZUMI 4 (*considering*): Hmmm. By the way, where're you going so early in the morning? You certainly don't look like the milkman.

NEZUMI 5: It's the death wish. You were right. I've been thinking of dying. I'm . . . I'm a very unhappy woman!

NEZUMI 4: I understand. I understand. But, er, it's sort of a waste, with a body like that and all. You eat yourself and you fatten yourself up. You're a veritable incarnation of self-perpetuation.

---

*The lines recited by the chorus in this scene and the next are Satoh's adaptation of one of the myriad descriptions of lovers on their way to kill themselves (*michiyuki*) found in *kabuki*. For other examples in English, see Donald Keene, tr., *Major Plays of Chikamatsu* (New York: Columbia University Press, 1961).

NEZUMI 5: I'm just tired. I've lost my dreams and desires. The umbilical cord of hope's been cut—snip!—just like that.

NEZUMI 4: Weep!

NEZUMI 5: What?

NEZUMI 4: Weep!

NEZUI 5: Yes, I suppose. . . .

NEZUMI 4: I could make you my leading lady. I'm a real honest to God *actor,* you know.

NEZUMI 5: What do I have to do?

NEZUMI 4: Lovers' suicide! We die together! A masterpiece, my falling star beauty! Just the two of us! Come on, let's take a fling at paradise, what do you say?

NEZUMI 5: Falling star? My name's Jenny.

NEZUMI 4: Look! Here in my left eye. See?

NEZUMI 5: What is it? Oh, my heavens! There's a star in your eye too!

NEZUMI 4: Now do you understand? On that blue and flickering star in the south sky this morning? I also made a pathetic little wish!

Music: The Brain Curd Aria. Nezumi 4 sings.

With blue skies shining overhead,
The thought occurred to me:
My brain is just a moldy curd.
Not a strand of muscle,
Or a single corpuscle!
O Brain fade away,
Moosh–a–goosh–a–moosh!

With blue skies shining overhead,
The thought occurred to me:
Put your brain on sale!
The spiritual, cerebral,
You don't need either one!
O Brain fade away,
Moosh–a–goosh–a–moosh!

How useless is a sardine brain,*

*Sardines and other fish products are a favorite organic fertilizer in Japan.

Chemically fertilized, too.
Where can I find,
Oh, where might I find
A little pure night soil?
O Brain fade away,
Moosh-a-goosh-a-moosh!

NEZUMI 4 (*supremely confident after his song*): To begin from the beginning, let me discuss with you the fundamentals of Agrodramatics. (*He ad-libs the following explanation in a virtual torrent of words.*)

NEZUMI 5 (*interrupting*): Yes, but I don't understand why we have to commit suicide. I am a very unhappy woman, but you're a man in search of fertilizer, right?

NEZUMI 4: Well then, what sort of man would be right for a very unhappy woman?

NEZUMI 5: Oh, very unhappy women die alone. They die lonely.

NEZUMI 4: How?

NEZUMI 5 (*with self-assurance*): Anyhow.

NEZUMI 4: Listen, I told you, didn't I? The female body, see, is made "For Life." You've got a ways to go before you let the air out of that one. You'll never get anywhere trying to improvise. You've got to have a systematic, analytic approach to the problem.

NEZUMI 5: If I wanted to, I could die just by dunking my head in a bucket of water, silly!

NEZUMI 4: Go ahead and try it. If it were just a matter of buckets, we wouldn't have this problem, silly!

NEZUMI 5: You're terrible. All right, watch. (*She pinches her nose and holds her breath.*)

Long pause.

NEZUMI 5 (*no longer able to hold her breath*): I want to cry!

NEZUMI 4: Listen, what did you wish on that star?

NEZUMI 5: I wished that my baby would be a boy. I'm a very unhappy woman. I wanted to raise a happy man to avenge me.

NEZUMI 4: But the child was a girl.

NEZUMI 5: That's right.

NEZUMI 4 (*with feeling*): You can't believe in willpower. Willpower's good for nothing. It's a pile of crap. You know what I wished? I . . . (*Suddenly, tears well up in his eyes.*) This broken-down junk heap wished for a hundred tons of gray matter! (*He collapses violently in tears.*)

NEZUMI 5: You're a very unhappy man, aren't you!

NEZUMI 4: I'm no good. I lack conviction. Oh! I'm just a three-penny actor. Agrodramatics is a flop! You see this leg? It's always rejecting good ol' mother earth! And this rotten bean-curd brain? It's forever putting on airs!

NEZUMI 5 (*sympathetically*): You studied with all your might, didn't you? Independently!

NEZUMI 4: Oh, shit! It's that goddam falling star. It showed me hope's sweet vision! I hate that blue star! I'll die out of spite! That's right! I'll give new meaning to the word failure!

NEZUMI 5 (*with determination*): Let's go.

NEZUMI 4: Whither?

NEZUMI 5: On a thoroughfare like this we might be seen. Come, I've decided to commit lovers' suicide with you.

NEZUMI 4: Rea . . . really!

NEZUMI 5: Really.

NEZUMI 4: Oh, thank you. At last I can hold my head up like a man. (*With feeling*): Thank you from the bottom of my heart.

NEZUMI 5: Call me Jenny!

Pause. They gaze into each other's eyes.

NEZUMI 4: Jenny!

CHORUS:
"Farewell.
The time has come
To end the pain
Trapped like mayfly dreams within our breasts."
A lonely couple's fate, perhaps.

The cuckoo's last dying cry resounds
Like the voice of a mother who has sold her child.

"By parting now in this world
We will be as one in the next.
But come, we mustn't meet the eyes of men."
And clutching each other tightly,
Hurriedly they depart.
They disappear.

THREE

As the lights come up, we notice Nezumi 1, "The Novelist," Nezumi 2, "The Pickpocket," and Nezumi 3, "The Samurai" intertwined and undulating in a corner. Their movements are listless and unenthusiastic. Monotony.

NEZUMI 1: Lovely are the fields! And a good day for sunbathing. Nothing like it. In the final analysis, I am nothing more than the obviously indolent concatenation of tepid inner organs; but nevertheless, lazing about like this, all sorts of disparate things somehow seem to take on a certain comprehensive credibility. (*He yawns extravagantly.*) The time?

NEZUMI 3 (*looking at the sky*): The sun has swept into the central heavens and . . . well, it's already noon.

NEZUMI 2: Fart!

NEZUMI 3 (*with his face in Nezumi 2's crotch*): It's stinky! Oh, it's stinky!

NEZUMI 2: Hey, don't rub your nose around so much!

NEZUMI 3: Stinky, stinky! Oh, stinky!

NEZUMI 2: Cut it out, I said!

NEZUMI 1: Slower . . . with heart . . . you've got to feel it . . . feel it, feel it . . . deeply . . . In truth, our's is a pipeline existence: mouth to anus, mouth to anus. Our's is an existence run through and through by this pipeline regimen. Such bliss! One's heart goes pitter-pat!

NEZUMI 3: Ohhhh! These warm inner walls!! Their sweet rhythm! Slimy, slimy! Heaven, heaven!

NEZUMI 2: Listen! I've been telling you to quit it. Your nose is too soft, goddamit! I can't stand pulpy noses! Quit it now. I said quit it! I'm . . . I'm going to get serious in a minute!

NEZUMI 3: Marvelous. Let's live happily ever after, just the two of us.

NEZUMI 1 (*correcting*): The three of us!

NEZUMI 2: No! Don't be surprised! From now on I'm changing my life. I'm gonna undergo a drastic character transformation. Watch and see. I'll be damned if I won't do it!

NEZUMI 1: Oh-ho! I'm not particularly surprised, but it is a new twist. Turnip! I found a turnip!

NEZUMI 2: Gimme a turnip!

NEZUMI 1: It looks delicious. Just ripe enough and crispy.

NEZUMI 2: Gimme it!

NEZUI 3: Nope, it's my turn. Anyway, aren't you the one that ate the remains of that box lunch we found? And all by yourself, too.

NEZUMI 2: But I'm still a child. A growing boy.

NEZUMI 1 (*nostalgically*): Ah, that box lunch. Actually, I'm the one who found it. At first, I thought it was empty. It was already pretty late. I thought the guys in that territory had already fingered it for sure. But when I opened the cover, there was a half-eaten egg, a whole piece of broiled fish, and more than half the rice with a pink imprint where the pickled plum had been. I was so happy. I thought to myself, "Boy, I've really struck gold this time!"

NEZUMI 3: Right. You really do find all kinds of things. We've got nothing but admiration for you. What can I say? Ah, yes. In other words, it's a kind of gift.

NEZUMI 1: You couldn't be more right. (*He starts to devour the turnip.*)

NEZUMI 2 and NEZUMI 3: Ah!

NEZUMI 1: Not bad. Not bad at all!

NEZUMI 3: Not bad indeed. But too bad! Ah, turnips! (*He suddenly draws his sword and slashes away aimlessly.*) Eiiiii . . . mmmmmmmm. . . . Turnips! Shit.

NEZUMI 2: I gotta change my life. Sunbathing, chronic hunger . . . . I've had enough!!! . . . My knife!

NEZUMI 1: Knife?

NEZUMI 2: Yeah, my knife. (*He reaches into the opening of his kimono.*) It's gone!

NEZUMI 1: Oh, knife! (*To Nezumi 3*): He wants his knife.

NEZUMI 3: Knife?

NEZUMI 2: Okay, goddamit.

NEZUMI 3: What is it?

NEZUMI 2: You pinched it! You gutter rats! What did you do with my knife? My genuine "Balls-of-Fire" brand knife!

NEZUMI 3: Okay, cut the kidding. Let's have another whiff of the stinky place. Sniff-sniff.

NEZUMI 1: That was a pretty good knife, wasn't it? No complaints about cutting edge. It glittered and had this real dangerous look about it.

NEZUMI 2: Give it back!

NEZUMI 3: How sweet it is! Up and up it goes, where it'll stop, nobody knows. Oh, stinky, stinky!

NEZUMI 2: Quit it! Goddamit! My knife! What'd you do with it? (*Throwing Nezumi 3 aside, he grabs Nezumi 2 by the lapels.*)

NEZUMI 1: That was your kinfe all right. No objections there. Let's agree on that completely. How about it? I suppose that clears things up pretty nicely. Right? Or maybe you're still not satisfied?

NEZUMI 2: You son-of-a-bitch! You think I'm gonna fall for that?

NEZUMI 1: Still not satisfied, eh? (*To Nezumi 3*): What shall we do?

NEZUMI 3: How about this? What if we were prepared to guarantee you, here and now, the ownership rights to all the knives in the world? That should make you feel better. Henceforth you shall be known as the "Knight of Kinetic Knifery." Okay?

NEZUMI 1: Okay?

NEZUMI 2: Metaphysical! The problem is my knife! If you think you're going to get away with this you've got another thing coming!

NEZUMI 3: But why do you doubt us?

NEZUMI 2: Because you're so damned dubitable, that's why!

NEZUMI 3: Reasonable, I suppose.

NEZUMI 1: By the way, I found another turnip.

NEZUMI 2: Gimme a turnip!

NEZUMI 1: Sure, I wouldn't mind giving it to you. Why, I'm already near to bursting myself.

NEZUMI 3 (*sword drawn but lowered*): It's . . . my . . . turn!

NEZUMI 2: Hold it, pops. I'm a young man with a future. And I've got a very demanding metabolism.

NEZUMI 3 (*painfully*): One cannot but admit . . . nevertheless!

NEZUMI 2: Gimme it!

NEZUMI 1: I'll give some to you, too.

NEZUMI 3: But how are you going to divide it? You've got to have something to cut it with. (*He looks at his sword.*) And as you know, old bamboo beauty here. . . .

NEZUMI 1: Your worries are over. Ta-ta! (*Smiling broadly, he reaches into his kimono and comes out with the knife.*)

NEZUMI 2: Ah! (*He starts for the knife.*)

NEZUMI 1: Take it easy. What are you going to do for a turnip?

NEZUMI 2: The knife, it's mine!

NEZUMI 1: Now, we've already recognized that. What are you going to do for a turnip?

NEZUMI 3: What are you gonna do? Huh? What?

NEZUMI 1: First let's eat.

Nezumi 2 squirms with frustration. Nezumi 1 cuts the turnip exactly in half with the knife. Nezumi 2 and Nezumi 3 eat the turnip. They savor it earnestly. Gradually, the three begin to feel at peace.

NEZUMI 1 (*putting the knife back in his kimono*): How is it?

NEZUMI 3: Wonderful. In the extreme. (*To Nezumi 2*): Right?

Nezumi 2, lost in eating, does not answer.

NEZUMI 1: The stomach and liver, the heart and lungs—in intimate relation they undulate toward toward ultimate life. As they swell and as they shrink in the . . . how shall I put it . . . .

CHORUS:
Dream! Dream!
With life as short as high-noon flower shadows,
Bask in its shade,
Tickle each other lovingly,
And dream!

Nezumi 4 enters. He is in a dire state. He has failed to die.

NEZUMI 4: This is crazy. Incredible! This sort of thing just doesn't happen. I strangle her, and she just keeps on breathing. Under water, she just breathes away like blazes. I slash her here, and she stabs me there. Blood gushes all over the place, but we don't die. We're just tingling with life. We can't die! We can't die! Ah, we can't die! I just didn't put enough feeling into it, that's it. This is a matter of a definitive deficiency of discipline.

NEZUMI 1 (*to no one in particular*): Shall I give you a turnip?

NEZUMI 2: Gimme a turnip.

NEZUMI 1: You seem somehow lifeless. One mustn't overlook the spiritually depleted. Poor boy.

NEZUMI 4 (*suddenly realizing he is not alone*): And whom might you be?

NEZUMI 2: Gimme a turnip.

NEZUMI Shh. I thought I'd eat again later, so I left mine from before. I'll give it to you, so just relax.

NEZUMI 4: More than spiritually, physically. You may not believe this, but I'm tired from dying. (*He laughs stupidly and collapses.*) This is crazy. And embarrassing!

NEZUMI 1: Heavens no. I sincerely believe you. I have no trouble coping with other people's misfortunes. Why, I'm even willing to sympathize with you. Rest assured!

NEZUMI 4: Thank you! You don't know what this means to me. Ah, and yet! The fact is, I have just failed at lovers' suicide! I cold-bloodedly ruined the crowning achievement of my aesthetic career! Wretch!

NEZUMI 3: The penalty for failure at lovers' suicide is death!

NEZUMI 2 (*immediately upon finishing Nezumi 3's turnip*): Gimme a turnip!

NEZUMI 1: There aren't any more turnips. Those were the last. (*To Nezumi 4*): But, if it was a lovers' suicide, there must have been another? . . .

NEZUMI 3 (*bending forward*): In other words, your . . . .

NEZUMI 4: I thought you'd never ask. Jenny!

Nezumi 5 enters.

NEZUMI 3: Damn, a woman!

CHORUS:

The trampled path through daffodil fields,
An endless approach to death.
A voice within their hearts benumbed
Hurries them on their way.
There is no appointed place, so
"Even this may be a spot for dying."

Nezumi 4 and 5 reenact their lovers' suicide as Nezumi 1, Nezumi 2, and Nezumi 3 look on.

NEZUMI 5: Looking as I do, I am unfit to meet with death. Please be patient while I retie my sash.

CHORUS:
Be this but a moment's liaison,
How far beyond the sweet reticence
A woman shows her husband
Is this respite to straighten front and back
Teetering on the brink of death.

Quiet and far away
Voices in prayer
Wander through the trees.

NEZUMI 1 (*chanting softly*): Namu Amida . . . Hail the Lord Buddha, Amida . . . Namu Amida . . . .

NEZUMI 4: Ah, joy of joys! I can hear prayers chanted in the distance. With those voices as companions . . . .

NEZUMI 5: Come, the road to death awaits.

NEZUMI 4: Hand in hand . . . .

NEZUMI 5: I am so happy.

NEZUMI 3: Hail the Lord Buddha, Amida . . . Namu Amida . . . Namu Amida . . . .

NEZUMI 4: Quiet your heart. Prepare yourself.

NEZUMI 5: Please bind my legs tightly with this piece of sash.

NEZUMI 4: Verily, you must not appear less chaste in death than in life. Here, I tie the knot. Ah! I fear it hurts you terribly!

NEZUMI 5: Be not concerned. Soon to be a corpse, my body no longer concerns me. Dear Actor, look at me just once more.

NEZUMI 3: Namu Amida . . . Hail the Lord Buddha, Amida . . . Namu Amida, Namu Amida. . . .

NEZUMI 4: Then . . . what of preparing our souls?

NEZUMI 5: I was ready long ago. Come now, here, straight to my breast.

NEZUMI 4: Don't rush me, don't rush me!

NEZUMI 5: No, we can wait no longer. Hurry!

CHORUS:
Woman's words are blades of tall grass
To a man of unsure footing.
Prayers in the wind sharpen the sword

To pierce the breast of human suffering.
And he lunges,
She thrusts,
He stabs,
She slashes.

Suicide has become routine to Nezumi 5, and her face betrays no emotion. Not so with Nezumi 4. He writhes with pain like a ham actor in a melodrama.

"Caw!" *a voice cries. It is Heh-heh. Cicadas buzz.*

Led by Heh-heh, the Lord of the Dawn's procession appears. Guardian enters next, a large wall clock strapped to his back. He carries the Lord of the Dawn wrapped in a purple cloth. So-so and Bo-bo follow. All three women wear air-raid hoods,* and the sleeves of their kimono are tied up with a cord that crisscrosses their back. Each carries a long sword under her arm.

HEH-HEH, SO-SO, and BO-BO *(singing an extremely well-known children's song):*

In and out and up and down
Knead and pound the dough.
The pestle's in the mortar going all around.
If it slips out all the fun is done.
The mice are in the storehouse eating up the rice.
Nice rice nice.
If your daddy calls you,
If your mommy calls you,
You must never answer back. No!
Who's the one who broke the cup
And left it near the well?
Was it you?*

The five Nezumis hurriedly kowtow. Their obsequiousness is infuriating. The procession passes and exits with great solemnity. The cicadas cease their buzzing.

---

*These are cloth hoods made of nonflammable material worn during the incendiary bombing of Japanese cities at the end of World War Two.

 *The song is *Zui-zui-zukkorobashi.* This translation may be sung to the traditional melody.

NEZUMI 5 (*rising to her feet*): Star! Falling Star! I knew all along—that I wouldn't be able to die. No matter how many times I've tried, I've never been able to die. It's not because I eat myself; it's because I betray myself. I'm not in hell, just dozing on its downhill slope, aimless and impressionable. Star! That's why I wanted a baby boy. I wanted my own son, with his fine little wee-wee all attached, to put an end to my life, my miserable existence. I wanted him to say, "Mother, prepare to die!" and drive his blade through my heart!

NEZUMI 2 (*looking up with the others*): Then you also . . . .

NEZUMI 5: What?

NEZUMI 2: It looks like you went and made a wish on that falling star this morning, too.

NEZUMI 4: Then . . . . (*He looks into Nezumi 2's left eye.*) It's true! The star's right there, big as life. That makes three of us! What an unexpected meeting!

NEZUMI 2: Wait a second! I'm not the only one. All three of us . . . . (*To Nezumi 3*): Right?

NEZUMI 3: Forsooth. (*Indicating Nezumi 1*): This gentleman recommended it to us. "That's the bright star of hope," he said.

NEZUMI 4 (*to Nezumi 1*): Is that right?

NEZUMI 1: Look for yourself. (*He brings his face right up to Nezumi 4 and exposes his left eye.*)

NEZUMI 4: No mistake about it!

NEZUMI 2: I wished to change my life.

NEZUMI 1: I see . . . . I wished that my life would never change.

NEZUMI 3: Myself, I wished for three sweet dumplings.

NEZUMI 5: What's this all about anyway?

NEZUMI 1: About? In brief, this is what.

Break. They look into each other's left eye and recoil in astonishment.

NEZUMI 1: But didn't you realize? That star was nothing but a disguise for the most notorious outlaw in all Edo, that great Nezumi. . . .

NEZUMI 4: Nezumi? You mean? . . .

NEZUMI 1: Hey, turnips!

NEZUMI 2: Gimme a turnip!

NEZUMI 1: This time there are five. Let's all eat them together.

NEZUMI 5: Nezumi? (*Realizing*) You mean . . . you mean that star might have been . . . .

NEZUMI I (*picking up the turnips*): Yes, that star was Nezumi Kozō, The Rat—our savior!

Blackout.

DREAM

The long whine of an air-raid siren. A banner appears with the word "dream" written on it in bold strokes. Heh-heh, So-so, and Bo-bo appear. Heh-heh is tightly hugging the Lord of the Dawn which is still covered with a purple cloth. The three women move around in the darkness, feeling their way with their hands. The sound of an airplane slowly approaches.

HEH-HEH *(screaming suddenly)*: Caw!!!!

An instantaneous flash of light. The three women prostrate themselves on the floor. The sound of the airplane fades into the distance.

A long pause. Then, Heh-heh cautiously gets to her feet. With great care, she removes the cover from the Lord of the Dawn. But under the cover is nothing but a hollow replica of the idol.

HEH-HEH: Yaaaaa!!!!!

Music.

SO-SO *and* BO-BO *(stentorianly)*: THE LORD OF THE DAWN WAS NOT THERE WHEN IT HAPPENED. BENEATH THAT SLOWLY FALLING STAR, BENEATH THAT BRILLIANT FLASH OF EN-ERGY, THE LORD OF THE DAWN WAS NOWHERE TO BE FOUND.

The music grows stronger, more violent. It suddenly stops and is replaced by the fierce wailing of a baby.

FOUR

A hundred waxed-paper umbrellas scattered about. From this point through the middle of Scene Six, these umbrellas proliferate unchecked. Actually, all nine of the characters are already on the stage but cannot be seen because they are hidden in the shadows of the umbrellas.*

The sound of a bell. First, Guardian appears. He is still carrying the wall clock on his back and clutches the Lord of the Dawn, still covered in the same purple cloth as before, to his breast. However, he is now wearing a quilted bathrobe.

GUARDIAN: Excuse me, I'd like to ask the way . . . .

Pause. There is no answer.

GUARDIAN: I am a man in search of a public bath! Isn't there a
    public bath in this neighborhood?

As a matter of fact, the cicadas have started buzzing again faintly in the distance.

> We ate the plum child.
> We ate the peach child.
> We ate the cherry child.
> Nen-ko-lo-ring.

Sing Heh-heh, So-so, and Bo-bo.

> Where is my eldest son?
> Where is my second son?
> Where is my youngest son?
> Nen-ko-lo-ring.

Sings Nezumi 5.

> The Lord of the Dawn
> Millions upon millions
> Of unfulfilled dreams
> A mountain of pebbles
> Nen-ko-lo-ring.

Chants the Guardian.

GUARDIAN: Please tell me the way! Which way do I turn for the
    public bath?

Laughter—as if someone were playing tricks on him. The voices belong to the five Nezumis. They do not show themselves.*

---

*Satoh did not use umbrellas as described here in the original production.

*In the original production, the lines spoken here by the Nezumis were delivered by Heh-heh, So-so, and Bo-bo.

NEZUMI 4: There is no bath, idiot!

NEZUMI 3: All the public baths have been remodeled as health centers—shit-head!

NEZUMI 4: They're under independent management and operate as liberated territory—bastard!

GUARDIAN: It must be the wind, the untutored wind.

NEZUMI 3: What wind?! Creep!

NEZUMI 4: Go find a sauna somewhere and roast to death! Middle-class ass-wipe!

GUARDIAN (*shaking his head*): This is madness, delirium. I've got to get a grip on myself. In the first place, I'm not middle class. I'm descended from a long line of bona-fide guardians, the elite of high society. In the second place, why should the public baths, playgrounds of the common people, up and disappear? As long as there are common people, the public baths will prosper. I will not succumb to the temptation of delirium. I am the captain of my destiny, the master of my fate! (*Shouting*): Whither lies the public bath!

Nezumi 2 pops up.

NEZUMI 2: I'm the untutored wind. Shall I tell you?

GUARDIAN: Thank you. I take back what I said before. After all, "the answer, my friends, is blowing in the wind," right? You must be one of the wind's star pupils.

NEZUMI 2: This is the public bath right here.

GUARDIAN: What? Where?

NEZUMI 2: Here. This is the "Floating World Public Bath."

GUARDIAN (*searching with his eyes*): I never would have recognized it. (*He pulls out a crisp, new ten-thousand yen bill.*) I'll have to get change.

NEZUMI 2 (*grabbing the bill*): No change, sorry. This will just cover it.

GUARDIAN: Hey, wait a minute. Why, just the other day, at the bath near my house . . . .

NEZUMI 2: Right, 35 yen is the going rate for adults, but we've got special prices for clocks and little pricks.

GUARDIAN (*pulling himself up to his full height*): Swine! What do you mean "little prick." With fear and trepidation, I'll have you know you are in the exalted presence of the. . . . (*He stops in midsentence, realizing that he must keep the Lord of the Dawn's identity secret.*)

NEZUMI 2: Fear and trepidation, eh? Can't say I know them. Anyway, I'll just keep this. Only see that the little prick doesn't pee in the bath.

Nezumi 2 disappears. In his place, Nezumi 3 and Nezumi 4 stand up. Nezumi 4 is completely swathed in bandages, but he is peppy as ever.

Seeing no alternative, Guardian removes the clock from his back, disrobes, and disappears behind one of the umbrellas. Obviously, the cicadas stop buzzing.

NEZUMI 4: What time is it, anyway?

NEZUMI 3: About five? (*Looking at the sky*): Mmm, about five o'clock, almost sunset.

NEZUMI 4 (*breathing deeply*): The air's nice. I feel like I could be content forever. For example, natural happiness . . . . See! I'm overflowing! I'm overflowing!

He jumps about like a grasshopper and then shakes all over spasmodically. In other words, he is demonstrating the fundamentals of Agrodramatics.

NEZUMI 4: See? Light as the wind. Physical aeration. A rather elementary etude.

NEZUMI 3: Like the wind? Interesting.

NEZUMI 4 (*still moving about*): Sing something.

NEZUMI 3: Huh?

NEZUMI 4: Sing something, come on. No, wait a minute. Don't sing. Singing! Unpardonable! First profound inspiration. Inspiration. Deep, broad, rich waves of inspiration extend outward, eventually gripping the diaphragm. Like this, see?

NEZUMI 3: No.

NEZUMI 4: The point is air! You take the primordial energy of inspiration transmitted from Mother Earth through your feet to your gut and transmogrify it into ethereal vibration. ZAP! You got that? (*At the top of his lungs*): GAAAAA!!!! GAAAAA!!!!

NEZUMI 3 (*feebly imitating*): gaa! ga.

NEZUMI 4: That's the essence. These ethereal vibrations will become the exquisite strains of song; they supply color and intricately delicate motion to physical locomotability that of its own accord becomes transparentized! Okay, sing!

Nezumi 3 sings something totally irrelevant. For a while, Nezumi 4 moves around in consummate bliss.

NEZUMI 4 (*overwhelmed*): That's it! We're perfect together! Just as I thought, you're . . . .

NEZUMI 3: Forget it. What a pain. As I've been trying to tell you, I have no interest in Art.

NEZUMI 4: But that's just it! You have a way of putting on airs, but the Agrodramatics I conceive is not mere entertainment or art. Comrade! It is a new style revolution!

NEZUMI 3: What?

NEZUMI 4 (*compromisingly*): . . . but we must be patient . . . .

NEZUMI 3: I'm all for revolutions. In fact, if you're saying you can carry out a fundamental revolution that will do something about the absolute state of vacuity characteristic of my stomach, you can count me in.

NEZUMI 4: But that's the whole idea! Indeed! All the more so! Yes! You and I together. We start out small but intense. We go big-time. New stars in the constellation of Agrodramatics! We take the lead and by ourselves becoming the salt of the earth, the world around us will be transformed into verdant fields! Ah! I can see it all now! If only I had realized sooner! The fertilizer of Agrodramatics is you and I. Come, we're off to the front. Now that we've decided, there's not a moment to lose!

NEZUMI 3: I haven't decided anything.

NEZUMI 4: You! . . . . (*He turns up the whites of his eyes and glares at Nezumi 3.*) You planning to spend the rest of your life in that sewer? Come on, you've got talent I tell you. I can see it. I'm counting on that wasted body of yours.

NEZUMI 3: Yeah, yeah. But I'm more of a man than you seem to think. Don't dismiss me too lightly as a wasted away old samurai. I've got hidden talent!

NEZUMI 4: Hidden?

Nezumi 3 suddenly draws his sword and lets out a bloodcurdling scream. A spray of blood appears on one of the umbrellas.

NEZUMI 3: Ambush!

NEZUMI 4: Not really! (*Looking at the sword*): But . . . .

NEZUMI 3: Of course, it's bamboo. It wouldn't cut paper. I just use it to threaten with. My specialty is young boys. For pleasure and profit. I don't make a bad living at it.

A groan.

NEZUMI 4: What's that?

So-so stands. She is dressed as a babysitter with a baby on her back. In her hands she carries a doll's bloody, severed head.

SO-SO: What are you going to do about this? It came off.

NEZUMI 3: This is a frame up!

SO-SO (*pointing to his drawn sword*): With that thing in your hand, how do you expect anyone to believe you?

NEZUMI 3: This is some sort of misunderstanding. This sword
. . . .

SO-SO: Humph. If you're going to make excuses, make them to the police. Or shall we settle it between us?

NEZUMI 3: Listen to me. Relax and look here. This sword is bamboo. See? Bamboo!

SO-SO: So what? With your foul sword play, you just . . . . My eyes aren't just a couple of knotholes, you know. (*To the doll*): Oh-oh! How sad! Before you could speak a word, you departed this world! Ah, how mortified you must be! Such bad, bad men. Inhuman monsters!

NEZUMI 3: Don't be unreasonable. And please don't raise your voice.

SO-SO: Who's being unreasonable! This is my normal voice. You got some objection?

NEZUMI 3 (*to Nezumi 4*): What shall we do?

NEZUMI 4: What do you mean, "What shall we do"? Let's get out of here before we get stuck in this up to our neck.

NEZUMI 3: Yeah, but somehow we seem to be pretty stuck already.

SO-SO: You're right there, you're right there. You'll never get away. Now, are you going to put this head back on where it belongs or are you going to pay me compensation?

NEZUMI 3: Er . . . how much is the compensation?

NEZUMI 4: Hey, forget it. She's some kind of con-artist. This is blackmail.

SO-SO: One million yen.

NEZUMI 3: That's expensive.

NEZUMI 4: What're you talking about? You know you haven't got a cent to your name.

SO-SO: And not a penny less.

NEZUMI 3: This is just great.

NEZUMI 4: All right, bitch, just take it easy. Even if we had the motive, how're we gonna cut anybody up with old bamboo beauty? Use your head. You keep this up, and we're the ones who're gonna go to the police. You'd better get the hell out of here while the getting's good!

SO-SO: I don't think I have to go anyplace. If that's the way you want it, we can go to the police right now. Let's go to the democratic, egalitarian police, how about it?

NEZUMI 3: You don't have to make things worse . . . .

SO-SO: Who's making things worse? I listen civilly to what you have to say and the first thing I know, you're taking advantage of me. Bitch? Who're you calling a bitch? Huh? You bastards aren't going to get out of this one so easily. Is this anyway to talk to a girl of my youth and beauty?

NEZUMI 3: I'd just like you to keep your voice down. It gets on my nerves. I haven't eaten anything but half a turnip since this morning.

Nezumi 1 appears suddenly, turnip in hand.

NEZUMI 1: Turnips again! Am I lucky with turnips or cursed by them? (*He eats and exits.*)

NEZUMI 4 (*to Nezumi 3*): Kill her.

NEZUMI 3: Huh?

NEZUMI 4: She says you murdered the kid with bamboo beauty, right? If it won't cut her up, then that's the end of her story. Either way, it'll settle things pretty nicely.

NEZUMI 3: Mmm. Resort to violence, eh?

SO-SO: Ha! You gonna cut me up? Okay, come on. Come on and cut me up. Go ahead. Go ahead. KILL ME!!!!!!!!!

NEZUMI 3: It's the only way, I suppose.

NEZUMI 4: So do it.

NEZUMI 3: But . . . .

NEZUMI 4: You're good for nothing. Okay, let me have the sword.

Nezumi 4 takes the sword and starts to slash away at So-so.

SO-SO (*screaming*): MURDER!!!!

NEZUMI 4: Die!! (*He stabs her again.*)

Bo-bo stands up. She too carries a baby on her back.

BO-BO: I saw that.

NEZUMI 3: Damn, another one.

SO-SO: Help! Murder! Police!

NEZUMI 4: Liar. You're not even bleeding.

BO-BO: It'll come, don't worry, it'll come. Spurting! You're a murderer!

NEZUMI 4: You're making a mistake. I'm a fully certified, genuine failed suicide. If I can't kill myself, how could I kill somebody else?

NEZUMI 3: That makes sense.

BO-BO: We've got all the circumstantial evidence we need. It'll be easy enough to prove motive. At the very least, you'll get sent up for attempted murder!

SO-SO: Murderers!

BO-BO: Anyway, come with us. Let's settle this once and for all.

The sound of a bell. Everyone exits. In their place, Nezumi 1.

NEZUMI 1: Another turnip! This makes 73!

Music: Turnip Blues. Nezumi 1 sings.

> Man is born of turnips
> And to turnips shall return.
> Turnips! Passionate vision of my soul.
> Witness of my dark devotion.
> Turnip, red turnip,
> You are my life!
> Turnip, white turnip,
> How I relish you!

NEZUMI 1: Nothing but turnips. The kid'll be all right, but the rest won't like it. Monotonous meals lay waste man's soul. Even if not a box lunch, I should at least be able to come up with a slice of moldy bread. If my talent for finding things were suddenly to change into nothing more than a talent for finding turnips, it would be a serious blow to my influence. That wouldn't do at all, not at all. This is where an organizer has got to have perseverance. A piece of fish sausage and a quarter of a rotten tomato would be enough. There's got to be something around here to eat!

Nezumi 1 disappears.

Carrying Lord of the Dawn and a towel, Guardian enters. He speaks as he scrubs what must be assumed to be Lord of the Dawn's back. Cicadas begin to buzz.

GUARDIAN: Oh, what a pity! What a pity! To think that the daily ritual of your bath has to be performed in a squalid place like this! I hate that Nezumi Kozō, that nasty Nezumi Kozō! But, I am the Guardian, the one and only duly appointed Guardian. So please rest assured. Even if I have to stake my life, I will watch over you through thick and thin. I'm not a man of many talents, but I've got backbone. What have I to fear from some sneak thief? You can count on me, yes indeed! (*Finished rinsing.*) Okay, let's get back in the tub again and soak. You mustn't get out until you've counted to a hundred. If you don't get all nice and warm, you'll catch a cold, you know.

Guardian and Lord of the Dawn disappear. The cicadas cease their buzzing.

Nezumi 1 reappears. In the vicinity where Guardian is hiding, a wall clock strikes five.

NEZUMI I: Ah! A turnip! This time it's a big one.

He pulls up the turnip, but it turns out to be the head of a doll.

HEH-HEH (*voice only*): Head-thief!

Heh-heh rises.

NEZUMI I: Huh? (*He looks at the "turnip."*) It's a head, not a turnip. And another babysitter-type!

HEH-HEH: You took it!

NEZUMI I: Sorry. I made a mistake. I thought it was a turnip. I was all caught up in my work. Don't take offense.

HEH-HEH: Give it back.

NEZUMI I (*innocently*): Of course.

HEH-HEH: Not the kid's head, his life. What do you think this is? You think he's gonna make it to heaven having been mistaken for a turnip?

NEZUMI I: Yeah, but . . . . The head's off and it's not going back on. That's obvious. You'll just have to resign yourself to the fact, that's all.

HEH-HEH: What are you, some kind of nut? Give it back! Give it back!

NEZUMI I: Don't be ridiculous. I'm sure you're speaking out of the grief of the moment, but you can't change the way things are. My sympathies. Well, if you'll excuse me. (*He starts to leave.*)

HEH-HEH: Hold it right there!

NEZUMI I: A fruitless discussion is a waste of time. As you can see, I'm extremely busy.

HEH-HEH: You're going to pay for this.

NEZUMI I: Oh, come now. How about a turnip and we'll call it even? (*He takes out a turnip.*)

HEH-HEH: No thanks.

NEZUMI I (*simply*): In that case . . . . See you around.

He starts to leave. So-so and Bo-bo block his path.

NEZUMI I: Ah-ha! So you came in force! Three women. You could have done better. I advise you to quit while you're ahead, ladies. Not only haven't I a cent, but I'm just the slightest bit provoked. It'll be time for supper soon, and I'm in a hurry. If I don't get home, my friends will starve to death. Let me pass!

BO-BO: No.

SO-SO (*threateningly*): You've got your problems and we've got ours.

NEZUMI I: Come on now! I'm pretty strong, you know. When I'm angry, I"m half crazy, see! I'm liable to go to extremes. Now get out of my way! Move!

BO-BO: Crazy? Good.

SO-SO: You're crazy and we're crazy.

And with this, So-so jumps on Nezumi 1. He is extremely weak after all, and she is able to finish him without the aid of her two compatriots.

BO-BO: Three down and two to go.

HEH-HEH: Don't worry about them, they'll get theirs soon enough. For the moment, let's take care of this one.

SO-SO: He didn't even put up a fight. How dull!

The baby on Bo-bo's back starts wailing.

BO-BO: There, there. Shhh-shhh.

HEH-HEH: Let's go, shall we?

HEH-HEH, SO-SO, and BO-BO:

We ate the plum child.

We ate the peach child.

We ate the cherry child.

Nen-ko-lo-ring.

Dragging Nezumi 1 as they sing, they exit. Nezumi 5 rises slowly, singing.

Where is my eldest son?

Where is my younger son?

Where is my youngest son?

Nen-ko-lo-ring.

Nezumi 2 peers out from beneath the umbrella immediately next to Nezumi 5.

NEZUMI 2: Dearest! I've waited so long!

Blackout.

FIVE

In the dim light, Nezumis 1, 3, and 4, like a procession of the blind,
pass through the performance area holding onto one another. All three
are blindfolded. Heh-heh follows them, teasing the headless baby on
her back with a pinwheel.

CHORUS:
　At the end of your long fall,
　The same old hell just waits for you:
　Vomit colored aspirations
　To whirlwind tour the womb.
　Flagellate malice
　Works its sterile way
　From Anemia Drive
　Into Shadow Alley where
　Illegible traffic signs read:
　No Parking! Slow Down!
　Morning-glory sickly faces
　Protrude through pickets,
　Murderers in pillory
　Trumpeting warning,
　"Don't piss on my feet!"
　Cannibal prostitutes
　Await their prey
　On dead-end streets
　Beneath banners reading
　"Through Traffic."

When they have passed, the lights come up a bit. There is the occa-
sional sound of water dripping. Nezumi 5 carries a small book. Nezumi
2 rests his head on her lap.

NEZUMI 2: It's cold . . . I'm hungry. When it gets dark, I get the
　shakes. I'm gonna catch a chill. I'm sorry.
NEZUMI 5: Why?
NEZUMI 2: Somehow . . . oh, never mind. . . . It's just that I
　shiver so much. It's always like this. I must be sick or some-
　thing.
NEZUMI 5 (*laughing gently*): It's all right. Don't worry yourself

over it. But you're right, evenings like this are unpleasant. Did you see the sunset?

NEZUMI 2: Uh-uh.

NEZUMI 5: It was probably black, anyway, and stagnant. Evening comes and then the morning. Tomorrow arrives and it's the same as today. It was probably overcast—yesterday was the same way. Last night I was groaning with labor pains. I felt so awful. I wonder how many that makes it? I've lost count. I just keep getting pregnant and having babies. Ten years? No, longer. It's been so long, I can't even remember. Every nine months bing! bing! just like that. Babies one after another.

NEZUMI 2: I'm gonna change my life. I'm gonna change my life. It's easy enough to say it. Can you remember what you were like ten years ago?

NEZUMI 5: It hardly matters whether I remember or not, I was the same as I am now. Nothing's changed. I've just produced baby girls one after the other, that's all. Not a single boy. I'd bring them into the world, then sell them one by one. All of them. They all looked just like me. All unhappy women. I'm everywhere. The place is crawling with unhappy women. Old Edo's going to overflow with them.

NEZUMI 2: Ten years ago. I was still a kid. Oh, goddamit! How did I ever wind up in a sewer like this. A damp room and pulpy noses. By now, I must be as unhappy a guy as they come. Won't you read to me? Anyplace.

NEZUMI 5: Anyplace?

NEZUMI 2: In that book.

NEZUMI 5: Oh, all right. (*Reading*): "Bang-bang! Bang-bang! Flame spewed from Georgie's twin pistols. 'This is extermination!' Winking his stoney eyes, Georgie was the perfect nihilist. 'My little lambs, too bad! I'm on the wolves' side!' Bang-bang!" (*She gazes off into space.*) Georgie!

NEZUMI 2 (*similarly*): *Balls-of-Fire Georgie: Knight of Liberty!*

NEZUMI 5: "Paling with fright as they tried to discover where they had gone wrong, one by one the lambs breathed their last. But this was useless reflection, for the lambs had made not a single mistake."

NEZUMI 2: Balls-of-Fire Georgie was our hero. When we played two-gunned Balls-of-Fire Georgie, everybody wanted to be the crimson-caped masked man. Georgie! Someday I, even I, will be like Balls-of-Fire Georgie!

NEZUMI 5: "This is hell, all right, but, lambs, I'll see you fall deeper still!' screamed Georgie laughing hysterically. Bang-bang! 'Not in hell but forever toward it—this is the policy I advance my followers. Lambs! Be not saved. Be lost!' Bang-bang-bang-bang!!"

NEZUMI 2: But actually, the story of Georgie galloping across the Great Plains was written in a tiny room in a corner of this very sewer. The Turnip King, he's the author. (*He embraces Nezumi 5.*) You're so warm. I can't remember how long it's been since I felt like this.

The two are silent. Guardian comes floating in.

GUARDIAN: Burble-gurgle-blurp-blurp. Burble-gurgle-blurp-blurp. Friends, this is incredible. However, I do not believe in the incredible. Therefore, I do not believe what is happening to me. I am not here. The me that is here is not real; and the me that is not me and someplace else is the real me. (*He sneezes.*) No mistake in logic, I trust. Individuals faced with incredible situations are usually too quick to accept that situation as "real," and they visit the most hideous confusions upon themselves. There we were up to our shoulders in hot water, and just as we'd counted to 90 the bottom of the bath fell out and we were washed down into this sewer. But I am the Guardian. I have the duty to protect the Lord of the Dawn through rain and sleet and hail. How could I possibly submit meekly to this kind of absurdity? Though my body may un-resistingly wallow in this stream of filth, I shall not allow it to muddy my reason! My reason is lily white! Why, it's virtually transparent! (*To Lord of the Dawn*): Please rest assured. My resolution is firm. I will find you a new public bath. Then we'll wash ourselves again all over and not get out of the tub until we've counted to a hundred—slowly. Okay? Well, burble-gurgle-blurp-blurp, burble-gurgle-blurp-blurp.

Guardian floats away and in his place Bo-bo and So-so enter. They approach Nezumi 2 and Nezumi 5, who are still locked in a warm embrace. So-so and Bo-bo pounce on Nezumi 2 and Nezumi 5 respectively, blindfolding them with strips of black cloth they carry.

BO-BO (*to Nezumi 5*): Aaaah! At last . . . .

NEZUMI 5: Who is it?

SO-SO (*to Nezumi 2*): You are Georgie!

NEZUMI 2: Huh?

SO-SO: It's Georgie, isn't it?

BO-BO: It's me, Jenny, Georgie. I, Georgie, to whom you bid farewell at the Bridge of Farewells, have returned just as I promised. Nine months to the day. Darling, what have you done with our child?

NEZUMI 2 (*quietly, testing*): Bang. Bang.

SO-SO: That's right.

NEZUMI 2 (*louder*): Ba-bang! Bang!

SO-SO: Good. Good.

BO-BO: Now, put out your hand. (*She takes Nezumi 5's hand.*)

SO-SO: You can escape. After all, you are two-gunned, crimson-caped Balls-of-Fire Georgie!

NEZUMI 2: Maybe . . . . No, but . . . Balls-of-Fire, I am . . . Georgie! . . .

BO-BO: Now, Georgie, your hand—your proud, strong hand. (*She takes Nezumi 2's hand.*)

NEZUMI 2: So, its finally changed. It's changed at last! My life's changed! I'm Georgie, you hear! Balls-of-Fire Georgie!

NEZUMI 5: Is it true? Are you really Georgie?

NEZUMI 2: That's me all right! Georgie, the one and only Georgie!

SO-SO: Georgie! (*She embraces Nezumi 2.*)

BO-BO: Oh, Jenny! (*She draws Nezumi 5 to her.*)

NEZUMI 5: Georgie! (*Hardly able to speak*): My love, my life! You didn't forget! You came for me! I'm so happy. (*She smothers tears of joy against Bo-bo's breast.*)

So-so and Bo-bo look meaningfully at each other.

BO-BO: At the end of your long fall . . .

SO-SO: . . . the same old hell just waits for you!

They throw Nezumi 2 and Nezumi 5 to the ground.

SO-SO and BO-BO: Ah-hah-hah-hah-hah-hah!!!!!!

The lights dim, leaving only So-so and Bo-bo illuminated. Heh-heh joins them.

CHORUS:
Three times for you
Three times for us
And then three times more.

Three times three makes nine times
Nine times makes a game
A game's a game of nine times.

You have your rules
And we have ours
And each will abide by his own.

You are the blades of a pinwheel
We set the pinwheel a-spin
Breathing for us is revolving for you.

Revolving you come to relative truth:
Clean is dirty, dirty is clean
And all is a limitless grey.

Once the spinning's started
There's nothing left to do
But wait your turn and suddenly

Fall one by one.

HEH-HEH: The wind's stopped.

The three women disappear.

SIX

Like the sound of the sea, now near, now far, a recording of the Emperor's World War II surrender speech is heard, mixed with the strains of a well-known popular song.

The five Nezumis are seated in a circle. They are all still blindfolded. They have just eaten and are reciting prayers on a long, communal rosary. A large, bubbling cauldron is placed near the center. The broadcast ends.

NEZUMI 3: I'm really sleepy. My first full stomach in a long time. Humph, it's natural enough . . . (*He heaves an exaggerated yawn.*) If we could only . . . .

HEH-HEH: Quiet! Silence is to be maintained at all times.

Nezumi 4 yawns loudly.

NEZUMI 1 (*in a small voice to Nezumi 3*): The time?

NEZUMI 3 (*sniffing with his nose*): Huh? You find another turnip or something?

NEZUMI 1: . . . no . . . .

NEZUMI 2: Gimme a turnip!

NEZUMI 3: How do you like that? He eats and eats, and it's still turnips! And tonight's meal was high-quality animal protein, too.

NEZUMI 1: It's just a habit. We should feel sorry for him. It's a sort of conditioned reflex. Turnip!

NEZUMI 2: Gimme . . . a turnip. . . .

NEZUMI 4: He's talking in his sleep. Kids are great, so innocent.

HEH-HEH: Quiet! I repeat, quiet! Thirty seconds. Silence is to be strictly maintained.

NEZUMI 4: Huh? Thirty seconds? Thirty seconds to what? (*To Nezumi 1*): Do you know?

NEZUMI 1: No.

NEZUMI 3: You think it's all right?

NEZUMI 1: What?

NEZUMI 3: You know . . . .

HEH-HEH: Twenty-five seconds.

NEZUMI 3: In other words, uh . . . twenty-five seconds before what? I mean, they say there's no such thing as a free lunch, right? I just have the feeling this is all too good to be true. I mean . . . the, er . . . .

NEZUMI 1: What are you whimpering about? And you call yourself a samurai!

NEZUMI 3: In principle.

HEH-HEH: Twenty seconds.

NEZUMI 3: You shouldn't discriminate against me just because I'm a samurai. Samurai get anxiety attacks just like anybody else. What's scary to you is going to be scary to me.

NEZUMI 1: Anyway, don't get so excited. Just keep your eyes pealed.

HEH-HEH: Fifteen seconds . . . ten seconds . . . nine . . . eight . . .

NEZUMI 4 (*to Nezumi 3*): You're shaking, aren't you?

NEZUMI 3: Forsooth.

HEH-HEH: Five . . . four . . . three . . . two . . . one . . . zero!

Nezumi 4 shrieks.

NEZUMI 1: Sh!

Silence. Nothing happens.

NEZUMI 1: See! That's what I thought. They were just bluffing. (*To Nezumi 3*): Right?

Nezumi 3 swallows down hard.

NEZUMI 5 (*to no one in particular*): My children. My new born babes.

NEZUMI 1: Huh?

NEZUMI 5: Triplet girls.

NEZUMI 1: I see. Females are rather repulsive. Especially three. . . .

NEZUMI 5: We ate them.

NEZUMI 4: What did you say?

NEZUMI 5 (*pointing to the cauldron*): They were in there. All three of them. Two without heads, one alive.

NEZUMI 4: . . . not . . . really . . . .

NEZUMI 3 (*again swallowing hard*): That . . . can't . . . be.

NEZUMI 5: I'm their mother. I know the taste of my own flesh and blood.

NEZUMI 4: Don't be . . . don't be silly.

NEZUMI 1 (*standing to give a speech*): To be perfectly frank, I have always had a deep sense of distrust in food. Food can never stray from the established one-way path from mouth to anus. Accursed fate! Nourishment to excrement—this is the normal, slow process of descent which forms my greatest concern. Shall I tell you my ideal? Shall I describe my dream? Shit to shit! Feces unlimited! What I am suggesting, ladies and gentlemen, is nothing less than the semiperpetual circulation of these feces! We of the pure pipeline races must unite! We must organize ourselves into communities of two and three people. And we must create the holy communion of mouth to anus, anus to mouth! Yes, my friends, we must move anew toward this goal: the creation of this Passionate Community!!! The end. (*He sits down.*)

Nezumi 2, fast asleep, claps.

NEZUMI 5: What did he say?

NEZUMI 3 (*still resisting the urge to vomit addresses Nezumi 5*): You mean . . . what we, er . . . I mean the soup of which we have just so greedily partaken was made out of . . . .

NEZUMI 5: My three babies, yes.

NEZUMI 3: You're kidding. Aren't you?

NEZUMI 1: Now that you mention it, it did bear a certain resemblance to human flesh.

NEZUMI 3 (*vomiting*): Upppphhh!!

The umbrellas vanish instantly.

Nezumi 4 stands, takes off his blindfold, turns it over, and ties it on again as a headband. This time it has the emblem of the Rising Sun against a white background.

NEZUMI 4 (*bowing*): Father, Mother, thank you for the food of which I am about to partake.

NEZUMI 3 (*similarly*): Thank you, Mr. Soldier. Thank you, Mr. Farmer. Thank you for the food.

They approach the cauldron. All but Nezumi 3 and Nezumi 4 disappear.

NEZUMI 3: Alka-Seltzer, Pepto Bismol, Carter's Little Liver Pills,* toothpaste, water color paints. Of all water color paints, red is the sweetest. Beans in my pillow.† Sweet beans. Throat lozenges.‡ Then frogs, grasshoppers, butterflies. I'll

---

*The patent medicines, all digestive aids, mentioned in the original text are *Ebios, Jintan, Wakamoto,* and *Seirogan.*

†Small beans are often used to stuff pillows in Japan.

‡*Asada-ame,* another over-the-counter medication.

eat anything. Then I'll get big and strong. I'll get big and strong, and I'll be chief of staff.

Nezumi 3 sticks his hand into the cauldron and slowly stirs.

NEZUMI 4: Sta-sta-sta-sta-sta-sta-sta. When the sta-sta priest* comes around, hang five and seven talismans from your belt, wrap your head tightly round; give up on life, give up on death. The Buddha is in life and death. Where there is the Buddha, there is neither life nor death. The cycle of life and death is nirvana. One should not eschew this cycle, but embrace it! Then the distance between life and death is the sole great Karma of all things. Ah, well, well. . . .

Nezumi 4 likewise sticks his hand into the cauldron.

NEZUMI 4: Ready!

NEZUMI 3: In the quiet countryside, resolutely we forge the mettle of our bodies and our souls.

NEZUMI 3 and NEZUMI 4: Get set! Go!

Dripping and decapitated, they pull one of the dolls from the cauldron and seize it violently from both sides.

They disappear and are replaced by Nezumi 1, who appears elsewhere on the performance area also wearing a Rising Sun headband and carrying a bamboo spear.

NEZUMI 1: Motherfucker!!! Say thirteen yen fifty sen!* Say it, say it! What's wrong, motherfucker, can't you say it? Thirteen yen fifty sen! Again! Clearer! Thirteen yen fifty sen!!!! Thirteen yen fifty sen!!! Motherfuckering son-of-a . . . . (*He plunges his spear into the cauldron and skewers a doll. This one has no head either.*)

Nezumi 1 disappears. Nezumi 2, also wearing a Rising Sun headband, appears in one corner sharpening his knife.

Suta-suta-bōzu were mendicant priests of a syncretic Buddhist-Shinto character who, during the early to mid-nineteenth century, wandered in the great urban centers of Japan dressed only in rope talismans (*shimenawa*) wrapped around their head and waist. *Suta-suta* is an onomatopoeic approximation of their steady, unrelenting gait.

*"Thirteen yen fifty sen" (*jūsan-en gojissen*) is a shibboleth used particularly in the prewar period to identify Koreans in Japan. They were supposed to mispronounce it *chūsan-en kochissen*. Koreans living in Japan have been the frequent object of discrimination and exploitation.

NEZUMI 2: Contradictions are universal and absolute, but the way in which contradictions are reconciled, that is, the form of struggle, differs in accordance with the quality of the contradictions themselves. There are contradictions which are characterized by outright antagonism, and there are others which are not. Based on our concrete discoveries concerning the nature of the world, we know that there are cases where originally non-antagonistic contradictions develop into antagonistic contradictions, and, furthermore, where originally antagonistic contradictions have developed into non-antagonistic . . . . (*He stops in midsentence, looks up at the sky and grins.*) I'm strong, I'm really strong. Balls-of-Fire Georgie! One-hundred million Balls-of-Fire Georgies! One-hundred million Balls-of-Fire,* attack!!!!! Yaaaaa!!!!

Placing his knife between his teeth, he reaches into the cauldron and pulls out the third doll, dripping wet. Then he plunges his knife into it. A baby's cry rings out. Nezumi 2 vanishes.

Nezumi 5 enters quietly, almost dancing. She too wears a Rising Sun headband. In her arms she carries an empty baby's gown which she teases incessantly with a rattle.

NEZUMI 5 (*cooing*): They'll die. They'll be killed. Every one of them will be killed. Never . . . never!!! I'll never give birth to a man! What's the point!?

Nezumi 1 through Nezumi 4 join her. Each has a mortuary urn hung around his neck.

CHORUS:

In swamps and quicksand marshes
Man's slipshod cityplanning
Explodes:

Glass shatters,
Asphalt ruptures,
Concrete crumbles.

White shadow ghosts
Saturate stones,

---

*"One-hundred million balls of fire" (*ichi-okunin no hinotama*) was the phrase used during World War Two to describe the transformation of the entire Japanese population into superhuman warriors.

A blood brotherhood
Till the end of time.
A siren reverberates through the room.
NEZUMI 1: A parting toast!
All drink together.
NEZUMI 1: Attention!
All line up at attention.
NEZUMI 1: Right face!
All do a right face.
NEZUMI 1: Our object is in the sky beyond: that falling star
  sparkling silver brilliant as it slowly describes its arc. Repeat!
NEZUMI 2-NEZUMI 5: Our object is in the sky beyond: that
  falling star sparkling silver brilliant as it slowly describes its
  arc.
NEZUMI 1: One! (*Responding himself*): Yessir! (*He takes one step
  forward.*)
The others follow suit.
NEZUMI 2: Two! Yessir!
NEZUMI 3: Three! Yessir!
NEZUMI 4: Four! Yessir!
NEZUMI 5: Five! Yessir!
NEZUMI 1: Salute!
All salute and then, holding that pose, take turns reciting the following.
NEZUMI 1–5: Please forgive us for preceding you in death.
  Mother, thank you for the jam and buns. They were deli-
  cious. Uncle, thank you for the grapes. They were delicious.
  Aunt, thank you for the stew you worked so hard to prepare.
  It was delicious. Great Uncle, thank you for the cigarettes.
  They were delicious. Great Aunt, thank you for the candies.
  They were delicious.
For a second time, the siren sounds. Gradually it darkens.
NEZUMI 1–5: Banzai! Banzai! Banzai!
By this time it has grown so dark it is almost impossible to see.
NEZUMI 1: The time?
Silence.
NEZUMI 3: Five minutes past . . . the Hour of the Rat.
*It is pitch dark. Cicadas begin to buzz. "In and Out," the children's
song sung earlier, can be heard and a procession becomes visible in the*

gloom: Heh-heh, So-so, and Bo-bo, in long, blond wigs and chewing noisily on sticks of gum; and the Guardian, in high spirits, laughing uproariously.

GUARDIAN: Advance! Forward! We're off to the hot spring! To Atami!* We'll rent a Roman bath big enough for a thousand people!

Again, it darkens. The buzz of the cicadas is all but deafening.

*Atami is a hot springs resort southwest of Tokyo.

SEVEN

Tympany. Heh-heh, So-so, and Bo-bo.

HEH-HEH: Be it day or dark of night.

SO-SO: Hot or cold, dark or bright.

BO-BO: Stars scattered through the heavens. Still a deep blue sky.

HEH-HEH: Mountain valleys, peaked space upside down. Or desert space, wide and open. Look!

SO-SO: Oh! The froth upon the waves. Multitudinous seas incarnadine! Red-red-red!

HEH-HEH: Time, a million miles per second. Stop motion! Listen!

BO-BO: Oh! The moaning earth voice. Surge, explode, shake, and tremble. Boom-boom-boom!

HEH-HEH: That is Great Japan. That is Edo old!

SO-SO and BO-BO: Meow!!

HEH-HEH: We're three cats.

SO-SO: Feline . . .

BO-BO: . . . all three.

HEH-HEH: We are the ones who give!

SO-SO: We are frizzly bearded . . .

BO-BO: . . . Santa Claus!

HEH-HEH, SO-SO, and BO-BO: Now is the time to give! Now is the time to give!

They strike a dramatic pose.

Laughter rocks the room. It's Nezumi Kozō: The Rat!

NEZUMI 1–NEZUMI 5 (*from off stage*): Now is the time to steal! Now is the time to steal!

Nezumi 1 bursts into the performance area in robber's gear. Percussion.* Heh-heh, So-so, and Bo-bo engage Nezumi 1. Nezumi 2, Nezumi 3, and Nezumi 4 next enter by turns and clash with Heh-heh and the others. They are dressed like Nezumi 1 in robber's gear. One by one they flee or chase the cats away until only Guardian remains. Then he too disappears.

_____

*This climactic scene was conceived and directed as a *tate* or traditional kabuki melee. It was to be accompanied by the staccato punctuation of the wooden clappers used in kabuki.

Nezumi 5 enters, reconnoitering.

GUARDIAN (*without showing himself*): Ma! . . . Mommy!

Nezumi 5 spins around, taken by surprise. The Guardian, still hugging Lord of the Dawn, is hanging upside down, spattered with blood. The hands on the clock on his back are fixed at midnight. It strikes ten times, twenty times, thirty times, on and on without end.

GUARDIAN: Take it off—take the clock off! It's heavy. It's so
   damned heavy. Please . . . Mother . . . take it off, take it off
   my back . . . Please, Mother . . . Mother! At this rate it will
   be the Hour of the Rat forever! Mother!

Nezumi 5 slowly turns to look at the Guardian. She hesitates—but then stabs Guardian. Blood.

   Music: The Jirokichi Theme. Nezumi 1-Nezumi 5 enter. They remove their robber's masks. Each has a horrible keloid scar across his profile.

A dim and steamy bath to wash away the past
Like slipping from the womb, naked slipping in
Only this time the markings of a man
Beneath the hot water, the silver blade of revenge!

Ah, just to strike once, to strike back just once!
To take the place of God
And strike back at all injustice!

A struggle to the death, how happy I would be!
To wallow in the gore, it would be pure bliss!
And then to cleanse myself all over again
In frothy sewers deep and dark and dank.

Ah, just to strike once, to strike back just once!
To take the place of God
And strike back at all injustice!

On the tip of my tongue a twattled jelly-bean,
Can't get no satisfaction, sweet though it be.
Out of drive and duty I crawl from hole to hole—
I can still remember the taste of my first true love!

Ah, just to strike once, to strike back just once!
To take the place of God
And strike back at all injustice!

It sparkles a steely blue, oh yeah.
It sparkles a steely blue, oh yeah.

Suddenly, the roof of the theatre becomes transparent, revealing a million stars twinkling in the midnight sky.

The Nezumis are nowhere to be seen. They have vanished as if they never existed.

Notes

INTRODUCTION

1. The following sources provide additional information on the shingeki movement. Eric J. Gangloff, "Kinoshita Junji: A Modern Japanese Dramatist" (Ph.D. diss., University of Chicago, 1973); J. Thomas Rimer, *Toward a Modern Japanese Theatre* (Princeton: Princeton University Press, 1974); A. Horie-Webber, "Modernisation of the Japanese Theatre: The Shingeki Movement," in W. G. Beasley, ed., *Modern Japan: Aspects of History, Literature, and Society* (Berkeley: University of California Press, 1977); Brian Powell, "Japan's First Modern Theatre—The Tsukiji Shōgekijō and Its Company, 1924–1926," *Monumenta Nipponica* (1975), 30(1):69–85.

2. Rimer's *Toward a Modern Japanese Theatre* is a biography of Kishida and an analysis of his work to 1939. On Kubo, see my translation of his *Land of Ash* (Ithaca, NY: Cornell East Asia Papers, forthcoming).

3. Tsuno Kaitarō, *Higeki no hihan* (Tokyo: Shōbunsha, 1970), p. 227 and passim. I discuss Tsuno's theory of the shingeki movement at length in chapter two of my "Satoh Makoto and the Post-Shingeki Movement in Japanese Contemporary Theatre" (Ph.D. diss., Cornell University, 1982). For another discussion of orthodox shingeki and the transition to postmodern drama, see Kan Takayuki, *Sengo engeki*, Asahi sensho 178 (Tokyo: Asahi shimbunsha, 1981).

4. This anthology is by no means exhaustive. There are many other plays that deal explicitly with Hiroshima and Nagasaki. Seven of these, including all of the plays in this volume except Satoh's, are collected in *Nihon no genbaku bungaku*, vol. 12 (Tokyo: Horupu, 1983). Others, like Murai Shimako's *Hiroshima no onna: sono ichi* (*Teatro*, July 1983), have appeared in magazines. In 1967, an English version of Miyamoto Ken's *The Pilot* (*Za pairotto*) was staged at the University of Hawaii in a translation by Jean S. King and Fujiko Chamberlain.

5. Robert Jay Lifton, *Death in Life: Survivors of Hiroshima* (New York: Random House, 1967).

6. Robert Jay Lifton, *The Broken Connection: On Death and the Continuity of Life* (New York: Simon and Schuster, 1979), p. 314.

7. Ōe Kenzaburō is a prime example. John Nathan reports that Ōe asked that his book *Hiroshima Notes*, Toshi Yonezawa, tr., David L. Swain, ed. (Tokyo: YMCA Press, 1981) be released by his publisher on the same day as his novel *A Personal Matter*, John Nathan, tr. (New York: Grove Press, 1969). Nathan writes, "Ōe was of course asking that the books be considered together; in one he chronicled the survival of an actual atomic bomb, in the other he sought the means of surviving a personal holocaust [the birth of his brain-damaged son]." "Introduction," Ōe Kenzaburō, *Help Us Outgrow Our Madness,* John Nathan, tr. (New York: Grove Press, 1977), p. xvii.

1. THE ISLAND: ORTHODOX REALISM

1. Details concerning the Self-Reliant Theater Movement may be found in Ōhashi Kiichi and Abe Bunyū, eds., *Jiritsu engeki undō,* Thespis Series 66 (Tokyo: Miraisha, 1975).

2. Mingei is described in detail in A. Horie-Webber, "Modernisation of the Japanese Theatre: The Shingeki Movement," in W. G. Beasley, ed., *Modern Japan: Aspects of History, Literature, and Society* (Berkeley: University of California Press, 1977).

3. Quoted in *Gendai nihon gikyoku taikei* (San'ichi shobō, 1971), 3:473.

4. *The Tale of the Heike,* Hiroshi Kitagawa and Bruce T. Tsuchida, trs. 2 vols. (Tokyo: Tokyo University Press, 1975).

5. Kenneth D. Butler, "The Textual Evolution of the *Heike Monogatari,*" *Harvard Journal of Asiatic Studies* (1966), 26:5–51.

6. Despite its long history, the Kiyomori Festival is no longer celebrated. Hotta suggests three reasons. First, a highway now encircles the island, and the police refuse to sanction the procession because it is too dangerous. Second, the majority of men on the island are no longer fishermen but work for business firms on the mainland and are unable to take a day off for the festival. Third, the custom of reimbursing participants for time lost when they do take part has become established in recent years, and the cost of holding the festival has become prohibitive. Personal correspondence from Hotta Kiyomi.

7. This is a paraphrase of Shinran's *Tannishō.* Selections from this work, including this pronouncement, are translated in Wm. Theodore de Bary, et al., eds., *Sources of Japanese Tradition* (New York: Columbia University Press, 1958). Pages 187–218 of this work deal with Pure Land Buddhism and can be consulted for further background information.

8. Robert Jay Lifton, *Death in Life* (New York: Random House, 1967), p. 21.

9. Saeki Ryūkō, *Ika suru jikan,* pp. 76–77; translated in "The Eternal Recanter," *Concerned Theatre Japan,* 2(1–2):112.

10. Examples of postwar shingeki plays written in this vein include Kinoshita Junji, *Fūrō* (Turbulent Times); Miyamoto Ken, *Meiji no hitsugi* (A Coffin for Meiji); and Fukuda Yoshiyuki, *Nagai bohyō no retsu* (A Long Row of Tombstones).

2. THE HEAD OF MARY: NAGASAKI AS THEOPHANY

1. Takashi Nagai, *The Bells of Nagasaki,* William Johnston, tr. (New York: Kodansha International, 1984), pp. 107–109.

2. For a more complete account of Tanaka's background, see J. Thomas Rimer, "Four Plays by Tanaka Chikao," *Monumenta Nipponica* (1976), 31(3):275–298.

3. Fukuda Tsuneari is another playwright deeply influenced by Christianity who has refused baptism. Fukuda is also a disciple of Kishida Kunio and a "literary" playwright. For a discussion of Fukuda, see Benito Ortolani, "Fukuda

Tsuneari: Modernization and Shingeki," in Donald H. Shively, ed., *Tradition and Modernization in Japanese Culture* (Princeton: Princeton University Press, 1971).

4. No such conspiracy actually existed. It is entirely Tanaka's invention.

3. THE ELEPHANT: THE ABSURDITY OF THE REAL

1. The significance of *The Elephant* seems to have dawned on early audiences only very slowly. See Tsuno Kaitarō's comments in his "Preface to *The Elephant,*" *Concerned Theatre Japan* (Autumn 1970), 1(3):60.

2. In September 1984, the troupe changed its name again to the Suzuki Company of Toga (SCOT). For more details on this troupe, see my article, "The Post-Shingeki Theatre Movement," in William C. Young and Colby H. Kullman, eds., *Theatre Companies of the World* (Westport, Conn.: Greenwood Press, 1985).

3. Betsuyaku's 1971 play *The Move (Idō)* is also available in English in Ted T. Takaya, ed. and tr., *Modern Japanese Drama: An Anthology* (New York: Columbia University Press, 1979), pp. 203–272.

4. Robert Jay Lifton, *Death in Life: Survivors of Hiroshima* (New York: Random House, 1967), p. 169.

5. Lifton, *Death in Life,* p. 187.

6. Lifton, *Death in Life,* p. 172.

7. Yamamoto Ken'ichi identifies this man as Yoshikawa Kiyoshi. Yamamoto visited him in 1984 in Hiroshima where he was hospitalized for a stroke. He was 72 at the time. Yamamoto Ken'ichi, "Engeki jūjirō," *Shingeki,* February 1984, p. 53.

8. Lifton, *Death in Life,* pp. 231–233.

9. *Asahi shimbun,* evening edition, July 31, 1970; Yamamoto, "Engeki jūjirō," p. 50.

10. Carol Jay Sorgenfrei, "Shuji Terayama: Avant Garde Dramatist of Japan," (Ph.D. diss., University of California-Santa Barbara, 1978), p. 78.

11. Senda Akihiko, *Gekiteki runessansu: gendai engeki wa kataru* (Tokyo: Libropōto, 1983), p. 109.

12. Tsuno, "Preface to *The Elephant,*" p. 66.

13. For a similar case, see my description of Satoh's experience in the demonstrations and its influence on his work in "Satoh Makoto and the Post-Shingeki Movement in Japanese Contemporary Theatre," (Ph.D. diss., Cornell University, 1982), pp. 98–102 and passim.

14. Robert Jay Lifton, "Art and the Imagery of Extinction," *Performing Arts Journal 18* (1982), 6(3):55–56. In *The End of the World: An Introduction to Contemporary Drama* (New York: Schocken Books, 1983), Maurice Valency also argues that modern drama, culminating in the work of Beckett and Ionesco, has its roots in precisely the kind of vision of the end of the world that Hiroshima presented.

15. Yamamoto, "Engeki jūjirō," p. 52.

4. NEZUMI KOZŌ: THE RAT: HOLOCAUST AS METAHISTORY

1. Mircea Eliade has explained this tradition:

Fire renews the world; through it will come the restoration of "a new world, free from old age, death, decomposition and corruption, living eternally, increasing eternally, when the dead shall rise, when immortality shall come to the living, when the world shall be perfectly renewed." . . . What we wish to emphasize is that in [this] Iranian conception, history (whether followed or not by infinite time) is not eternal; it does not repeat itself but will come to an end one day by an eschatological *ekpyrosis* [cosmic fire] and cosmic cataclysm. For the final catastrophe that will put an end to history will at the same time be a judgment of history. It is then—*in illo tempore*—that, as we are told, all will render an account of what they have done "in history" and only those who are not guilty will know beatitude and eternity. Mircea Eliade, *The Myth of the Eternal Return or, Cosmos and History,* Willard R. Trask, tr., Bollingen Series 46 (Princeton: Princeton University Press, 1971), pp. 124–126.

This apocalyptic vision was taken over and reformulated in secular terms by Marx, who substituted "revolution" for "apocalypse," and "the proletariat" for "the elect." Eliade elaborates on the correspondence between Marxism and classical theology.

Whatever we may think of the scientific claims of Marx, it is clear that the author of the *Communist Manifesto* takes up and carries on one of the great eschatological myths of the Middle Eastern and Mediterranean world, namely: the redemptive part to be played by the Just (the "elect," the "anointed," the "innocent," the "missioners," in our own days by the proletariat), whose sufferings are invoked to change the ontological status of the world. In fact, Marx's classless society, and the consequent disappearance of all historical tensions, find their most exact precedent in the myth of the Golden Age which, according to a number of traditions, lies at the beginning and the end of History. Marx has enriched this venerable myth with a truly messianic Judaeo-Christian ideology; on the one hand, by the prophetic and soteriological functions he ascribes to the proletariat; and, on the other, by the final struggle between Good and Evil, which may well be compared with the apocalyptic conflict between Christ and Antichrist, ending in the decisive victory of the former. It is indeed significant that Marx turns to his own account the Judaeo-Christian eschatological hope of an *absolute goal of History;* in that he parts company from the other historical philosophers (Croce, for instance, and Ortega y Gasset), for whom the tensions of history are implicit in the human condition, and therefore can never be completely abolished. Mircea Eliade, *Myths, Dreams, and Mysteries* (New York and Evanston: Harper Torchbooks, 1967), pp. 25–26. Cf. *The Myth of the Eternal Return,* pp. 149–150.

The coincidence of Marxist revolution and Apocalypse, such as Satoh is depicting (and criticizing) here, is by no means alien to the theater and is in fact at the heart of agit-prop theater. See Tsuno Kaitarō, *Mon no mukō no gekijō* (Hakusuisha, 1972), pp. 74–90, for a discussion of this issue. Mayakovsky, for example, believed quite literally that the Russian revolution would conquer death, and his play *The Bedbug* concerns what happens when, fifty years after the Russian Revolution, "The Institute of Human Resurrection" brings one Ivan Prisypkin and the bedbug who died with him back to life. Prisypkin died, appropriately, in a conflagration, one that began when his bride's veil caught fire at their wedding party. See Guy Daniels, tr., *The Complete Plays of Vladimir Mayakovsky* (New York: Simon and Schuster, 1968).

2. For additional information on the Japanese religious tradition underlying the activities of Heh-heh, So-so, and Bo-bo, see Carmen Blacker, *The Catalpa Bow: A Study of Shamanistic Practices in Japan* (London: Allen & Unwin, 1975).

3. Blacker, *The Catalpa Bow*, ch. 6, especially pp. 115–126, gives a discussion of the varieties and implications of this myth in Japanese religion.

4. *Nukeraremasu* ("through traffic") became a euphemism for red light districts because misleading signs to this effect were placed at the entrances to a red-light cul-de-sac to lure "the unsuspecting" into its precincts.

5. Tsuno Kaitarō, "Of Baths, Brothels, and Hell," *Concerned Theatre Japan* (Spring 1970), 1(1):142. This article, which provides a wealth of detail concerning *Nezumi Kozō: The Rat,* may be read profitably in conjunction with the present discussion.

6. Walter Benjamin, "Theses on the Philosophy of History," *Illuminations,* Harry Zohn tr. (New York: Shocken Books, 1969), p. 26. Satoh quotes the paragraph from which this phrase is taken in the epigraph to one of his later plays, *Abe Sada no inu* (Abe Sada's Dogs, 1976).

7. *Onna-goroshi abura no jigoku (Murder in Oil Hell),* in *Atashi no biitoruzu* (Shōbunsha, 1970), pp. 64–65.

8. Eliade, *The Myth of the Eternal Return,* p. 88. Emphasis in the original.

9. See, for example, *My Beatles* and my "Notes to Encourage a Production of *My Beatles*" in *The Canadian Theatre Review,* Fall 1978.

10. Eliade, *The Myth of the Eternal Return,* p. 88. Emphasis added.

11. Tsuno Kaitarō "Of Baths, Brothels, and Hell," p. 143.

12. Benjamin, "Theses on the Philosophy of History," *Illuminations,* pp. 253, 264, and 262–263, respectively.